Louisa Waugh was born in Berlin and grew up in Liverpool. She didn't go to university; instead, she spent several years working with young homeless people, before moving to Mongolia where she wrote for the *Guardian*, the *Independent*, the *New Internationalist* magazine, and was a regular BBC World Service contributor. She now lives in Edinburgh.

HEARING BIRDS FLY

A Nomadic Year
in Mongolia

Louisa Waugh

An *Abacus* Book

First published in Great Britain as a paperback original
in 2003 by Abacus
Reprinted 2004 (twice)

A CIP catalogue record for this book
is available from the British Library.

ISBN 0 349 11580 X

Typeset in Adobe Garamond by
Palimpsest Book Production Limited,
Polmont, Stirlingshire
Printed and bound in Great Britain by
Clays Ltd, St Ives plc

Abacus
An imprint of
Time Warner Book Group UK
Brettenham House
Lancaster Place
London WC2E 7EN

www.twbg.co.uk

To the people of Tsengel
For sharing your stories
Танд баярлалаа

If an ass goes travelling, he'll not come home a horse

Thomas Fuller (1606–1661)

CONTENTS

CHARACTERS

Abbai – Tsengel village councillor, brother of Addai, Quartz and Oraz

Addai – brother of Abbai, Quartz and Oraz, the postmaster

Algaa – clinic chief with gold teeth

Alibi – the man who killed his friend

Amraa – local teacher

Apam – mother of Abbai, Addai, Quartz and Oraz

Bash-Balbar – father of Sansar-Huu

Deri-Huu – mother of Sansar-Huu: matriarch

Dorj – Gerel-Huu's rascal husband

Gansukh – village teacher

Gerel-Huu, Shinid and Bagit – 'gang of three': the school cooks

Gerele – Tuya's lover: the rogue

Greg – friend and Peace Corps teacher

Guul-Jan – Abbai's wife: the midwife

Kalim – the man who died

Kultii – village DJ

Lashun – Kalim's wife

Menke – school director

Merim-Khan and Aimak – Abbai and Guul-Jan's neighbours

Princess – Dr Janner-Guul

Oraz – brother of Abbai, Addai and Quartz

Quartz – brother of Abbai, Addai and Oraz: a widower

Sanak Sailik – charismatic village Imam

Sansar-Huu – Gansukh's husband

Shilgee – Deri-Huu's daughter

Sistem – relative of Abbai and patriarch

Szandrash – Addai's wife

Tuya – village teacher and rebel

Zulmira – village teacher

GLOSSARY

Aaruul – dried cheese curds
Ail – settlement of several *gers* or cabins
Aimag – province
Airag – fermented mare's milk
Arikh – vodka
Backo – there is none
Bagsh – teacher
Balakh – fish (Kazakh)
Bayartai – farewell
Büjig – dance
Buuz – steamed mutton dumplings
Buurtzug – deep-fried sticks of dough
Darakh – boss
Deel – calf-length embroidered tunic
Dombra – two-stringed Kazak guitar
Düü – little brother/sister
Eej – mother
Ekhner – wife
Emch – doctor
Esgii – felt
Gaa – get lost
Gadaad-neen hun – foreigner
Ger – traditional Mongolian felt tent
Gutal – traditional Mongol boots
Haj – pilgrimage to Mecca
Halkh – majority Mongol ethnic group
Hasha – yard
Hortlaa – liar
Ikh Khural – Mongol Parliament
Jolooch – driver

Kasgur – wolf (Kazakh)
Khar – black
Khadag – sacred silk scarf
Khamaagüi – it doesn't matter
Khetsüü – difficult
Khurim – wedding party
Makh – meat
Mal – livestock
Malchin – herder/nomad
Margaash – tomorrow
Muu – bad
Muukhai – horrible
Odoo/odocken – now
Okhin – daughter
Saikhan – beautiful
Sain – good
Sain bainuu? – How are you?
Shimin-arikh – home-brewed vodka
Shuudagiin salbar – Post Office
Sogtuu – drunk
Suutei-tsai – milk tea (served with salt)
Taivan – peaceful
Tarvag – marmot
Tarvag takal – marmot/bubonic plague
Togrog – Mongol currency
Tomagaa – blindfold for eagle
Tsaatsun – full (of food)
Tsagaan Idee – dairy produce
Tsai – tea
Tsai oh – drink tea (invitation)
Tsengel – delight
Tsoivan – flour noodles fried with meat
Ulaanbaatar – Mongol capital (Red Warrior)
Yamar? – what kind of?
Yamani-noluur – cashmere
Yari! – let's go!
Zowan – dirty/horrible

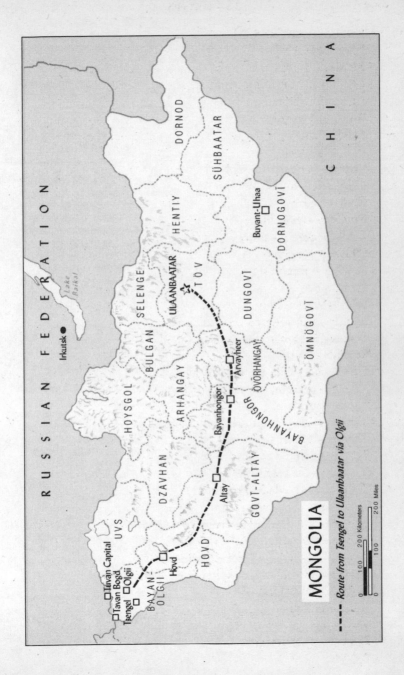

MONGOLIA

----- *Route from Tsengel to Ulaanbaatar via Ölgii*

INTRODUCTION

The word *tsengel* means 'delight'. This still seems a bizarre, almost mocking name for my former home: an unlit, windswept village where death and life were so raw, crude and compelling. The winter livestock massacre, carried out so the villagers could survive until spring, is the most explicit example of how people live with death out here in the arid central Asian steppe. But there's far more to living, and especially dying, in Tsengel, than the carcasses produced by the annual slaughter.

Whenever I talk about my time in Tsengel, I recall anecdotes and stories with loving attention to detail. So much of what happened there is still so vivid, each memory evoking its own emotions, contours and colours. I could draw you a map of the village right now – its dirt tracks, the dusty central square and the lovely, shoddy old 'klub' where we danced so much throughout the spring. I could identify many of the log cabins, tell you who lives there, what they do and where they herd their animals in summer. I'd add an illustration of the spooky clinic where I stayed for the first week or so, because no one knew where else to put me. Then I'd talk about the beautiful, treacherous Hovd river, which flanks Tsengel and drowns at least one or two of its people every year . . . but I'm racing ahead. Of course, I didn't arrive in Tsengel by accident: it's not that sort of place. And I wasn't stranded or enticed there either. I sought the village out. I'd already spent two years in Mongolia by then, but I still didn't really know anything about the other half of its small population – the villagers and the nomads who herd their livestock across the steppe.

*   *   *

Ten years ago, in 1993, I was on my way from London to Latin America, to spend six months teaching in Honduras. But a couple of weeks before our flight, Georgia, the friend who was coming with me, rang up and glumly confessed that her marriage of convenience to a rich, gay Moroccan had suddenly become extremely inconvenient – and now she didn't dare leave Britain. Our plans were flattened. The school wanted two English teachers, but I didn't know anyone else who would be prepared to come to Honduras. So I reluctantly cancelled the contract.

Having already resigned from my job at a youth homelessness project and given my landlord notice, I was at a complete loss. I'd been in London for three years and had started talking with increasing restlessness about the journeys I wanted to undertake, the cities I longed to explore. Now that Georgia couldn't join me, my plans were my own.

I'd love to say that I quickly rose to the occasion, carelessly flinging a few old clothes and a leather-bound journal into a small battered suitcase, and fleeing the country in sunglasses, never even glancing back over my shoulder. But I'm not made of such stern stuff. The truth is that I was scared.

Instead, I spent days in my attic bedroom gazing up at my creased world map while my friends were out at work, and carved bizarre, circuitous routes across the continents. I felt as though I had to go somewhere now, and not for anyone else's sake. My grimmest prospect was of waking up a year or five years later, and still being in London, still snared in the same work and still talking about travelling. That actually felt more frightening than setting off alone. It was a paradox: I was more afraid of staying than leaving.

I discarded Africa and South America for no particularly good reasons, and finally stood in front of Asia, glaring at a continent I knew almost nothing about. Asia and the Orient. My imagination easily evoked a headful of seductive colours and clichés. Cascades of silk. Languorous trains of camels crossing unnamed deserts. Raucous open-air markets laden with succulent fruit and the pungent smoke of frying spicy meat. Conical sun hats and Chinese characters. I had heard of the Trans-Siberian railway, which offered an epic dry voyage from Moscow through Siberia and then Mongolia to the Chinese capital. (I get terribly seasick and am scared of flying.) The very little I knew of China included its apparent legendary safety for women travelling alone. Once I was there I'd build up my confidence and the rest of my trip would sort itself out afterwards. The only thing of which I was certain, was that I needed a life beyond London. I booked an itinerary of tickets before I had a chance to change my mind, held a farewell party in the local pub and packed my bags. I teetered on the brink, left three weeks later, and cried half the way to Moscow.

After forty-eight hours in the Russian capital I boarded the Trans-Siberian. Still nervous, but dry-eyed. My allocated four-berth second-class compartment was already occupied by a friendly couple from Leicester, who'd just retired from running a knicker factory. Hank and Gwenda were on their way to visit their daughter in Hong Kong.

'We don't fly,' said Gwenda, splashing vodka into plastic beakers. 'We had a terrible experience on a plane once, and that was it for us. Actually, we'd still be working, but the Chinese undercut us. Their knickers are cheaper. Still, that's business for you – would you like a drink?'

After my weeks of edgy anticipation I didn't know whether to be relieved or reticent about sharing my maiden solo voyage with a middle-aged English couple who'd spent their working lives flogging knickers. But I swallowed my trepidation with our first toast, and the three of us quickly fell into travelling camaraderie. Hank, Gwenda and I spent several blissful days together as we trundled across the Ural Mountains into Siberia. I understood nothing of Russia, and felt cosseted from the often bleak landscape by the thick panes of glass that air-brushed our journey as we weaved from Europe into Asia.

Our days were absorbed like rain on parched earth and the time zones changed so frequently we stopped altering our watches. We parted company when they disembarked for a few days' detour at

Irkutsk, capital of Siberia and gateway to the world's largest lake, Baikal. Irkutsk was once known as 'the Paris of Siberia', but we arrived in the middle of a whirring summer blizzard.

'Now have a splendid time, dear, and don't forget to give us a call when you get back,' urged Gwenda, as they dragged their luggage and cameras away with them. I waved goodbye and blew kisses from the open train door. Then I settled back into the compartment, feeling bereft but strangely glad to be without them. They'd been wonderful company. Maybe that was why I wanted to spend the last day of the train journey alone. Now I knew there would be other people like them along the way: it was reassuring.

While arranging my Trans-Siberian ticket to China, I had also booked a detour en route. I'd arranged several nights accommodation in the Mongol capital Ulaanbaatar, then passage on to the next Beijing train. Two phone calls to travel agencies in London had secured the Mongol hotel room at a price that had made me gulp. But I was curious about Mongolia. I'd never met anyone who had been there, and was fascinated enough to want to spend a few days in this remote capital, and glimpse the enigmatic steppe nomads in their felt *ger* tents. This was an interlude before the Orient, then I'd be on my way.

Early on a Monday morning, while other worlds of people were reaching for the doors of their cars, offices and classrooms, I stretched my stiff back and swung my heavy pack over my shoulders. I queued briefly at the carriage door and then clambered down on to the platform in Ulaanbaatar, a little wary, excited and, above all, intrigued.

Men and women strolled along wide, pocked pavements. They wore *deels,* calf-length embroidered tunics belted with yellow silk sashes. Their long boots were frescoed in a medley of primary colours, the leather toes upcurled towards the bright sky. A small group of florid middle-aged male drinkers sat on concrete steps swigging at a bottle. One of them choked and coughed up a mouthful of blood. The concrete steps led through a narrow doorway and into a cold store with almost empty shelves, where women in fur hats handed over pink ration coupons for loaves of withered-looking bread.

A windburned herder cantered his stocky horse past the parliament building in central Sukhbaatar Square. The deserted, cloistered temple across the road had a fringe of wild grass and seeds writhing on its pagoda roof. I crossed the road to the temple, looking right and then left. But there were no cars.

My hotel was called the Bayangol. It was brightly lit and gaudy and the food was terrible. When I wandered from its glass-fronted doors towards the city centre, I thought at first that Ulaanbaatar held the terse atmosphere of another destitute Soviet metropolis, with its lofty theatres, parliament and cultural palace, its vacant stores and hideous army of scarred apartment blocks. But it was somehow compelling. It was as though the city had been accidentally built for a much larger population who had suddenly succumbed to a radical change of heart, and fled to live out their lives as herders on the steppe. The Bayangol gift shop sold tacky models of the traditional *ger* tents. They looked like minute circus big tops, a wooden frame insulated with felt and sheathed in white canvas.

I'd unwittingly acquired a driver and a pale, anxious-looking guide called Mandakh with my overpriced room, and after two days of museums and temples I asked if we could please drive outside the city and see the nearby countryside, the nomads and their *gers*. It was my last afternoon in Mongolia. Mandakh nodded cautiously.

'We are not allowed to take you more than twenty-five kilometres from the centre,' she confessed. When I asked why, she said she didn't know.

As we rumbled out of Ulaanbaatar, the apartment blocks fell away, revealing an immediate secondary city of *gers*, where thousands of urban Mongols raised their families in sprawling patchwork districts of fenced yards, crisscrossed by dirt tracks as gouged and pitted as bad skin. Obviously you didn't have to be a nomad to live in a tent.

After 15 or 20 kilometres I stood on grass scorched the colour of hay, and gazed across the silent landscape of steppe and low rolling hills, to the moment where it all dissolved into a brilliant clean sky. Here, even within sight of the capital, there were clusters of nomads. Settlements of *gers* and scattered herds of horses, sheep and goats. A horseman astride a narrow saddle carved from wood and branded with silver hurtled past us clenching his *urgaa* – a long noose snared to a wooden pole that the men use to lasso rebellious geldings. Beyond the clouds of dust and fragments of dry earth kicked up by the hooves, I could spy the rise of Bactrian camels in the distance. I turned my back on the capital, already quietly and totally smitten by the steppe.

Mandakh took me to drink tea in the nearby *ger* of an elderly herder called Enbisch, his wife Badamaa and their five daughters. We ducked through the short, open doorway, and the whole family rose to their feet and directed us to a thick rug at the rear of their small, spherical home. It looked dim and cosy, with narrow beds in a semi-circle round the walls, and a tarnished stove in the centre.

'This is where the guests sit,' whispered Mandakh as we knelt down. 'Look, he is giving you something. Sniff – and then give it back with your right hand.'

Enbisch solemnly pressed a cool stone tablet into my palm. His parched, thickly veined hands were like the roots of ancient trees. His daughters giggled and nudged each other as they trailed my movements with their eyes. It took me a moment to realise I was clasping a tiny carved stone bottle of snuff. Having never tried the stuff before, I just tipped a teaspoon-sized mound on to the base of my index finger, pressed it to my nostril and inhaled full strength.

OH MY GOD.

I choked like a greedy infant on a boiled sweet, tears streaming down my face, my nose singeing and tonsils screaming in rage. Colours flashed before my eyes and I snorted like a horse in shock. Enbisch, Badamaa and their daughters erupted into loud, careless laughter. They were still chortling when my sight resumed in watery focus, and even Mandakh was shaking her head and smirking.

'Maybe too much?' She tried to soothe me without giggling again. I caught her eye and we sniggered and then bellowed together with the nomads until we were all gasping and clutching our stomachs.

Laughter makes friends easily.

'*Tsai, tsai?*' Badamaa wiped her eyes and, her whole face smiling, offered me a steaming bowl of tea with her right hand. In the *ger* everything was offered and served this way. The tea was strong and milky, laced with salt. I drank it slowly and smiled at the five girls who were staring and smiling at me, and wondered why on earth I was going to China.

I didn't want to leave Mongolia. But my visa was expiring and I'd booked and paid for my train to Beijing, so the next morning I obediently climbed aboard and rolled off towards the Orient as scheduled. I kept looking back over my shoulder.

I returned to Ulaanbaatar in the spring, three years later. After my first, brief visit to Mongolia, I had spent the best part of a year travelling across Asia before returning to London and picking up my old life almost where I'd left it. But even though I had spent less time in Mongolia than any of the other half dozen countries I'd visited, I had carried my impressions of it with me the whole time, like a vital piece of luggage. They came home with me too, and remained at the fore of my mind, vivid and almost disturbing. All I knew was that the few days I'd spent around Ulaanbaatar had left more of a mark than anywhere else I had ever been. This half-empty land of nomads was going to preoccupy me until I went back.

I began to talk about returning to Mongolia. I didn't do much about it at first, but I talked a lot. Then, a few months later, I had one of those strokes of luck or fortune or whatever you call it when someone makes you an offer, and forces you to make up your mind whether to leave or stay. Through a friend of a friend I met a Mongol monk who was spending six months in London perfecting his English. The monk's name was Baatar, which means Hero. He was an insightful man who listened far more than he talked, and he invited me back to Mongolia, to teach in his monastery in Ulaanbaatar. I booked another Trans-Siberian ticket, and I didn't shed a tear.

Baatar had arranged for me to live with friends of his, an earnest dentist called Jargal-Saikhan and her twenty-two-year-old son, Sodnam. Sodnam spoke good English and a few days after I'd arrived took me dancing to a glitzy new disco called Hollywood. We sat with a crowd of his smart young friends, our bottles of cold beer rattling against the chrome table.

'This place is very good,' one of the women enthused, offering me a Marlboro. 'Before Hollywood, there was no good disco. We had nowhere to go. Now there are nice new places opening and we can go to enjoy.' I joined them on the strobed dance floor, and marvelled at the transformation of the barely habited city I'd visited three years earlier.

The most vivid indicators of how much life had changed in Ulaanbaatar during my three-year absence were people's clothes. The older generations still wore the traditional *deels* and hand-painted *gutal* boots. Some wandered stoically through the nowadays more crowded streets, while others stood patiently on corners, vending single cigarettes. Their children, however, dressed in smart, conservative Western-style clothes, imported cheap from China. The women cut or bobbed their hair short. The entrepreneurs coveted their mobile phones. Ulaanbaatar was a living mosaic of history and ambition.

I wasn't disappointed by this metamorphosis: it was utterly fascinating to witness, like a fast-forwarded stage of evolution. It also didn't take me very long to realise that many of the recent changes were a shiny veneer, lacking any real substance. There were power cuts at least once and usually twice or three times a day. The four flights of stairs leading from the apartment block entrance to Jargalsaikhan's front door were always unlit. The residents carried torches at night because the light bulbs had been stolen.

Local supermarkets were beginning to sell imported luxury foods, but they were expensive and most urban Mongols still lived on staples of mutton, rice, potatoes, turnips and bread. Prices rose frequently.

For the first few months, while I was teaching at Gandan Monastery, I co-existed happily between two worlds. My classes at Gandan were the antithesis of this urban frenzy to reinvent Mongolia as Asia's newest democracy. Here, instead, the remnants of an ancient Buddhist empire lingered.

Gandan was a complex of gold and crimson pagodas with pavilion roofs, rows of groaning copper prayer wheels plastered in written requests and pleas, and a cloistered Buddhist university. Pensioners rotated the wheels together, or circled urns of smouldering incense, perpetually threading necklaces of prayer beads through stubby fingers. I once saw a young man in a *deel* staggering like a drunk as he circled one of the temples, a frail and crumpled relative clinging round his neck like a barnacle to a rock. The young man was panting, the crippled older man chanting aloud from the Sutras.

In my classes, the young *lamas* (monks) sat cross-legged on narrow benches painted the colour of lemons. They called me *bagsh,* which means teacher, and brought me bowls of steaming black tea laced with salt. I became very fond of them. In the late afternoons, as I wandered out of the cloister and down the dusty hill that elevated Gandan above the restless city, men with burnt, creased faces from the steppe would tell fortunes by casting the ankle bones of sheep across squares of faded cloth.

In June 1996, the day after my classes at Gandan finished, there was a general election that changed Mongol history. The reigning Mongolian People's Revolutionary Party (MPRP) was spectacularly defeated by a coalition of young, North American-trained Mongol democrats, the United Democratic Coalition. It was the first change of government in Mongolia for seventy-five years.

Back in 1921, a young warrior named Sukhbaatar had appealed to the Russian Bolsheviks to assist the Mongols in repelling Cossack 'White Russian' soldiers who had entered the Mongol capital, then known as Niyslel Huree (Monastery capital). The army of Mongol revolutionaries and Lenin's troops drove the Cossacks out and a revolution was heralded. But the Bolsheviks themselves never retreated from the Mongol capital, which was renamed Ulaanbaatar (Red Hero) in homage to Sukhbaatar. Though the Mongolian People's Republic declared total independence three years later in 1924, it didn't make much difference. Mongolia quietly became the world's second communist state: garrisons of Russian troops were barracked across the Republic and the classic, vertical Mongol script was abandoned in favour of the Russian Cyrillic alphabet. Until the Democratic Revolution almost seventy years later, the Soviet Union was Mongolia's cultural, economic and political dominatrix.

It would be easy to assume that, having brought down their government in a bloodless revolution at the beginning of 1990, the Mongols would then enthusiastically vote the opposition straight into office. But they didn't. Although there was a host of democratic and independent parties canvassing for support, the MPRP regained a majority of seats in both the 1990 and the 1992 general elections. They shrewdly initiated social and economic reforms, and courted foreign investment and diplomatic relations. It wasn't until this year, 1996, that a combination of fervent US backing for the United Democratic Coalition and a languishing Mongol economy finally slew the MPRP.

During this election I found paid work as editor of a new independent English language newspaper called the *Ulaanbaatar Post*. The local ex-pat community was a slowly expanding crowd of UN consultants, VSO and American Peace Corps teachers, plus a swarm of evangelical US Mormons.

I eventually parted company with Jargal-Saikhan and Sodnam, though we remained good friends, and moved into a small, warm flat, which I shared with a colony of cockroaches. The building electricity supply was so erratic my neighbours and I referred to our block as 'the disco'.

In spite of the cockroaches, power cuts and ferocious long winters, when the temperature hovered at -20C for months, I loved living in Ulaanbaatar. I slowly learned to speak decent Mongolian, schmoozed in brand new nightclubs several times a week, and thrived on a chaotic work schedule. I had spent several years dreaming of another life out on the steppe, living amidst nomads, but, almost two years after I'd arrived back in Mongolia, I was still comfortably marooned in the realm of the Red Hero.

My turning point came swiftly and quietly. I was slumped in the crowded carriage of a broken train early one evening at the beginning of my second Mongol winter. We were stranded halfway between Ulaanbaatar and a city called Erdenet. The sun was dying and the silhouette of a lone *ger* glowed on the grasslands like a flare of magnesium. Nearby a camel stretched its neck and placidly sucked from a dark ribbon of water. I'd seen these languid sunsets before during previous trips and they were always poignant. But now I felt a sudden cold sadness wash over me, as I realised I was in grave danger of leaving Mongolia without ever having seen more than a glimpse of the nomadic life that had brought me back here in the first place.

The morning after the train limped back to Ulaanbaatar I began searching for a new home in the countryside. Realistically, I knew the only work I'd find in a village would be teaching English. With the tunnel vision and limited rationale of someone who is suddenly totally desperate, I convinced myself that I could exchange school lessons for the rural basics: a felt *ger*, meat, flour and salt. I wouldn't need much money in a village, because there wouldn't be much to buy.

I talked to everyone I knew and everyone they knew, contacting village governors, schools and friends of friends across Mongolia. But circumstances conspired against me. Letters were returned unopened, no one answered the static rural post office telephones, the governors were always sick or at home or somewhere else. I had already resigned from the newspaper, and though I continued going through the motions of socialising, my mind was finally elsewhere. I sensed that a unique opportunity was quietly slipping beyond my grasp. My Mongol friends shrugged nonchalantly when I fretted that I was getting absolutely nowhere.

'People are very slow in the villages,' my friend Javhlan told me. 'You have to be patient. No one hurries there. Wait.'

More than three fruitless months later my resolve was eroding when a friend called Greg flew into Ulaanbaatar for a few days. Greg was physically short, wore thick, aviator-style glasses, and though he was often as serious as his appearance implied, he could also make you laugh out loud with a wit so dry it set his stories alight. He worked for the Peace Corps in Bayan-Olgii province, more than 1,700 kilometers west of Ulaanbaatar. The previous summer he had briefly met a man called Abbai, who was the local government chief of a village called Tsengel.

I had never heard of Tsengel. It was, Greg explained over frothy beers at a rowdy bar, a settlement of about a thousand people, surrounded by mountains and flanked by a wide river called the Hovd.

'If you want remote, that's where you should go.' He drained his glass. 'It's the furthest west village in Mongolia. I was there for a couple of days last year. It's barren but beautiful. Great mountains. Interesting area to write about, you know. Quite out there on its own. There's a local Shaman and lots of Muslim Kazakhs. The Mongols are actually a minority. You could teach at the school, but winter would be very tough. Go at New Year, in February.'

'How would I contact Abbai?'

'Just send a telex to Tsengel, to the village post office. He'll get it — it's a small place. If you do come out west, be sure to bring plenty of food with you, and a stack of books. There won't be anything to do. Oh, and toilet roll — take lots of that. You know what the countryside is like — they never have that stuff.' He leaned forward and grinned. 'Louisa, don't look so worried — I think you'd have an amazing time.'

I wired the Tsengel post office in my slightly erratic Mongolian, suggesting the same arrangement once more. Ten days later a telex from Tsengel arrived: one smeared line of typed Cyrillic.

We need a teacher. Come to the village. Abbai.

PART ONE

Walking on Water

CHAPTER ONE

Tsengel, February 1998

The woman standing in front of me was the thinnest person I'd ever seen. Everything about her was long and undernourished. Layers of snagged cloth hung from her rakish shoulders in dark folds, and she appeared to have neither breasts nor hips, but a mere frame of bones and tight, dry skin, swamped by these clothes that couldn't possibly be hers. She offered a glancing smile through lips spare as blunt knife edges, but she didn't speak.

'This is Baddie-Guul,' said the hunchback who'd just brought me across the mountains and into the village. 'She will stay with you tonight. You have a good talk with her – she will tell you everything.' He and my other escorts left the room swiftly, slamming the door behind them.

Baddie-Guul and I stood in silence for several long moments, looking over at each other and then averting our eyes. We didn't even say hello. She returned to the corner of the candle-lit room, stooping over a tarnished pot simmering on the wood-burning stove. I glanced around. There were two narrow, full-length beds with shiny headboards, and a couple of wooden chairs, but the chipped desk between the beds engulfed most of the space. A glass door at the other end of the room was so filthy I couldn't see through it. The walls were all smeared flaking white, each tacked with a grimy selection of archaic United Nations posters promoting indigenous-looking young mothers serenely breast-feeding plump, cherubic baby girls. I couldn't understand the faded Cyrillic characters.

Oh God. I sat down on one of the beds and heard the small

sound of something tear beneath me. I desperately tried to think of something to say because the silence was making me cold and doubtful, but instead found myself wondering where the toilet was.

'Where are we? What is this place?' I eventually called across the room, much too loudly. Baddie-Guul flinched. I shrugged my shoulders, forcing myself to smile like a fraud.

'This is the clinic,' she said, turning back to her pot.

I shifted in my seat and sank deeper into the punctured springs. I wanted to be somewhere else, somewhere warmer and much more familiar than this ugly concrete ward, with its dingy furniture and broken floor. This was further than I'd imagined from Ulaanbaatar – in every sense.

The eight o'clock flight that morning from the Mongol capital to Bayan-Olgii province had not been an auspicious start to my new rural life. My friends and I had been so distracted toasting my departure with a bottle of lukewarm *arikh* (vodka) that I almost missed the plane.

The pitiful sight of a shrieking, half-sozzled Englishwoman pelting across the tarmac in pursuit of the gliding aircraft, flinging down several large bags – and a plastic bucket full of toilet rolls, which bounced and unravelled around her as she screeched and waved like a demented cheerleader – did at least alert the air traffic controller. He waded through the fuel mirage with his walkie-talkie clamped to his lips, and calmly stopped the plane on the runway.

It was -32C that morning, but I was sweating by the time I'd rescued everything except the toilet rolls, and climbed shakily up a wobbling ladder and into the cabin. I sat down with my face flushed and head bowed in shame, feeling extremely unsteady and very, very stupid. But this was the last flight out west for two weeks, and I knew if I'd missed it I would never have got my £100 back. No one even glanced at me when I slumped back in my seat and began to laugh quietly and hysterically to myself. Mongols can be sublimely deadpan.

When we landed at Olgii airport around noon, Greg was waiting for me. I flung my arms around him, triumphant at having even arrived.

'Are you OK? Tired? Scared?' he asked, taking a bag and the empty bucket from me.

'No. I've just realised how much I wanted to come here after all.'

That night I stayed in Greg's spartan but somehow comfy apartment. We bought beer from a drab store and drank until the power cut out at 10.30 p.m. Then we went to sleep.

'Greg?' I turned over and sat up, making the mattress curl. 'What's the worst thing about living in the countryside?'

'Why are you asking now? Look, it'll be fine.'

'But I want to know – what will be the worst part?'

'For you? Probably having drunk men banging on your door at two in the morning, demanding sex.'

I shook my head and grimaced in the dark. He proved to be unnervingly accurate.

Greg had a telephone he shared with the neighbours and the next morning someone rang just as Abbai had arranged, to say that a jeep would arrive at four o'clock to take me to the village. We wandered round Olgii for a couple of hours, and ate lunch in a trailer that had been converted into a shoddy café. The river that coursed through Olgii had already been frozen for three months, and the mountains surrounding the city, which was really just a large town, were the colour of sandstone and coal, their crests glinting white in the strong sun.

Mongols popularly claim that, for them, visiting Bayan-Olgii *aimag*, or province, is like entering a foreign country within the parameters of their own land. They regard their most westerly province as uncharted and dubious territory, an annexe settled by Muslims they neither know nor welcome. The Mongol Kazakhs make up just over 5 per cent of the entire Mongolian population, but represent 95 per cent of the 120,000 or so people living in Bayan-Olgii. On this barren cusp, at the remote juncture of Mongolia, China and Russia, the Kazakhs live in diaspora, the inheritors of a turbulent nomadic history of trekking back and forth over the mountains, firstly fleeing Russian and Chinese wars and finally being rejected by their own Republic. Here in the extremities of western Mongolia they eventually forged an enclave, a nomadic nation within.

After two years of living amidst the Ulaanbaatar Mongols, I too felt as though I'd just crossed a border into a harsher, more archaic land. Trees seemed to be an endangered species in Olgii and there was no grass, just mountains, rock, ice and piercing sky. The *gers* were outnumbered by antediluvian whitewashed homes built from wood and plastered in mud, the roofs flat like thick slices of bread. The whitewash was a pale silt of chalk and water, and the ground on which it dripped was dust and stone. Greg and I kicked up small clouds as we trailed the streets, serenaded by the lingering sad wail of the muezzin from the central mosque.

I felt distracted and skittish all day. My stomach is my emotional barometer and it gurgled and contorted into knots as I checked my bags and we waited for the jeep. I had no sense of what Tsengel looked or felt like – I was moving to a village I had never even seen on a map. After hearing Greg's initial description, I had deliberately chosen to learn nothing about Tsengel and its people, because I didn't want to expect anything – I wanted my impressions to be immediate and spontaneous, created *in situ*. However, I instinctively felt this wouldn't be an indifferent or mediocre time. I was moving into an extreme environment. I would either love or detest life in Tsengel, flee or thrive.

The driver beeped at about half past five. Greg and I hovered as my luggage of clothes, dried food, books and a wheel of cheese was forced into a jeep already bulging with sacks and half a dozen men and women with several children balancing on their wide knees. The driver was a malevolent-looking hunchback, whose cracked upper lip curled into a sneer when he suggested, '*Yavi?*' Shall we go? He made it sound more like an ultimatum than a question.

'Call me if you want a visitor,' said Greg quietly as I kissed him goodbye. I winked gratefully, because I knew he understood exactly how I was feeling.

I shared the carpeted front seat with a young woman carrying a swaddled baby, clenching my buttocks as we lurched from pitted tarmac on to an unpaved track that wavered through a sandscape strewn with clots of spiked yellow grass.

Olgii dissolved behind us as we drove through dust, snow and sand. The horizon was framed with muted mountains. My travelling companions, skull-capped men and headscarved women, all spoke to me in Mongolian but talked with each other in Kazakh, as guttural and alien to me as the unfurling scenery.

I stared through the smeared windows as Bactrian camels loped from the edge of the track when we roared past, their hairy, flaccid humps wobbling like breasts. But soon the trail faded like footprints in sand and the mountains began to submerge in the dusk, as herds of haggard horses stood their ground and stared under the immense, bruised sky.

I panicked quietly, even calmly, as we lurched west, wishing we would never actually arrive at the village, but continue driving across this uninhabited wild silence until my courage and the daylight returned. When the jeep did finally brake, just before a decrepit, rotting bridge straddling a wide river of ice, I gazed at the shadow of a ramshackle hamlet amidst the barren treeless river valley, and silently prayed this wasn't Tsengel – *anywhere but this desolate, godforsaken place, please, anywhere but here*. My companions shook their covered heads. 'No. One more hour.'

The men wandered off to urinate discreetly. Soon we all folded ourselves back inside the jeep and drove towards darkening sand dunes.

It was another three hours before we arrived in Tsengel. The jeep engine rasped, died and was slowly coaxed back to life by one of the stocky Kazakhs, squinting and coughing loosely as he worked, the smoke from his acrid cigarette wafting up into his thick eyelashes. I talked quietly with the woman who sat next to me in the jeep clutching her child. Her name was Aimak. She didn't live in the village.

'Oh, my home is nearby, in the mountains,' she told me casually. 'You'll find it. Someone will bring you.'

I didn't have time to say goodbye to her when we finally arrived. The hunchback was in a great hurry.

Inside the clinic at Tsengel, Baddie-Guul beckoned me over to the desk and poured steaming white tea into chipped bowls. The brew was salty and burned my lips, but the liquid trickled into my cramped stomach and my fingers began to tingle.

'Do you eat horse meat?' was the only question she asked me all evening. She spoke Mongolian hesitantly, like a language rarely practised. I said of course I did, though I'd never tried it before. She served it in small chunks with rice and it tasted fine, soft and oily. These days I found it hard to believe I'd ever been a vegetarian. While we were spooning our food, locals began to arrive alone and in pairs: men in padded, black winter *deels* and stiff, brown fur hats, who pushed open the door without knocking and stared at me intently, before railing Baddie-Guul with questions in Kazakh, then leaving as abruptly as they'd entered. It was completely unnerving. Occasionally Baddie-Guul handed one of them a bowl of food, which he ate in rapid silence, placing the empty bowl on the desk to be refilled with tea and departing without a word the moment he finished. No women came.

The final visitor, a pale, broad-shouldered Kazakh smoking a cigarette rolled in a shred of newspaper, was obviously Baddie-Guul's boyfriend. He perched on one of the chairs and glared at me without speaking. His name was Maram-Khan and he didn't speak Mongolian he finally informed me – in Mongolian. 'Why don't you speak Kazak?'

I scowled as he turned his back and spoke with Baddie-Guul as tenderly as he'd just been brusque with me. Feeling weary and unwanted I rubbed my aching eyes, and remembered I still needed to go to the toilet. We left Maram-Khan eating as Baddie-Guul guided me out into the yard and round several dark corners. I smelled the toilet before we reached it, and squatted awkwardly over the hole I found with my foot, holding my breath.

*   *   *

When Maram-Khan woke us at dawn the next morning by beating on the door with what sounded like his heavy boots, the room was dark and freezing as a vault. I pulled my hat on before I sat up in the sagging bed and hoiked open the curtains to invite some light inside. Baddie-Guul had slept fully clothed in the other bed and rose the instant she opened her eyes. She smiled at me carefully, greeted Maram-Khan and knelt before the dead stove, rekindling it in moments.

When she picked up her heavy coat and made to leave with her man, I also rose, knowing I was overreacting, that I wasn't being abandoned even though this was exactly how I felt.

'Where . . . are you going?' I asked miserably.

She smiled and Maram-Khan closed the door quietly behind them.

I stood poised in the centre of the room for several minutes after they'd gone, and then laughed out loud. I had to. I had never lit a fire, chopped wood, cooked on a wood-burning stove or coped without electricity in my life. What the hell was I doing here? Pulling on my jacket and boots (I'd slept in everything else) I too abandoned the clinic.

CHAPTER TWO

Tsengel was a long and sprawling village. A few ugly, breeze block buildings stood in the central square, just down the track from the clinic, but everything else was built from wood and mud: the homes, the *hashas* (fenced yards), the trench toilets, and a series of small buildings with low, padlocked doors, which I guessed were stores and kiosks. Dirt tracks trailed through the village, coated in dust, pitted with stones and roamed by packs of rancid, limping dogs. I paused to stare at a tiny, whitewashed building set back from the houses amidst torrents of rubble, a collection of rickety antennae balancing precariously atop its roof. I read the plaque on the metal door – *shuudangiin salbar*, post office.

It was bizarre; there was no one about. But I walked on in the brilliant cold sunshine, because there was no reason to return to the lonely clinic. Dark, low-lying mountains surrounded the village on three sides, their crests smeared in snow. On the other, a wide hill displayed an outlandish-looking settlement of ornate quadrangles and white conical turrets. I wondered who on earth lived there.

I followed several gaunt cows to the edge of the river. Its waters were frozen so solid they reminded me of huge, uneven slabs of white marble. I gazed across the frozen vista. I suddenly realised I'd never seen a sky like this before: a startling, cloudless cobalt sky, which soared across the roof of this desolate valley, and gave the village a sudden, silent beauty.

People. I finally saw some villagers. Five pensioners tottered towards me, their faces creased as scrunched brown paper. We exchanged Mongol greetings.

'*Sain bainuu?*' How are you? Literally, are you good?

'*Taivan.*' Peaceful.

They smiled at me toothlessly, clasping my hands but asking no questions, and hobbled on. I walked the rest of the length of the village without seeing anyone. Every doorway was closed; there were no children playing outside. Tsengel was silent. I couldn't think where everyone in the village might be. It was all very strange.

Eventually I followed the solid river vein back to the clinic, which, I could now see, was a hideous U-shaped building with large cracked windows and a derelict courtyard strewn with rubbish and ash from the stoves. A jeep was parked outside my door. A short, slender man with the taut features of a hawk gestured to me enthusiastically.

'Ah, hello!' he said in English, then immediately reverted to Mongolian. 'How is your room? Fine? Good, good. Has the school director visited you? No? Oh, he will come soon. I am Abbai, Chairman of the Tsengel District Government.'

I smiled and held out my hand. It was Abbai who'd sent the telex offering me food and accommodation in return for teaching at the local school. It was good to meet him.

'Now . . .' Abbai ran a blackened nail down a list of words in his open notebook and switched back into painstakingly rehearsed English. 'Do you need . . . a pillow, a cushion, a maid?'

'A maid?' I wasn't expecting room service.

'Yes. Very difficult for you here,' Abbai said confidently.

I asked for the pillow but declined the cushion and maid, feeling in turn bewildered and amused by the unfolding plot of my arrival.

Abbai beckoned over a tall, bespectacled man in his fifties, still handsome in spite of a patchwork of creamy-coloured skin staining his brown face and neck. 'This is Zultan.'

'*Sain bainuu, bagsh.*' Zultan grinned as though trying to suppress raucous laughter. 'Today is *Tsagaan Sar*. Shall we go to the country-side?'

Of course. I clicked my fingers, remembering the date and why Tsengel appeared to have been evacuated. *Tsagaan Sar*, Mongol New Year – the ancient rite celebrating the gradual retreat of the five- or six-month Mongol winter, and the beginning of a fresh cycle of the seasons. The dates are dictated by the oriental lunar calendar, so they fluctuate between early and late February every year. In Ulaanbaatar *Tsagaan Sar* officially lasts just three days, but rural celebrations famously linger for several weeks. Everyone in Tsengel must be visiting friends and relatives in the mountains, consuming the traditional New Year *buuz* (steamed mutton dumplings) and *arikh* (vodka) in terrifying quantities. Most Mongol families make and freeze more than a thousand *buuz* to steam for guests throughout the celebrations. Wherever we were going now, it was to eat mutton and drink *arikh*.

An hour later I felt woozy. Four hours later I had chronic indigestion and an afternoon hangover, Abbai and Zultan were completely smashed and we were careering across the steppe en route to yet another feast.

Every settlement we visited reflected the one before it in all but the most intimate of detail. A discreet valley in the nearby mountains, where a cabin had been erected so close to the rock it might have evolved from the seam itself. Inside, there was inevitably one dim room with a low ceiling and several immaculately made beds. A cauldron of snow was melting on the stove in the centre. A scarred chest or trunk emblazoned with hand-painted, leering orange dragons, fleecy clouds and flowers with enormous pale-blue petals, squatted at the rear, beneath a frame of sombre black and white family photographs. A woman was tending the stove, always surrounded by several lean, windburned children.

Mounds of *buuz* were laid before us at every stop. The oil squirted down our chins as we ate. *Arikh* was splashed into wooden bowls inlaid with beaten silver, which were passed from host to each guest and back again using only the right hand.

Whole families of visitors arrived while we were feasting, unwrapped their winter clothes, shared the rugs or leaned against the beds, and stared at me until everyone, including me, started laughing.

'They don't know who you are, *bagsh*,' chuckled Abbai. 'Now eat – eat meat!'

We wandered from one home to the next in a cheerful, greedy New Year haze. I watched a crowd of nomads playing cards in one home, everyone shouting and bantering as they tossed down their hand, people joining in and ducking out throughout the game. It didn't seem to matter who won. It was a chaotic, noisy and disorienting first day in the mountains. I absolutely loved it.

We finally drove back to Tsengel as dusk was thickening to darkness. It was only when I waved goodbye to Abbai and Zultan that I remembered the clinic would be freezing and that even trying to light a fire was beyond me, because I was too tired and a bit drunk. Just as I was crawling into my cold blankets Baddie-Guul arrived, and I was embarrassed but relieved when she wordlessly rekindled the stove, then lay down on the other bed.

Abbai didn't return to the clinic, and the school director never appeared, but over the next few days it felt as though the rest of the village came to visit. From early morning until late at night the door of my ward would swing open, and one or two or three men or women I had never seen before would come on in, sit down and have a good look at me. Crumpled pensioners came in with their grandchildren, mothers with their daughters, small gangs of teenagers and pairs of those stern-looking, silent men. Everyone arrived with someone else. Mongol hospitality dictates that doors are never closed to guests, and that visitors are always offered tea. I drank gallons as I exchanged greetings with tens of smiling, shy people – and the odd, swaying, late-night drunk, who was harmless but had to be persuaded to go home. It was truly surreal: whole afternoons evaporated in bowls of tea and introductions. Women gazed at me, beaming and nodding, but usually saying little. The men uttered almost nothing. They all spoke Mongolian, so it wasn't a problem of language. They didn't seem wary, only bashful, and unable to resist visiting the foreign *bagsh*, but lost for words upon arrival. I constantly asked people's names, their children's names and ages, where they lived and what they did. They in turn all asked me my name and where I came from, but no one queried why I'd decided to come and live in Tsengel.

The only visitors I didn't welcome at my door were the shadows who frequently rapped on the ward window with their fists late at night, startling me out of sleep and then fleeing back down the track as I lay alone and uneasy in the dark.

During one brief afternoon respite from this onslaught of guests, I decided to visit the clinic staff, whom I'd never seen. I thought this would make my bleak ward seem less remote, and help me feel more connected to the life of the village. I circled the building twice before I found the main entrance – a mean doorway that led into a corridor black and cold as a tunnel. Inside, the air was so damp it almost dripped. I waded towards a shaft of sunlight at the far end of the tunnel, my arms outstretched, and almost trod on a fat, slithering, white cat, which hissed spitefully at me in the dark. I yelped and banged straight into a large, very dead-looking bundle laid out on a trolley. Shit – what was *that*? Fleeing down the rest of the tunnel, I swung round a sunlit corner and almost collided with two women in clean white coats, who stared at me blankly, then opened a door between them and hollered inside.

A young woman, also in a white coat, stepped outside and smiled as though she had been expecting me. 'You are the *bagsh*,' she said, in a voice as crisp as her uniform. 'I am Doctor Janner-Guul. Come in, please.' I stared at her. With her clear, pale skin and long brown plait draped over one shoulder, she looked like a classic English rose.

Inside her busy surgery the young doctor talked to me in Mongolian as she wielded a pair of pliers towards a nervous-looking teenage girl, who was sitting on a bench and clutching her mouth.

'I want to learn English. I am very happy you are here. Can I have lessons from you?'

She gestured for the teenager to remove her hand, swabbed the offending tooth, clamped the pliers on to it, and then wrenched with her entire body weight. I flinched, as did the young girl and the dozen or so other people in the surgery. But the tooth did not come out.

A man sitting behind the only desk stood up purposefully, flashed his own impressive set of heavily gold-capped front teeth, and took over the extraction. We all stared silently together like a crowd witnessing a gruesome accident, as he reinserted the pliers into the girl's reluctantly open mouth – and tore the tooth from its root. My eyes watered as blood spurted into the petri-dish. The victim actually looked relieved.

'Hello, *bagsh*,' said the man with the gold teeth. 'I am the clinic director, Algaa.'

'Will you teach me English, *bagsh*?' repeated Dr Janner-Guul. I quickly learned that she was a very tenacious woman. I said yes of course, and invited her to come over for a cup of tea whenever she liked.

An hour later she was perched in my ward, sipping tea, flicking through one of my text books and arranging her private English classes. From then on Janner-Guul would visit me two or even three times a day on her own, strolling in for tea and a chat, and tutting under her breath when anyone else arrived to distract my attention. Just once she arrived with a friend, another woman her age who smiled and frowned simultaneously, and, instead of coming inside, greeted me warily at the clinic ward door.

'I am Zulmira. I am a Kazakh teacher at the school. *Sain bainuu*?' She glanced around the room. 'Is this your home?'

I nodded unenthusiastically. The ward was damp and draughty. I was warm only when I sat within reach of the stove. The clinic was set apart from all the village cabins and, despite my constant guests, felt very isolated. After dark the hovering candlelight shadows, the faceless prowlers and leaden silence made it plain spooky. Zulmira and Janner-Guul chatted together in Kazakh for a few minutes, before the young doctor nodded, and strolled back towards her surgery. Zulmira fiddled with her hat for a moment, unable to meet my eyes.

'*Bagsh*, shall we walk together, go to the river and skate?'

I clasped Zulmira's bare hand when we first clambered down on to the ice. We didn't have skates, just our boots, but soon we were coursing together across the wide Hovd, where rare trees were embalmed to their waists, and at moments our rink was transparent enough to gaze straight down to the rocky river bed. We sped and explored across the river together, laughing out loud, and finally resting flat on our backs on the shining ice, flushed and breathless.

A small crowd of children whizzed towards us, whooping as they circled and wove around us where we lay. Zulmira leant on one elbow and finally grinned at me, through solemn, dark-blue eyes. A pelt of black hair was braided at the nape of her neck.

'I was away from here for six years,' she said, as though sharing a secret or thinking aloud. 'I was studying and teaching in our Kazakh city, Alma-Ata. I came back last year, and now we all live together – my parents and ten brothers and sisters. I'm the oldest, you know.' In spite of her lingering smile, her voice carried an undertone of bitterness or regret, I wasn't sure which.

'Are you married?' I asked without thinking. In Mongolia women usually marry young, especially in the countryside.

She shook her head. 'My friend is in Kazakhstan,' was all she ever told me.

As we skated back towards the village with our entourage, a man lounging on the ice and watching his children play greeted us with 'Happy New Year' – it was still *Tsagaan Sar*. I tried not to stare at his son, whose radiant young face had been ravaged by a ferocious cleft palate. It had left a cruel, wide-open gorge straddling his milk teeth.

Yet another guest was patiently waiting outside my door when we returned to the clinic, weary and thirsty – a young woman clad in a sheepskin jacket, who greeted us warmly. A birthmark blazed across her left cheek. Somehow it suited her. '*Sain bainuu, bagsh*, I am Gansukh,' she beamed. 'Will you visit our home now?'

Until I gratefully moved out of the clinic ward, my time in Tsengel drifted from one spontaneous visit or invitation to the next. I hosted guests, visited people whose homes I could find, and wandered around and beyond the village, hating only the concrete ward and my incompetence in fending for myself inside it.

Gansukh, her handsome, bashful husband Sansar-Huu and their two young children were the first Tuvans I met in Tsengel. Their ancestral homeland, the Republic of Tuva, borders north-western Mongolia and was originally a Mongolian province called Urianhai. When the Bolsheviks began their domination of Mongolia in 1921, they immediately claimed Urianhai as an addition to their vast Soviet empire. Five years later, in 1926, the province was renamed the Republic of Tannu Tuva, although it remained under complete Soviet jurisdiction. Tuva, which gained nominal independence in the early '90s but remains an obscure republic, is best known for an obelisk in the obscure capital, Khyzl, which is built on the geographical centre of Asia.

I spent the spring and summer living alongside Gansukh, Sansar-Huu and their Tuvan friends and relatives, and came to realise that Tuvans and Mongols have remained homogenous peoples, strongly resembling each other physically, culturally and religiously. They're both central Asian nations of traditional nomadic herders who live in *gers*, and revere Tibetan Buddhism tinged with Shamanic lore. They eat the same food, observe almost identical festivals, rituals and taboos. Only their languages are truly distinct from each other. Tuvan is a lyrical voice; Mongolian is harsher and more guttural.

The Mongol Tuvans all spoke fluent Mongolian, and could cross the border from Mongolia to Tuva whenever they desired, and for as long as they wished. But many Mongol Tuvans had never visited their motherland. They were settled, integrated and apparently happy in Mongolia, with no compelling reason to return to another home. It was their neighbours, the proud and distinct Mongol Kazakhs, who were the outsiders, the outcasts and exiles here.

CHAPTER THREE

Zulmira and Gansukh looked at me expectantly as Sansar-Huu poured more tea.

'We are your students, *bagsh*,' said Gansukh. 'We both need to study English. I know a little and Zulmira too. When can you teach us?'

I paused, a *buuz* cooling in one hand. I didn't know anything about training two local teachers. But with the school director nowhere to be seen, it seemed a good idea.

We started lessons in my ward the following afternoon, Gansukh and Zulmira skilfully deterring visitors by turning their backs and loudly asking me questions whenever we heard foot-steps treading towards the ward door. Dr Janner-Guul would listen in to part of most lessons, scribbling in her notebook and hissing questions at Zulmira before reluctantly returning to her surgery.

Baddie-Guul still appeared at my door early every morning, before either the first guests, Janner-Guul or Gansukh and Zulmira arrived. She would silently kindle the stove, haul buckets of water, brew tea – and then hover as though waiting for orders. Although I genuinely appreciated her assistance, we were both uncomfortable with this arrangement. Baddie-Guul rarely addressed me directly, and I knew she just had nothing to say to me. I suspected she was the maid Abbai had suggested. But I didn't want a servant, and anyway couldn't justify being anyone else's burden. The next morning she came, I quietly thanked her, and said I would now light my own stove and fetch my water from the river. Baddie-Guul nodded, evaporated from the ward, and I had to begin fending for myself.

After several dismal attempts at kindling the stove, which involved using every scrap of available paper and blowing on the damp sticks until I was light-headed and spluttering, I finally got it right. Once or twice I had to resort to my jacket, hat and gloves inside the ward because I also managed to put the fire out again. But Gansukh and Zulmira quickly showed me the trick of dripping candle wax on to the kindling to make it more flammable. There were scores of these subtle and quietly satisfying innovations to be learned. I also trudged outside with the two empty pails, filled them from a narrow well smashed through the river ice, and slowly slopped back home. I really had to take a bath, though the only tub in the ward was my red bucket. I did wash my hands and face every morning, but the rest of my body was going to start putrefying if I didn't scrub myself down soon.

As I ladled water into the kettle one morning, I looked around the spartan ward, and despised it. Someone had noisily yanked off the outside door handle the night before, kids were constantly taunting me, spraying pebbles at the windows, or scaling each other's shoulders to gawk through the glass. I felt like a public freak show. Waiting for Abbai or the school director to arrive was proving as futile and frustrating as trying to communicate with elusive spirits. But it was when I idly opened one of the desk drawers while waiting for the kettle to boil and found the key to the cloudy glass door at the end of my room, that I reached the point of no return. The lock was stiff, but I cranked hard, and stepped into another, smaller ward, dark and filthy as a cellar, where, in the corner, one gruesome, smeared hulk of furniture languished.

A gynaecological chair, complete with wide, stiff stirrups.

There was something about that room and that chair that reminded me of every sordid late-night thriller I'd ever seen. Zipping up my jacket I went in search of Abbai and the unseen school director. There had to be somewhere better to live in Tsengel than next door to *this*.

*   *   *

Menke glowered like a bull straining to charge. A squat, hairy man in his late forties, he ruled the Tsengel school from a dingy wooden office, heated, like the rest of the rooms in the cramped narrow building, by a tarnished stove.

'Thank you, *bagsh*, for coming to our village,' he growled, ignoring both the stream of teachers now noisily crowding inside his room to greet me, and the fact that I'd already been in town for more than a week. He explained my school teaching schedule in a barrage of rapid Mongolian. I sat and nodded passively. I would teach both the school students and the teachers. Zulmira and Gansukh would attend my English classes whenever I taught their respective Tuvan or Kazakh students. This was my first hint of the apartheid that divided Tsengel. The Tuvan and Kazakh pupils were taught separately – and the few ethnic Mongol students at the school inevitably studied with the Tuvans.

'Erm, Menke *bagsh*, is there another room, or maybe a *ger* I could live in?' I asked when he had finished, and told him of the cold and the late night intruders.

Menke paused for a moment, then shrugged. 'I don't know. We have no rooms.'

For a moment we looked straight at each other, then I nodded, lips pursed, quietly dismayed.

'*Bagsh*, Menke *bagsh*.' Gansukh spoke up from the doorway, where half a dozen teachers were still hovering and talking amongst themselves. 'Maybe Louisa *bagsh* could live in my *hasha*, in our *ger*?'

Four or five days later I moved into a *ger* in the corner of Gansukh's *hasha*, her yard. A whole troupe of village men had converged at the ward without warning while I was drinking tea with Dr Janner-Guul, bundled my possessions and almost every piece of furniture (including the stove) into an open truck, rumbled over to Gansukh's home and deposited the whole lot, including me, next to the newly erected *ger*. Then they all left as swiftly as they had arrived. I'd never moved house so fast in my life.

A Mongol *ger* looks like a small version of a circus big top. The wall is made of four or five sections of crisscross latticed wood that are bound together with rope. These sections are collapsible, and can be easily strapped on to the back of a camel when the nomads move on.

The *ger* roof consists of forty or so poles, each about six feet long. The bottom of each pole fits into one of the lattice V crosspieces, while the top slots into a wooden crown that supports the poles and raises the roof height. Once the wooden frame is in place, felt is wrapped round the inside and the outside of the *ger*, before the white canvas sheath is fitted over the top and secured with canvas strips like long apron strings.

Gansukh and I spent the afternoon arranging the *ger* into my new home. I watched her bind the bed legs tightly to the latticed walls, as though they might otherwise escape while I was sleeping.

'We always do this,' she said, smiling at my intrigue. 'It helps the walls not to fall down when there is a strong storm. It stops the *ger* from . . .' She mimed some sort of implosion. I raised my eyebrows as her young son and daughter, Yalta and Opia, gazed at me without blinking and fumbled for their mother without turning their heads away from this strange new guest.

When Gansukh and the children crossed the yard back to their cabin at dusk, I lay down on my shackled bed and heaved a huge, glad sigh of relief. I was delighted to be away from the clinic and finally in the realm of the village. Now there were families next door and around me, children and animals in the street outside: the noise was a quiet buzz of reassurance. I liked Gansukh, her husband Sansar-Huu and their shy toddlers. The *ger* itself was a domed capsule of privacy, the felt walls thick and comforting. No one could see what I was doing inside or who I was with. The only window into my new shell was a wide slit in the canvas roof, which acted as a skylight and revealed a bold sliver of the blue universe above. Sansar-Huu had already offered to suspend a light bulb through the skylight, and connect the wire to the frayed cable dangling just outside the yard. Tsengel was connected by a host of these inert cables, which looped around and across the village like slack washing lines.

But we never bothered with the bulb and it would have been

a wasted task. There was no electricity in the village for the next nine months anyway.

With my housing resolved and school lessons due to begin in another week, I wandered around and beyond Tsengel every afternoon, exploring the village and its frontiers.

To the north the mountains were steepest and darkest, and the Hovd at its widest, sprinkled with minute islands afloat the impenetrable ice. A track followed the course of the river and then rose high above the banks, meandering into the wilderness beyond, where I could still glimpse occasional cabins and herds. The nomads wouldn't be moving into their *gers* until the summer.

The only people I ever met on these slow rambles were young boys herding goats, a nomad or two cantering by, clad in a rumpled *deel*, and once, an ancient, shrivelled woman perched on a hillock and peering through a monocle.

'I can't find my camels,' she told me earnestly, her milky cataract eyes seeming blind to my being a *gadaad-neen hun*, an outsider. 'Here. You look. Can you see them?'

We searched and found them together, and she teetered off on half-crippled legs to claim her beasts.

I stood in her place on the hillock and spun round slowly. In the other direction, beyond the village to the south, the Hovd entered a wide gorge, its walls gradually rising into crusted towers of fierce black rock daubed with snow, beckoning towards even lonelier and more barren land.

I am a city girl at heart. I like good food, noise and distractions. Constant hot water and bright lights. I've always hated drudgery and manual work, getting caked in dirt or sweat. I already despised hauling my pails of water every day, and my fingers were sore, constantly ingrained with tiny, evil splinters from the wood Gansukh had taught me to split.

But I was already in the thrall of this village and these wild, dark mountains.

CHAPTER FOUR

Dr Janner-Guul became a frequent visitor to my *ger*. I privately nicknamed her Princess. She was a very regal young woman, invariably robed either in her scrubbed white clinic coat, or a smart brown *deel* and a sleek fur hat. Princess had just finished studying at the Olgii city hospital, and now had to spend three years practising in Tsengel to complete her training. She was from Olgii and hated living in the village. She frequently told me that, more than anything, she wanted to be back in the city with her friends and family, dancing in the Friday night disco and living in a house with a TV and part-time electricity.

'This place is horrible,' she would state, dramatically sweeping her hand in front of her, as though gesturing to a silent crowd. 'There is nothing here. No electricity, no market. Nothing to do. I have no friends except Zulmira.'

I never met anyone who hated Tsengel like Princess. Throughout my time in the village people gradually opened up to me about how difficult life was, but surprisingly few said they actually wanted to leave Mongolia's furthest west village, and none with her royal vehemence.

She would stride into my *ger* any time during the day. 'Can I have an English lesson *now, bagsh*?' she would demand, opening her notebook regardless of what I was doing. She was an amazingly quick learner – having already spent a year in Kazakhstan, where she had gleaned a little English – and always asked me to give her homework, although she never did it. She would also arrange lessons with me in advance, which was fine, except that she rarely turned up when she said she would. 'I was busy working. I was in the countryside, *bagsh*,' she would tut if I asked her why she hadn't arrived two days earlier. I would occasionally tell Princess off, though I quite liked her cheek, and I felt for her. After all, I had chosen to move into the village, but she was stranded here for far longer than I would ever stay. Three years in Tsengel could have the bearing of a life time in purgatory, if you'd never wanted to be here in the first place.

When I did bemoan the fact that she frequently kept me waiting, was unreliable, and that I did actually have other things to do, Princess knew exactly how to placate me.

'Do you want to go to the countryside?' she asked, almost triumphantly, knowing that of course I did. 'When someone in the mountains is very sick, a *malchin* [herder] rides here on his horse to tell us. Then our jeep has to go to bring them back to our clinic. We can take you with us. I will tell the driver.'

I smiled at Her Highness, knowing whoever he was, the driver would undoubtedly carry out her orders.

Princess rushed into my *ger* one morning, while I was scribbling about her in my journal.

'Quickly, Louisa,' she commanded, poised in front of my desk like a monarch before her scribe, 'we're going to the mountains to collect my grandfather, who is very sick. His heart. We will come back tonight, I think, but it's very far away so we must go Now. *Yavi?* Are you coming?'

'Yes, I am!' I closed my journal and reached for my jacket and gloves. This was too much of an adventure to miss, and I was only taking one class at school that day. Gansukh nodded casually when I shamelessly suggested I could teach it the next morning. I bundled up and clambered into the jeep, squeezing in next to an ancient Kazakh clad in a thick *deel* and a gorgeous, floppy, red felt hat lined with fur.

I assumed we would immediately tear off across the steppe to rescue the patient, but instead we sat in the jeep outside Gansukh's *hasha* for an hour or so, waiting for two more passengers who both eventually scrambled aboard: a sickly looking young woman with a large bundle in her arms, and a young man whose upper front teeth had been heavily gold capped just like Algaa's at the clinic. Here it seemed even emergencies had to wait their turn.

The doors were finally slammed and the jeep accelerated straight out of the village and on to the frozen Hovd.

'Are we really going to drive on the river?' I fretted, clutching at the front seat as we roared upstream, as though this would somehow prevent the vehicle from plunging through the ice. Everyone guffawed with laughter.

'This is the winter road, Louisa *bagsh*!' grinned the driver, Jarkan, a convivial, chain-smoking Kazakh with a constant, winsome smile. 'In your country, there is black road; here we have our ice!' I found myself chuckling too.

The crumpled Kazakh sitting beside me was so old his face was almost concave. His withered insides began to produce the most amazing noises, like a decrepit engine fighting for its life. I winced each time he emitted another belch. The pale young woman was rocking her bundle, which I eventually realised was a baby when it gurgled, although it was so thickly swaddled I couldn't actually see any skin. The snow thickened as we drove and skidded into the river gorge: its dark snow-splattered walls rising on both sides, and the gorge narrowing as we sped upriver. I felt as though I was being spun into a new dimension: a portal of ice and rock, with a sky above us that was so rich it was almost indigo.

Princess pointed out *ails* (settlements) in narrow valleys, which had splintered off from the gorge like branches from an artery. Occasional cabins were poised on natural ledges way above us, and tiny specks of black were scaling the almost vertical walls in search of exposed grazing. Life was raw here, the terrain unyielding.

'Many people and animals die here at the end of winter,' Princess told me calmly over her shoulder. 'The winter is too long. My grandfather is very ill now.'

But despite our waiting invalid we paused at several settlements en route. The jeep lurched up from the Hovd and through a white ravine, disturbing a herd of camels grazing nonchalantly amidst the snow drifts, a sight that made me smile and shake my head. Jarkan braked in front of a low wooden cabin backing on to sheer rock, where a big ugly dog was baring its broken teeth in front of the door. A nomad restrained his baying hound as we quickly entered. We all crouched near the stove on tiny, hand-made stools, and drank tea and chewed on deep-fried sticks of dough called *buurtzug*. The nomads and I stared at each other, smiling and saying hello while Princess was examining a pallid-looking patient. I was quietly amazed that all the men seemed robust and healthy, with tanned necks, and cheeks the colour of sandstone.

'Our winter is very difficult,' one or two of them told me almost cheerfully. 'When the snow is very deep only our horses can climb up here. It is very dangerous for the *mal* [livestock].'

This interminable struggle to survive and raise a family amidst windswept, snowbound rock was taking a heavy toll on their women and children. One young mother, who I instinctively knew was no older than me, looked particularly dry and haggard, surrounded by half a dozen babies and infants. Her splayed fingers, which cupped her bowl of tea, were embedded with bruised, rotten-looking nails. Rocking on the ball of her heels, she didn't even raise her head when one of her infants howled as Princess placed her cold stethoscope on his scrawny ashen chest. My elation shrivelled as the boy rasped while inhaling. His chest was rattling like coins in a tin. Princess turned to his father and quietly shook her head. This kid was going to die.

When we lurched back down on to the frozen Hovd I relaxed in my seat, finally convinced that our bypass *was* solid and safe. Sadly this was more than could be said for my unhealthy back seat companions. The elderly Kazakh was now hawking into a spittoon discreetly placed between his thin legs. I tried to distract myself from his flying gobs of drool, but then the mother beside him began to throw up silently into an empty jar and we had to stop. When she got back in she carried on gently vomiting, passing her sleeping baby to the young man with the gold teeth, and refilling the jar again and again. I have never seen anyone puke so much. Each time the jar was full we paused while she emptied it into the snow at the river's edge.

I had no idea how long we'd been travelling when we finally swung off the Hovd and into a huge white valley. It looked gorgeous – untrodden and chaste. There were no tyre or animal tracks, no footprints, cabins or *gers* to be seen. We drove straight into a snow-drift. Gold Teeth placidly unearthed a shovel from under the back seat, Jarkan one from under the front, and they started to dig. We slowly baled ourselves out of this valley – and straight into another, with thicker snow and taller peaks.

Princess and I perched on the frozen drifts as the men toiled, and gossiped in our dialect of Mongolian and a few words of English. She immediately asked me about my boyfriend, which was a more complicated question than she probably thought as I had left them both in Ulaanbaatar. So I gave her a simple, evasive answer – 'He's in England.'

Her fiancé was studying in Turkey for the next three years. 'So I have to stay here before he comes home and we can marry, and then I can go back to the city with him,' she said, raising her eyes mockingly into the cobalt heavens.

As we took our turn with the shovels, a procession of camels began to glide into the valley. They waded towards us, swaying gently, each beast tethered to the one in front by a leather thong threaded through a pierced nose peg, all of them burdened with a section of a nomad's *ger*: blood-red poles, the trellis walls, long, fat rolls of felt with the blue *ger* door strapped on top. I floun-dered over towards them, thrilled by the contradiction of this train loping not through a desert, but a snowscape. The young herder leading the cavalcade on horseback shrilled with laughter when he saw me.

'Photo! Photo!' he hollered. In my experience most Mongols love having their photographs taken, and will demand that you snap them, even if it's virtually impossible to send them a copy. In three years I never met a camera-shy Mongol. I took several pictures of his smooth flushed face, and of his first camel, which was carrying three young calves swaddled amongst its cargo.

'The little animals cannot walk because the snow is too deep,' explained Princess. 'His family is moving to a new valley. Here there is too much snow. He says the *mal* are dying.'

Princess talked about death with the apparent ease of someone who had witnessed, studied, poked and dissected corpses. I found her tone unnerving. Her familiarity with mortality was intimate – she seemed to think of death not simply as an adversary to be conquered, but as a keen and potent presence with whom she lived.

Was this how the nomads survived here, in the thrall of death? A battle that lasted as long as each of them, pitched against the bitter elements, the land and rock? I stood there wondering if you *could* spend your whole life in combat against death. Surely the battle itself would erode and wear you down, leaving you weak, sullen and vulnerable? There would have to be a ceasefire, a truce sometimes, just so you could relax your vigilance and reclaim the pleasure of living for its own sake. But if you allowed yourself, and your family, to be careless or nonchalant here, even for a while, would that be your nemesis?

I'd never once thought of death, or even life, in these terms. This extraordinary landscape and its people were leading me towards awkward and passionate questions that had never occurred to me before.

An early extract of my Tsengel journal, written just after this trip, bears the heavily underscored words:

Don't be sentimental. It's not what I expected – there's no romance here. I've never seen people struggle so much just to survive. It *can't* be like this all year – the mountain women blank and jaded, the animals emaciated, the kids sick and stunted. Life must get easier.

In retrospect, it read like a plea.

We waved goodbye to the young nomad, watching as the procession coiled across the valley towards the western frontier mountains. Jarkan and Gold Teeth were still digging.

'Are you OK, Louisa?' asked Princess suddenly. 'Is this very difficult for you? We've still got a long way to go. I think maybe we will have to stay in the mountains tonight.'

'No!' I told her. 'No, don't worry. I'm very happy.' And I really meant it.

We eventually arrived at a lone cabin somewhere in the valley, where the young mother, her baby and the belching Kazakh disembarked. Gold Teeth stayed with us. This snowbound cabin was the loneliest home I'd ever seen.

'Do they live here?' I asked Princess, gesturing to our companions as a headscarved woman and three children appeared at the door.

Princess shook her glossy head. 'No. They are taking their horses from here. They will ride,' she pointed into the white mountains, 'maybe six hours that way to their home. She was sick in the jeep because she's pregnant again.'

The wind began to thrash against the jeep, which groaned to the lip of the valley. Beyond us a series of wild, boulder-strewn hills were smeared in shallow snow and driving got easier. We rumbled downwards, dodging the boulders and the odd herd of ragged sheep and goats. I inhaled loudly as an immense lake of opaque ice rose into view, backed by barbed white peaks and pine forest dark as bitter chocolate. If landscapes were music this would have been a drum roll. I had no idea where on earth we were, and when I asked Princess she said just one word, 'Tsergal,' which left me none the wiser.

There was no track or trail ahead, but Jarkan obviously knew where he was going. The land was now suddenly pitted with a series of huge, snow-filled hollows, as though dinosaurs or some other primeval monsters had lain gargantuan eggs that had compressed the frozen ground before hatching. Nomads had erected their *gers* in these indentations to protect themselves and their animals from the gale that screamed around and across us now, rocking the jeep.

We stopped a raw-faced child to ask for directions, then drove on. It was getting very cold in the jeep and my feet were numb. Suddenly Jarkan tipped us over the edge and into one of the hollows, where a tall Kazakh *ger* flapped in the freezing wind. It was like sliding into a bowl of icing.

Princess's grandfather lay on a metal cot, a black and white skullcap glued to his head, and a tapered metal pipe clasped between thick, gnarled fingers. His family stared at me, bewildered. Princess explained who I was, and I practised my Kazakh, which didn't take long because I only knew how to say hello and how are you.

A headscarved woman brewed tea on the stove, which was a tarnished oil drum. She served it brown and stewed, laden with salt. Despite the bitter cold and the onslaught battering the felt walls, the *ger* floor was only half covered: the entire front portion was frozen brown earth. But a wide ream of crimson cloth embroidered with gold thread had been woven around the high ceiling, lending a fantastic slash of imperialism to this crude, half-furnished home.

Grandfather spoke slowly, in a voice as cracked as his fingers and face. His legs were bound in thick, black jodhpurs, and he moved so stiffly I expected him to creak. Everyone was speaking in Kazakh, which still sounded garbled to me. I shrank inside myself: I had no points of reference here and felt as though I was crouched at the edge of the world.

Princess rose to her feet. '*Yavi.*' Let's go.

'Where?'

'To another *ail* for food.'

'Is it near?' I feared another epic journey.

She smiled. 'It's OK – you can ride a horse.'

Everyone but Grandfather crowded out of the *ger* to watch me mount a horse the colour of the tea we'd just drunk. Leaving Jarkan and Gold Teeth behind, Princess and I clambered to the rim of the icing bowl just as the sun was falling into the lake far below us. I gasped.

The mountains ahead looked as though they were on fire, consumed in flames of violet, orange and scarlet. The sky above them was a riot of dark, dark blue, purple, yellow and saffron, colours of wild laughter. The lake itself was molten silver, and in the far distance, God only knows where, a lone pyramid of rock or ice glowed translucent pink like an immense suspended crystal. Elemental fireworks. At that moment it was as though Princess and I were the only people in this world: everyone else had vanished while the earth and skies were ablaze.

There was no sound. Nothing.

It was like looking at the earth for the very first time.

Moments or minutes later the flames began to subside and merge into the darkness. Princess called to me and I rode on, knowing I'd never see a sunset quite like that again in my life.

In a cabin sheltering behind overhanging rocks our dinner hosts were a young Kazakh couple, Toktalbek and Kamar, who were playful and even affectionate together. He looked like a herder should – ruddy in the face, stocky and strong. His wife was elegant and smiling. They looked good together – and very happy. They were the first couple I'd seen actually touch each other since I'd arrived in Bayan-Olgii. Mongols, Tuvans and Kazakhs are not very tactile people. We sat in a circle on the felt rugs with several other visitors, and blessed our meat by raising our hands, palms inwards, to eye level, then slowly lowering them over our faces and murmuring, 'Allah.' I copied everyone else. The cabin was cosy, much warmer than the draughty *ger*. Its walls were festooned with joints of drying meat, and several early lambs bleated from their pen in the corner. Princess was relaxed and chatting. She looked tired but surprisingly happy.

'This is my brother,' she told me, nodding to Toktalbek. He gave me a wide grin and immediately asked if we had *malchin* (herders) in my country. Mongol *malchin* live nomadically, packing up their *gers* and driving their herds to fresh pasture five or six times a year. Their lives are dictated by the seasons, and extended families often live together in order to manage the livestock between them. Satisfied by my answer that, yes, we do have some herders left in Britain, though they're not nomads, he turned back to his sister. During my first couple of months in Tsengel this happened frequently. People wanted to know certain information about me and my world, they asked their questions, and then that was usually it. It took me quite a while to gauge how to talk to locals with whom I shared almost no mutual experiences, to learn how to banter and chat easily with them. When I finally cracked it, this made all the difference in the world to my life in the village. But I can still vividly remember sitting in that cabin reeling from the utter foreignness of my surroundings. I had spent two years doggedly learning Mongolian because I wanted to be able to talk to the Mongols in their own language, but these people were Kazakh. I couldn't share more than a word with them.

When, a while later, another woman entered the cabin, I was still sitting alone in a roomful of people talking to each other.

This new woman was older, middle aged, and looked very weary. Her black hair was heavily streaked with white, which was unusual for a woman here who looked as though she was only in her forties. She beamed at me and fired questions at Princess. She sat down in front of me, and via Princess, asked me to speak, so she could hear the sound of my voice. Then she wanted me to sing. Feeling embarrassed, I cleared my throat and half-heartedly crooned 'Yesterday'. Everyone clapped and laughed casually. Afterwards she and I looked each other in the face, smiling and shrugging at our mutual fascination and lack of common words.

I wanted to thank her, because I suddenly felt fine again. It doesn't take much – just a glint of inclusion or a little attention – to make you feel as though you could eventually belong anywhere. If we'd spoken the same language I bet she and I would have sat and talked together all night.

Toktalbek unhitched a *dombra*, a Kazakh guitar, from the wall, and its elegiac tone echoed round the cabin as he sang about something sad and precious.

'We had a foreign visitor here once,' Kamar told me in slow, clipped Mongolian.

'Really?' I felt disappointed. Of course, I'd hoped I was the first.

'Yes. A man from Holland on a bicycle. Three years ago.'

I wondered where on earth he'd been going, but she didn't know.

My new friend, whose name was Ak Butta (which I later learned means White Camel), invited us all to the cabin next door, where we consumed another pot of boiled mutton and bowls of liver-coloured tea. My stomach began to churn. It felt late and was bitingly cold outside when Princess and I finally stumbled and shivered our way back down to the icing bowl under a star-soaked sky. A radio was crackling inside Grandfather's *ger*, and a steaming sheep was being heaved on to a platter for our third supper. I picked at the grey flesh, feeling steadily more queasy, and lumbered outside to pee and groan next to several camels kneeling in the snow.

Ten of us slept in the *ger* together, buried under thick *deels* and sheets of felt. I was given one of the three narrow beds, and lay on my back watching shadows tremble on the faded wall hangings. I tried to ignore my aching acid stomach and drifted through the events of the day one more time, as the stove cooled and the *ger* walls shuddered as though they too were breathing.

When I awoke at first light, a fire had already been rekindled – and I felt absolutely wretched. At breakfast I begged for boiling water instead of tea.

'No, no.' Jarkan shook his head, beaming broadly. 'Drink tea and eat meat, *bagsh*. That is what you need!' The remains of the sheep were served up cold for breakfast. I staggered outside and threw up in front of the camels.

We left the *ger* mid-morning, with Grandfather in tow. He was so frail Jarkan practically carried him to the front seat of the jeep. My stomach was curdling as we lurched out of the icing bowl and back towards the barren hills. Jarkan suddenly accelerated, flinging the jeep and all of us forward as Gold Teeth grabbed a rifle from underneath the seat and unwound the back window.

'*Kasgur*! *Kasgur*!' Everyone was shouting, Grandfather suddenly upright in his seat. I held my breath as the jeep swerved insanely and Gold Teeth aimed the barrel at a shadow streaking ahead of us. But four wheels were no match for this prey, which melted into the rock and snow like an apparition. Gold Teeth lowered the rifle as we braked in front of another cabin.

'What was it, what was it?' I pestered Princess as we crowded inside.

'A wolf. They are taking the *mal*, so we want to kill them.'

'Are there many wolves here?'

'Yes – and now they are so hungry they come very near the *ails*.' She looked at me sternly. 'You do not know the countryside, Louisa – it is very dangerous. Now, at the end of winter, is the most difficult time. All the people and animals are weak and hungry. *Muukhai* – it's terrible.'

When we crouched inside the cabin I rudely refused tea, and asked instead for hot water, because I thought I was about to throw up again. Princess handed me a bowl of frothing camel's milk, which is scarce in winter because milk yields are very low. The generosity was wasted. Two minutes later, I was outside the door, heaving in the brilliant sunshine. A young girl in a dark-blue *deel* watched with utter fascination as I retched myself dry, and then silently handed me a kettle of warm water to rinse my hands and mouth. After that I felt almost fine. God, it'll take some time, I thought, as I dried my hands and face on a clean rag, but me and my guts will have to get used to this.

We took a different route home, speeding to the centre of the marbled Tsergal lake so Jarkan and Gold Teeth could go fishing. While they were baiting at the edge of wells somehow forged by previous anglers, Grandfather struggled from his seat clutching his prayer mat, knelt arthritically towards Mecca and worshipped Allah on the ice. When he had finished, he hailed Jarkan in a surprisingly loud bellow, which Princess, giggling coquettishly, translated for me.

'Ey! You two boys! I am a sick old man! I need to go to hospital. Come here! I don't need fish – I don't even like fish! Do you want me to freeze to death before we get to the clinic?' Good for him.

It took all day to get back to the village, because we stopped on the way to collect various adults, children, and a very agitated goat, which was casually slung in the back and howled constantly in dismay.

By the time we had swung back on to the Hovd there were

eleven people in the jeep, including two young boys squashed in the boot with the goat. Every journey I made into the mountains evolved like this: drive, *ger*, tea, drive, *ger*, meat, tea, drive . . . my internal clock took months to adjust to Tsengel's rhythm.

We accelerated down the Hovd at dusk, shadows rising up the river gorge walls like an incoming tide. Tsengel straggled into view, looking oddly familiar now.

When Jarkan finally dropped me off in front of Gansukh's *hasha* I thanked him and Princess warmly. Courteous to a fault, he thrust half a dozen limp fish into my hands. I dragged myself heavily towards my *ger*, wanting nothing more than my sagging cot, sleeping bag and pile of blankets. I was exhausted. Unlacing my boots I suddenly clapped my hand over my face, remembering my students, who'd now been waiting for me for two days.

'Louisa *bagsh*,' I berated myself out loud, 'you've only just got here, for God's sake. You'll have to make it up to them, and stop skiving.'

PART TWO

Hearing Birds Fly

CHAPTER FIVE

Spring is the most fickle season of the year in Mongolia.

The villagers didn't like it. They said you couldn't trust this weather, that it was 'as unpredictable as the moods of women'. Sansar-Huu and his friends joked about this ancient metaphor, but the climate was grim. Winds blasted, snow flurried, and the sun struggled to pierce the ice. From every visible angle, Tsengel looked pale and desiccated, as though it had been stripped of all excess and whittled down to its essence like the core of a fruit. Nothing was growing, and the soil looked like frozen sand. Winter had drained the blood even out of the stones. The temperature was low but some mornings it hovered flirtatiously, and then Sansar-Huu assured me that warmer weather, the thawing of the glacial Hovd, and maybe even rain would soon be on their way.

I was standing on the river, searching for water. Since moving into Gansukh's *hasha* I'd found several winter wells smashed through the thick ice, but though the sun was shining now, the previous night and this particular morning were bitterly, bitterly cold, and the nearby wells had all resealed. Squinting across the bright ice, I spied a young boy with an axe, patiently chipping away at a depression in the centre of the river, and skated over to join him.

'I also need water,' I told him, and he nodded, his small hands clasped around the axe handle. He didn't look startled, just preoccupied. After these first few weeks, people were starting to get used to me being here. It was a relief not to be stared at all the time.

The boy and I knelt down together on the Hovd and dug our own well: hacking through the ice and slowly scooping out slush with our ladles, taking it in turns to rest and warm our freezing wet hands with our gloves. Eventually we had to tilt ourselves right over the hole just so we could carry on. The slush froze to the scoop of the ladle, my trousers froze to my knees and the wind howled over us. My God it was grim. It was too cold to speak, too cold even to think. My fingers were solid and stiff as metal when water finally bubbled up into the basin of our well.

'*Sain bain*!' we exclaimed together, smiling numbly up at each other. Good!

We slowly filled the four pails and trudged off to our own *hashas*. I didn't spill a drop on the way home. I couldn't believe it had taken me so long just to fetch two buckets of water, and now I had to get ready for school. Inside my *ger* I realised my face was flushed but my body was shivering. I stripped off the wet clothes, shoved fistfuls of kindling into the stove, and wondered once again where on earth Gansukh and Sansar-Huu fetched their water. I'd never seen either of them at the river. That afternoon, after school, I finally asked them.

Sansar-Huu shrugged. There were several brimming pails in the corner of their cabin. 'We go to the well round the corner. Why? Do you need water?'

I closed my eyes, shook my head and tried to laugh it off. I was learning a whole new way of living here, and had to ask for advice and directions just to finish the simplest tasks. Sometimes it felt like I just couldn't do anything for myself.

'I will take you there now,' he said. 'We also need some more water.'

Sansar-Huu knew I floundered sometimes, and he offered the kind of help that meant I could usually fend for myself afterwards. He escorted me to a *hasha* two dirt tracks behind ours, where a communal well had been drilled into the stony brown ground. There was a heavy wooden lid over the top, and a truck tyre, inner tube bucket dangling down the shaft. (I couldn't help thinking it looked like an industrial sized condom.) The coarse rope was frozen and had to be hauled up hand over hand, burning my fingers even through my gloves. But, as Sansar-Huu wryly commented when I winced, 'It's easier than going to the river, *bagsh*.'

We were all getting used to each other now, Sansar-Huu, Gansukh, the children and I. For the first week or so after I'd moved in, it had, understandably, been a little awkward: we three adults had all self-consciously been on our best behaviour, using the polite '*ta*' (you) to address each other, instead of the informal '*chi*' that was now gradually slipping into our conversations. At first young Opia and Yalta were fascinated but rather scared of me, and wouldn't venture into my *ger* on their own. But soon Yalta boldly brought his little sister in to visit me, and to rummage through the plastic bag I used as a rubbish bin. He was a quiet and serious little boy, but I remember he used to cheer gleefully to himself if he found any empty tins, which he instantly hid inside his jacket and coveted as toys. Once she overcame her shyness, I realised little Opia was actually a fearless toddler, who got up to all sorts of mischief. She laughed and howled with equal passion, and soon I affectionately nicknamed her 'Hooligan'. It stuck.

Gansukh and I were also beginning to spend time together. She observed as many of my classes as she could, we strolled to and from school, and had our own daily English lessons, which Zulmira had suddenly stopped attending. She wouldn't visit the *hasha* or my *ger*, and seemed to be avoiding me – I had no idea why. I couldn't fathom Zulmira at all. When I did see her she either looked at the ground or over my shoulder. She never caught my eye. I didn't quite have the confidence to ask her if anything was wrong – there was anger smouldering beneath her avoidance, a bit like one of those supposedly dormant volcanoes that suddenly erupt, wreaking total chaos and sending everyone fleeing for their lives. I was at a bit of a loss with Zulmira, so I took the coward's way out, and was polite but also distant towards her, and instead concentrated on my friendship with Gansukh.

During the long dark evenings Gansukh often came to see me when the kids were asleep, or invited me over to their cabin for a candlelit mutton supper. We sat and ate, then drank bowls and bowls of tea in the warm shadows of their home. Sometimes we stayed up and talked till late as the candle melted the evening away, or Gansukh strummed her guitar, and crooned lilting old Mongol songs while the children breathed steadily. Sansar-Huu and I watched her and dreamed.

I always enjoyed watching Gansukh and Sansar-Huu together because they obviously adored each other. Their mutual desire was displayed in subtle gestures and light-hearted banter: an interlocking of the eyes that lasted all of two or three seconds, a brief smirk in response to a private joke, an occasional playful spank across the shoulder, constant small efforts to make each other's lives easier. They continually welcomed me into their home, and I never felt uncomfortable or excluded. Actually, they rarely touched each other in front of me, or, I guess, anyone else. Mongolia's wild landscape sustains a surprisingly conservative population. Men and women have their staunch hunter-gatherer roles, and rarely seem to deviate from what is expected of them, from the rules laid down even before they were born. I never saw a couple holding hands, linking arms, even kissing each other hello or goodbye on the cheek. In fact, unless they were actually parting for a long time, they didn't even say goodbye, just silently walked away from each other, often without a glance. The word *bayartai*, meaning 'goodbye', is only uttered when someone isn't coming back.

Gansukh and Sansar-Huu were both from Tsengel. Gansukh's parents lived just down the street, while Sansar-Huu's family were nomads out in the cold mountains. They knew each other as children because Sansar-Huu boarded at the village school, but got together while they were both studying at university in the Tuvan capital, Khyzl. As soon as they graduated, they got married.

'We wanted to stay in Tuva,' Sansar-Huu told me, 'but I am the only son in my family, you know, and my parents are getting older. We came back so that I could help them with the *mal.*'

Nowadays he was a part-time herder and house-husband, and often stayed at home with the kids during the day while Gansukh was out at work. They took turns with the housework and cooking, or did it together, which was fairly unusual for a couple anywhere in Mongolia. Here in the village, where only men drove jeeps, built cabins or herded livestock, and only women looked after the kids, cleaned the house, scrubbed the clothes and cooked, their teamwork was a local act of rebellion.

'Our Mongol food is not so good, very few vitamins,' tutted Gansukh as we were polishing off a pot of *tsoivan*, meat and flour noodles, in their cabin one evening. 'We have no vegetables, and now even the winter *makh* [meat] has all finished, and we've got to eat this dry *makh*. You must boil it for one hour even before cooking. Look!' She reached over and showed me what looked like large tufts of grey felt hanging by thick snagged threads to a bleached bone. I nodded in a noncommittal sort of way, and felt mightily glad I hadn't seen it before we ate. 'Two or three years we can keep this, Louisa, because it's hard, tough meat. And there is only black tea now,' she added, wearily. 'The children need milk. But Sansar-Huu is going away to help his parents with the *mal* again. He will be in the countryside for weeks, and when he comes back to visit us he'll bring milk and yoghurt, and then we won't have to drink black tea any more.'

The Mongols cherish their milky tea, but there was hardly any local milk at the moment. The livestock had dried up like the land.

'When are you going?' I asked him.

'Oh, tomorrow or the day after. Very soon.' He smiled at his wife, then looked directly at me, frowning. 'Many men are going away, so it is good to have two women together in the *hasha* . . . you two can help each other while I'm gone. In the countryside our *mal* are struggling because there's too much snow in the mountains. They have nothing to eat. We will have to move them and try to find pasture where they can feed, and then maybe I can bring home fresh meat and dairy to eat.'

I tried to be polite about the local cuisine, and deliberately kept my opinions to myself. But the villagers happily told me what they thought – 'Our food is *muu* [bad]' – and I silently, wholeheartedly agreed. The food in Tsengel was dire. Meals were bland, seasoned only with salt, and, worst of all, were utterly, relentlessly monotonous. Grey mutton was boiled up with extra chunks of pure white fat (to keep you warm through winter), and terminally served with rice or flour noodles day after day after day after day for ever. There was, it must be added, a respite in summer to look forward to, when milk would be simmered, fermented, curdled and clotted into every dairy food possible. But even then, I knew from past experience that Mongol herders stoically chewed on meat and bones every evening, and dosed their milky tea with salt and a little glistening fat. For a change of diet they ate goat or sometimes beef instead.

Knowing there would be little chance of buying any provisions once I was here, I'd dragged a hefty load of supplies to Tsengel with me. My *ger* cupboard was stocked with diminishing packets of Russian coffee, eastern European pasta and Chinese tomato paste, bulbs of shrivelled garlic, tins of German fish, bottled Bulgarian salad and packets of Czech soup. A barrage of cheap imports. Mongolia produces meat, flour and dairy, but very little else, and that, in essence, is why rural Mongols eat a mere handful of ingredients for most of their lives. The climate, especially here in the arid, semi-desert steppe of the extreme west, is hostile to crops, and the growing season notoriously brief. Since the communist regime collapsed in 1990, even the collective flour mills have been neglected, and, exacerbated by the misfortune of several poor harvests, domestic grain production has almost halved. The sacks of flour and rice in Gansukh's cabin bore the trademark characters of Chinese goods. The pasta, paste and tinned fish in my cupboard were luxuries that had never reached the kiosks of Tsengel. They could only be found in the city.

This, of course, made them all the more precious to me, as they were literally irreplaceable. But I was also quietly ashamed of my stockpile and guiltily hoarded it in the back of the cupboard. I was happy to share my Ulaanbaatar bounty with anyone who visited while I was cooking, and I sometimes made dinner for Gansukh and the family. But I quietly dreaded people witnessing this unprecedented food stash, because, in the face of this leaden local diet, just having the option of local meat or tinned fish, pasta or rice made me feel guilty of the crime of privilege.

My agreement with the local school was that I taught the pupils in exchange for somewhere to live, plus wood and the food staples. There was no cash transaction involved, which made it all very simple. Whenever I saw the school director, Menke, he scowled his greeting even when he smiled. '*Sain bainuu*, Louisa *bagsh*. Do you need anything? *Makh*? Flour? If you do, go to the kitchen and tell them. They have everything.'

I would nod and thank him as I headed off to my next lesson. I still wasn't sure where the entrance to the school kitchen was, but Menke intimidated me, and I never felt very comfortable asking him for or about anything. I'd have to find it myself.

Tsengel was a labyrinth of unmarked closed doors that had to be swung or dragged open, revealing maybe a cramped classroom with low narrow desks and rattling windows taped to the panes, a tiny spartan shop where locals lingered over a roughly hewn counter but rarely seemed to buy anything, a draughty coal cellar, or the steaming sauna of the school kitchen – the warmest room in the whole village.

The kitchen was ruled by three headscarved women: Gerel-Huu, Shinid and Bagit. When I knocked, peered inside and entered for the first time, it was warm, noisy and crowded. Gerel-Huu, who was very short and bow-legged, was scolding a couple of pupils who'd just sneaked in to pick at scraps from the last meal; Bagit, the oldest of the three, had several missing teeth and a tired stoop. She was stirring a vat bubbling on the stove, while Shinid grinned at me, revealing a mouthful of crooked, gleaming teeth, and paused from kneading a Himalayan-sized mound of dough to offer me a bowl of tea. 'Hello, *bagsh*! *Tsai oh*!' Drink tea!

Two of the teachers were sitting at a table, sharing a newspaper between them. I sat down on the other stool and immediately had to peel off my jacket because of the lovely, fierce, damp heat.

Shinid swept rivulets of sweat from her wide forehead. 'Hottest place in the village, this kitchen! You come here whenever you have time. All the teachers come in here for tea!'

The two *bagshes* glanced up from the small print and agreed, smiling. Outside, a young posse squashed their faces up against the clouded window to get a better look at us, and Gerel-Huu spotted them and roared, '*Gaa!*' Get lost! with the inflamed passion of a statuesque diva, brandishing her small clenched fist and a huge, lethal-looking wooden ladle. The posse chortled and fled like sheep.

'How many students do you feed?' I asked, looking round. The kitchen featured a large wood-burning stove, on which presumably they cooked everything, two sturdy tables for pounding dough and hacking slabs of meat, and an impressive assortment of large pots and cauldrons, which were constantly being refilled with icy river water by pairs of wiry children with bare red hands and dripping boots. The kitchen was almost aesthetically spartan and absolutely immaculate, apart from half a dozen goat heads gently rolling round under one of the tables.

'One hundred and ten children every day,' said Shinid, raising her arms to attack the mass of dough. '*Tsai* and bread in the morning, then lunch, and dinner in the evening.'

'All year?' I squeaked, startled by the treble figures.

Gerel-Huu laughed out loud. She had a great laugh, which engulfed the whole room like a blast of heat from an oven. Everyone in the kitchen echoed her, chuckling gently in her wake.

'Yes, *bagsh*! They all come from the mountains in September and stay till summer. Their parents bring us meat and wood, and the children sleep up there.' She nodded towards the ceiling. 'We have dormitories.'

After draining another bowl of salty tea I stood to leave, then remembered the actual reason for my visit. Could I have some meat as Menke *bagsh* had said?

Gerel-Huu disappeared into another room, and returned clasping what looked like a large white cudgel with several dark streaks running through it like grains of wood. She thrust it into my arms. '*Makh, bagsh.*'

It was several kilos of mutton fat with slithers of meat in between. I gulped slightly, knowing I'd never eat it. Maybe I could give it to Gansukh. My dismay must have showed, because Gerel-Huu placed her hands over her wide hips and eyed me shrewdly for a moment.

'*Bagsh* – do you prefer *khar makh*?' Black meat, meaning lean meat.

'Yes, yes, I do.' I smiled hopefully.

'*Sain bain*. We still have some fresh *khar makh* at my home, but not mutton. Beef. We don't like it so much. I will take this meat and give you *khar makh*. My girl will bring it to your *ger*.'

I beamed and gratefully handed back the cudgel. The next morning her young, moon-faced daughter, who was called Badamtsetseg, came over to see me, giggling and clutching a frozen slab of dark lean beef.

It tasted absolutely delicious.

CHAPTER SIX

On April Fool's morning the rising sun blazed so suddenly and fiercely that the Hovd finally seemed to thaw a little and glittered like wet fish scales. I happily shed my thick jacket, gloves and hat, and set off exploring again before my afternoon classes. On impulse I turned towards the hill on to which the village backed, with the ornate settlement poised on top. I could stroll up and greet whoever lived there.

The hill wasn't very high, but still offered me a fresh view of Tsengel and from the upper slopes I could oversee the village layout: the square in the centre, with the clinic on one side, the school on the other and the tiny post office at the rear, nearest the river. The crooked rows of cabins expanded out from the nucleus, with their narrow alleyways between the individual *hashas*. On one quiet corner there was the small, unadorned local mosque. It looked just like any of the other houses except for the star and crescent icon staked into its roof like a weather vane, glowing molten in the new-born sun.

White smoke plumed from every chimney, a jeep spluttered in the distance like a smoker's cough, cows, goats and dogs were scavenging for food. On the gleaming white river beyond I could see two men skidding, and hear them whoop as they played ice hockey together, their laughter ricocheting against the rock. Further upstream a camel was being led to drink at a large well, while figurines with wooden poles across their shoulders supporting a bucket on either side were staggering back across the slippery ice towards the river bank. Remove the tangle of dead cable wires, the hacking jeep, the two-storey breeze-block monstrosity from the central square, and the age and era of this village would be indefinable. I already knew that this was what I really loved about Tsengel and what made all the struggling and drudgery worthwhile: that I wasn't living under my own sky, but in an older starker world, where the elements wielded their chaos like unrestrained deities.

The summit of the hill was wide, stony, and deserted. Nothing stirred as I approached a settlement of large, adobe quadrangles with solid wooden gates and ornate crenellations. I wove quietly between them, touching the rough texture of the walls and peering cautiously through the closed gates, not quite sure what I'd see inside. They all seemed empty. The interiors were low mounds of pale brown earth: baked, frozen and sealed by the seasons. Ah, now I suddenly understood where I was. So I walked on carefully, because I didn't know *who* I was stepping over.

Beyond the quadrangles there were four broad white pyramids, all at least eight feet high. Each was crowned in a canopy of clay so intricately sculpted it looked as though they could have been draped in thick embroidered white cloth. There was something ominous about these pyramids, or perhaps I felt guilty for trespassing. I scuffed my feet as I walked towards them. The lower walls were cracked with hairline fractures where the whitewash was beginning to flake. They all contained a single window pane, which held metal bars but no glass so there was no way of getting in – or out. Above the bars there were black and white framed photographs of elderly women and men, smiling benignly.

I stood back and decided I liked this place. After all, the living are far more frightening than the dead, and here the keepers of the earth had been graciously entombed in their own serene hamlet. It was only when I noticed several more shallow mounds clustered at the edge of the hillside and identified only by anorexic posts with a name and two dates gouged on to thin, wooden-nailed plaques, that I felt uneasy. These last few looked pitiful, the ugly remnants of swift and crude burials, as though the relatives were somehow ashamed or appalled and were trying to forget the woman, man or child who had just stopped breathing. One of the mounds had been smothered by a nest of rusty barbs, which must have been to prevent dogs from burrowing down to the body just underneath.

When Gansukh spied me wandering through the village without my jacket or hat on, she hurried over and told me off. 'Louisa, what are you doing? You must not go out like this – it will make you sick.'

Zulmira echoed the sentiment when I saw her coming out of school. '*Bagsh*,' she could never bring herself to use my first name, 'you need a hat – your head will get very cold.'

I promised to fetch my hat, asked her how she was, and slowly steered the conversation round to our next English lesson together. Zulmira shifted her gaze to an object over my shoulder. 'I am busy, *bagsh* . . . too many Kazakh lessons. I will tell you when I have time.' Her tone didn't encourage any debate, and we soon said goodbye. I wondered what I'd done to offend her.

Despite both these warnings about wearing a hat I stubbornly, stupidly continued wandering around bare-headed for the rest of the day, because the sun felt promisingly warm all afternoon even though the wind still held icy threads. By dusk the air had cooled, and my head was beginning to thrum gently, as though there was a draught whistling through my ears. Then my forehead began to tingle, and within a couple of horrible hours, I was slumped over my desk, catatonic and groaning, my hands clutching at my splitting skull. I couldn't eat anything that night. I felt sick and half-blinded with agony, but eventually managed to fumble for several painkillers and wash them down. I knocked over the candle as I clambered on to my bed and slumped face down, miserable, nauseous and shivering. I knew it served me right, but that didn't help at all. I couldn't hoist myself back on to my feet until late the next morning, and even then still felt as though my eyeballs were bruised and my head was rattling like a gourd.

As I was blearily making coffee, Gansukh came in with Amraa *bagsh*. All the local teachers were called bagsh after their first names, in the same way the doctors were called *emch* and the drivers *jolooch.* Anyone who was paid for work in the village was immediately identified by what they did.

Amraa limped inside and sat down heavily. She inhaled the steam from the bowl of coffee I offered her, savouring the rich dark waft. 'Mmm, *sain bain!*' I'd been introduced to all the teachers, but hadn't had the chance to speak to Amraa till now. All I knew of her was that she, her little sister and their parents were one of the few ethnic Halkh Mongolian families in the village. The Halkhs are the Mongolian ethnic majority, and make up about 80 per cent of the overall population. Amraa's parents came from Ulaanbaatar, but ended up here more than a decade ago, because they were both Mongolian language teachers and were offered work teaching the Kazakhs to speak Mongolian. Now Amraa also taught Mongolian, and worked at the school alongside her mother. Her father lived in Olgii and visited at weekends.

'I never wanted to be a teacher. I wanted to study as a doctor,' Amraa told me as we were draining our bowls and chewing on *buurtzug*, 'but a kettle of tea was knocked over me when I was young, and I can't use my arm properly.' She placed the bowl in her lap, rolled up her sleeve and calmly displayed her ruined limb. Blistering red welts trailed from her right shoulder down to the wrist, as though lines of thick cable had been badly welded just beneath the skin. Her shrivelled right hand looked like papier mâché: the layers of waxy epidermis stretched tight over joints that had been curled into a claw by the callused webs between her fingers and palm. Her nails were torn on both hands, chewed into ragged dirty stubs. I was momentarily lost for words. The scars were hideous, her hand crippled and useless.

I imagined, though she made no effort to show me, that Amraa's legs were also maimed, because she walked with a pronounced limp that tilted the whole of her small body to one side. But I didn't pity her. It's impossible to pity anyone who bares their deformity while looking straight over at you, keen, smiling and unabashed, calmly demanding that you acknowledge her disfigured flesh.

'We've come to tell you about the disco at the klub tonight,' said Gansukh, her voice shrill with excitement. She ignored Amraa's wounds.

'Disco?' I repeated, like an unknown foreign phrase. 'What disco?'

Words about pleasure – like disco, music, fruit, wine, comfort, sex – had no context for me here. These days I only seemed to use words from the language of survival: hard, cold, wood, ice, meat, flour.

I had no sensual life in the village and no energy to pursue one. I was beginning to feel as though I was sexually bankrupt, celibate and unavailable because of who and where I was. I think the only reason I didn't find this frustrating, yet, was because I was so tired most of the time. My definition of pleasure had been totally inverted: a long, hot, foaming bath, fried chicken, avocados and a cold beer were the extent of my fantasies now.

Anyway, how could you have a disco in a village without electricity? But Gansukh and Amraa were nudging each other, giddy like adolescents. 'Yes, it's tonight at the klub. They have power, a motor. We can all go together. Have you got any lipstick?'

Sansar-Huu had already left for the mountains, so Gansukh had to find a baby-sitter before the three of us could get out the lipstick, then storm off to the klub for the evening. Eventually we set out in the dark, stumbling back towards the school. The klub was in the central square, though I hadn't noticed it before. A small boisterous crowd was surging towards the back entrance, and even from the outside, the muffled music was loud and inviting. A spotty teenager asked us all for Tg 200 (about 15p) entrance fee. We climbed up the steps and waded inside.

The dance floor looked like a crowded hillside. It tilted down to a wide stage, where a motley DJ crew in *deels* were huddled round a tape deck. One naked light bulb dangled over the stage and another above the 'hillside', casting a dim, atmospheric glow. A huge wood-burning stove at either end of the stage kept the venue snug.

I was thrilled. It was a great dancing klub because it fulfilled the basic requirements – was large, dark and noisy – but the real pleasure was watching the villagers relax and party for the first time since I'd arrived. They were, almost without exception, wonderful dancers, waltzing gracefully to their own traditional music, and shimmying to any other in huge circles of twenty or thirty revellers. The motor shuddered and the bulbs flickered between numbers, but the dance floor never emptied.

Amraa and Gansukh introduced me to a host of new people that night, including their mutual friend and teacher Tuya, a Tuvan with glossy hair thick as a horse's mane, and a careless easy smile.

'*Saino!*' Hi! She greeted me casually, chewing gum and sitting close to the good-looking man at her side. 'This is Gerele,' she added, nudging her companion, who grinned lopsidedly at her and then me. I liked Tuya straight away and knew I wanted to be a friend of hers. There was a sense of the rebel about her, in the way she chewed her gum, wore blood-red lipstick and flirted recklessly with Gerele in the dim, public klub. A refreshing streak of irreverence. A headful of impatient ideas. She looked like a woman who loved to laugh. We all whirred together with the crowd to dated American and Mongol pop until we were beginning to sweat. When someone boogied across our wide circle and passed a white knotted scarf into my hands, I held it up and glanced over at Gansukh, bewildered.

She laughed and shouted over the distorted lyrics, '*Büjig!* Dance! You have to dance there in the middle, then give it to another person!'

So I did, laughing as the circle cheered and stamped. Several other women spontaneously joined me in the centre and we strutted together.

As soon as we paused for breath, Amraa, Gansukh and Tuya were in constant demand by men, who extended their hands and inclined their heads chivalrously whenever they asked a woman to dance. The women also waltzed up and then down the dance floor together, looking deft and gracious even in their heavy winter boots. Several women beckoned me on to the floor, where I stomped heavily on their small feet because I've never learned how to waltz. They grimaced and giggled, and gave me brief, impromptu lessons as we spun unsteadily. It was only at the end of the evening that one of the men invited me to be his partner. He was incredibly tall for a Mongol, and held me round the waist and by the right hand with outsized, hot, sweating palms. As we tried to waltz, he shook with constant nervous laughter, and every time I looked up towards him or tried to ask a question, he was arrested with giggles and we would trip up over each other again, while all the onlookers tried not to snigger. I think his friends had dared him to ask me.

The steaming hot klub air erupted outside into the night as the music finally finished and we bundled up again and headed off home.

'*Yanaa*! It's freezing,' shivered Gansukh, linking her arm through mine and recoiling slightly as a troupe of men raucously passed by. 'Those boys in the klub are always drunk after the disco,' she hissed, 'all they want to do is drink and then fight.' She shivered again. 'Ah, *margaash* [tomorrow] it's going to be very cold.'

She was right. Overnight the temperature plunged and torpid white clouds brooded over the nearby mountains, shrinking our landscape to myopic proportions. I zipped up my bulky jacket, pulled my hat down low over my freezing ears, and begged the school for a sack of coal. Some of the men who had ridden out to the mountains to save the *mal* returned on their weary horses, and warned us about deep snowdrifts and relentless blizzards heading our way.

First, we endured an onslaught of dust in Tsengel. I was woken violently from a lurid dream a few nights after the disco, startled into consciousness by what sounded like a pig being killed outside my door. It was actually a violent dust storm that screamed around the village and battered the felt walls of my *ger* until dawn. There was another storm the next night, and I sat up in my narrow bed clutching at my blankets, swearing under my breath and hoping the felt could withstand the fury.

'This is very dangerous wind in spring, you must sleep in my house,' insisted Gansukh. 'Your *ger* could topple.' I gratefully spent several cosy nights in her warm and rigid cabin, while outside the telegraph poles lurched as though reaching towards each other. In the mornings we often couldn't even see to the other side of Tsengel. Jaundiced dust clouds obscured the cabins, the mountains and the hazy ball of sun.

But despite these ferocious storms and the freezing weather, the classroom stoves were cold and unlit. The cleaners always stopped kindling the fires on 10 April – and that was that. It was a blatant hangover from the long communist era, when collective decisions couldn't be reversed, even if it was going to make life easier for everyone. (In Ulaanbaatar the central heating was controlled by the power stations and went on and off at pre-determined dates, regardless of the weather.) It did amaze me that the Tsengel teachers never complained and that Menke saw the chilly classrooms and shivering pupils and teachers, yet never relented. The school wasn't short of wood or coal.

Amraa and I battled home from our classes during one vengeful storm, clinging to each other and reduced to staggering backwards as others shielded their eyes and tried to wade blindly forward through the stinging dust. Children crouched behind rattling *hasha* fences, people shrieked in the gale as they clenched hands and inched their way home. We were all caked in spring debris. I could taste the grit in the back of my throat, feel it plastered to my hair and skin. Amraa and I finally made it back to my *ger*, which was the nearest shelter. We drank black coffee and shared a nasty, taste-less bar of Chinese chocolate from one of the kiosks. As we talked, the felt walls swayed around us as though to thumping music.

'Ey, this is the worst time of year,' Amraa exclaimed, raising her voice above the dull roar outside. 'Winter is OK. We know it will always be cold. But this spring is dangerous because we never know what the weather will do. The air pressure is low, so everybody is very tired all the time. This dust is everywhere, the *mal* are starving, and where is the rain? *Khetsüü*. It's difficult.'

Princess had visited the day before and told me exactly the same thing. I hadn't seen her much recently. She said she'd been very busy and had no time for lessons at the moment. She had just driven deep into the Altai to collect a patient, and had been stranded there for three nights. Even the veritable Jarkan hadn't been able to navigate his jeep through the storms and drifts.

'Allah, I am exhausted,' she'd complained as I made her some strong coffee. 'I have no time to do anything, you know. Just sleep and work. Because now the clinic is full of sick people – and the mountains are full of dead animals.'

CHAPTER SEVEN

It was five to eleven on a Wednesday morning, and the tiny Tsengel post office was heaving. The mail came once a week, at about eleven o'clock. By quarter to, you could hardly get in the door.

The man from Olgii who delivered the mail had a slow indulgent smile, a moustache thick as yak hide, and the stomach of a well-fed cow. His bulk was exaggerated by the fact that everyone else in Tsengel was either stocky or skinny. He was the only fat person I'd ever seen in the village, and he didn't even live here.

He passed over the sack of mail to the grateful crowd and rumbled off minutes later. Then the post master, Addai (brother of Abbai), and his assistants, Nina and the sublimely named Buyan-Tok-Tok, set to work. Everyone would push forward, trying to attract their attention as newspapers were grabbed, telegrams, letters and parcels handed over. People who hadn't ordered papers and weren't expecting mail turned up by the dozen just to see what was going on, and enjoy a brief glimpse of the world beyond their own.

I was always deflated if there was nothing in the post for me. I would bow my head and retreat from the mêlée, feeling a momentary pang of almost dizzy loneliness. Damn it, this sack of crumpled paper was my only contact with anywhere or anyone else beyond Tsengel. Although I'd been in the village for a couple of months now, I still needed to know that my absence from the world outside was being noticed. If Nina caught my eye and shook her head I felt acutely aware that my family and friends were obviously all doing very well without me.

Nina, who was small, windburned and smiled like a dirty joke, did try to soften the blow. 'Your post will come next week, *bagsh*,' she'd assure me, and I appreciated her gesture, but still skulked back to school with a long face and the unloved air of a temporary orphan. If, however, she handed me an envelope, I thanked her as though she'd written the letter herself. A parcel made me cheer out loud and the villagers paused from sharing their news with each other to shake their heads and smile indulgently as I squeezed back out of the door so I could lean against the crumbling back wall, and read whatever it was quickly and quietly to myself. Then I read it again very slowly, word by word. Once or twice I tried to save opening my letters until I could get home from school, light my stove and brew a bowl of tea (the coffee had just run out), but couldn't wait that long. I would last until the end of my next class, and then read the sheets of pale-blue paper while perched on top of my wobbling desk, my heels drumming against the side.

One Wednesday I received three letters, which definitely made up for a disappointment the week before. It was much too cold to stand outside, and I raced to the school kitchen for a bowl of tea and a quick read before my second class.

You can tell so much about people's attitudes towards what you're doing and how you're living by the tone of the letters they write to you. My Australian friend Ktima was a journalist in London, and scribbled detailed questions, trying to extract specifics so she could form her own image of this archaic world I'd moved into. '*How is the food? I bet the weather's freezing – isn't it? Is there any night life out there?*' She wanted a reply of brevity: facts spiked with intrigue. I smiled and imagined sending back a postcard saying only, '*Hello, Ktima! This is Tsengel in four words: ice, dust, dried meat, disco.*'

My twin sister, Ami, always wrote very brief letters of just half a dozen lines. She wanted to know what I'd be doing on our birthday, and said in the same breath that she was appalled by my recent description of the outside toilets. I was well used to them by now. Anyway, frozen trench toilets don't usually smell, and most people swept out their cubicles and kept them incredibly clean. Greg was right, though: there wasn't a shred of loo paper around. We used last week's newspaper instead, torn into almost minute squares. Ami had just offered to send over a bulk of luxury toilet tissue to ease my plight.

Her husband, my brother-in-law, cracked jokes about washing with yak soap. Friends from Ulaanbaatar asked if I needed medicine, or more food. My mother sent cards with bright illustrations and flat bundles of magazines that I read, reread with Gansukh and then used either in the toilet or to light the fire. Ma asked me to write to her with descriptions of our lives in the village, and of how the landscape was changing *'now that spring is definitely with us, and must be arriving even where you are, Louisa.'*

That evening I sat at my desk and wrote her a long letter.

I am getting used to it all, Ma. The quiet life. I get up and go to bed very early, and still spend lots of time just looking after myself: chopping wood and fetching water never ends. The teaching's fine, and nowadays I have quite a lot of visitors after school. In the evenings I write my journal – which is turning into epic daily postscripts. I want to record all the details of this life unfolding around me.

I spend lots of time just talking to people because I want to hear their stories. Sometimes I actually feel like I don't have enough time alone, which I know must seem a very odd thing to say in a place like this! Here we are surrounded by all this wilderness, and yet there really isn't any sense of privacy. People literally live on top of each other, families all sharing one room together or at the most two. Sleeping, eating, everything together. I know for certain I'm the only person in Tsengel who has her own bedroom. But living alone here is something to be pitied and Gansukh always thinks that if I'm on my own

I must be lonesome and need company. The kids who live next door watch me from the roof of their house – even when I go to the loo! They just clamber up and stare until I shout at them to get lost.

But the most profound change is in the noise, or rather the silence. The sounds I've been inundated with all my life, you know – TV, the buzz of the fridge, doorbells and telephones – all gone. Like they never even existed. I never hear radio or TV broadcasts, flick switches, run a bath, answer the phone or drive a car. When there are no visitors and it's just me here in the *ger*, it's so utterly silent that I can hear the wings of a bird flying over the roof.

You asked about spring. Well, the weather is still bloody cold, but the Hovd river is thawing and splintering as though she's made up her own mind, and now there are thin streams coursing between bergs of ice floe, which sometimes rise up more than a metre and a half from the bank and are inlaid with some sort of lime-green-coloured mineral. Seriously! The whole river is strewn with this emerald and white ice, like sheets of broken stained glass. It's just extraordinary.

On my walks I see local men perched on frozen ledges overhanging the river, fishing. They don't even look up when another slab topples into the waters, though you can hear the crack of the ice echo across the valley. A few nomads are still riding their horses over the river, but it looks treacherous now, and the banks are mires of frozen mud. Dust storms still rage and our well is so clogged with dust and slush that we've resorted to hauling and boiling this infested-looking river water. It tastes OK, though a bit gritty, but it looks rank.

I didn't want to tell Ma that I also stumbled over carcasses on my walks. The river bank was now littered with bloated, decomposing calves, sheep and goats. The Hovd was beginning to melt, but the ground was still cracked and fissured, parched like a fossil. There was no pasture anywhere for the animals to eat, and they were starving to death. The little meat on them would never be eaten, because it was thought of as tainted. So the cadavers were left to rot and stink. What a waste.

'Rain, rain,' the worried villagers told me, one after another, 'we need rain now.' Cascades to douse the earth and revive the surviving animals. Mountain herders arrived in town and sat in Gansukh's cabin, shaking their heads and furrowing their brows as they recalled losing hundreds of beasts.

'This has been the worst spring for a decade,' Sansar-Huu told me on one of his fleeting visits home, bringing a small feast of dairy goods. Yields were still very low in the mountains, but the yaks were being milked, so we drank sharp fresh yoghurt and melted enormous thick wheels of frozen milk over the stove. They tasted rich and luxuriously creamy. Gansukh always gave me a small pail of milk to take back to my *ger*. She would hand it to me without ceremony just as I was about to leave. I would smile as I took it but say nothing. Because that's what you did. You didn't say thank you, just remembered that you too had things to share. I made half a pan of sweet rice pudding one afternoon. It tasted stodgy and fabulous.

Sansar-Huu usually stayed just one night to see his family. He was gone by dawn the next morning, cantering the 70 or so kilometres back into the Altai, where his parents were still struggling to salvage their herds. Since he'd been spending most of his time away I'd shared my city supplies with Gansukh and the children, because it just seemed the fairest thing to do. After all, we were all in the same predicament. Now these supplies had just about finished, and we endured dried meat, rice, flour and salt every evening for supper. During the day I lived on tea with bread or *buurtzug*, because I just couldn't be bothered to cook up another chewy, bland meal.

When I mentioned to Gansukh that it was my birthday at the end of April, I presumed that we'd probably just get a bottle of vodka in and have a sing song, as Mongols don't really tend to celebrate birthdays. But Gansukh immediately told Amraa and Tuya, and Amraa insisted she would organise a party. We all agreed and then said no more about it.

When 23 April dawned I was washed and dressed before I remembered that I was now thirty years old. Somehow it didn't feel very significant. I was brewing a kettle of tea and wishing it was coffee when Amraa burst in with a bunch of plastic flowers and a home-made card.

'Happy birthday! No, I can't drink tea, I have a class now. Don't forget your party is in the klub tonight!'

Sansar-Huu had also arrived back from the mountains the night before. He and Gansukh treated me to a big chunky bar of German chocolate from the black market in Olgii, and together with Opia and Yalta we drank *suutei tsai*, milky tea, and ate fresh bread and the chocolate for breakfast. It was almost continental.

Then, at my instigation, Gansukh and I went in search of beer, which could occasionally be found in one of the stores or kiosks. We scoured the whole village for alcohol. Every shopkeeper offered us a biscuit or pressed a couple of sweets into our hands as we browsed. We loitered at the counters, chewing and chatting and I wondered how they ever made any money, as they all seemed far too generous, handing out little treats to customers like us who didn't usually buy anything, and selling most items on tic. They each kept detailed lists of local debtors in small notepads under the counters. I rarely got anything from the shops simply because there wasn't much to buy. They all sold almost identical goods – candles, flimsy note books, small packets of biscuits and mounds of glistening, misshapen boiled sweets, which tasted awful. They had orange packets of Chinese yeast and bulbous sacks of Chinese grey rock salt, flour and rice leaking across the wooden boards. Only one place had any booze, and that was bottles of unlabelled local *arikh*, balancing on a stack of garish sweaters and a few pairs of cheap Chinese training shoes. The *arikh* was also very cheap, and you could smell the fumes even before you unscrewed the cap. I bought two bottles anyway.

As we wandered round and sheltered from blasts of dust, people crossed the street to shake my hand and wish me happy birthday. Locals I was sure I'd never even seen before dismounted from their horses or came out of their *hashas* to greet me. Tuya, Gerel-Huu, Zulmira, Princess, Nina and several of the teachers all pushed more bunches of flowers, small bags of glistening sweets and miniature bottles of perfume into my hands while we were wandering through the square.

It's a staunch Mongol tradition not to thank people for gifts, but to slip them into a bag or pocket and open them when you're alone. Thanking someone for a present is rude because it implies you were actually waiting for the gift. Opening it in public is a real personal affront. You just silently accept what's given, and put it away until later. But I really wanted to thank everyone, and struggled to keep my mouth shut as my arms filled. Eventually I had nowhere left to conceal the presents, and I felt quite tearful because everyone was making such an effort for me.

One of the men who came over to shake my hand stood in front of me at an awkward, sideways angle, looking at me with one dark eye. Until he swung round to retrace his steps, I could see only one half of his face. Then I gaped and immediately tried not to stare at the other half, which was completely smothered in neat, coarse, black hair, from just beneath his left eye all the way down to his chin. God he's a werewolf! I thought, then immediately felt ashamed of myself. Gawping fools like me were no doubt the reason he turned his other cheek in the first place. I felt myself blush.

Shrewd as ever Gansukh read my expression. 'That's Selik-Khan,' she said quietly. 'He's always looked like that. With that face. He was born like that, we don't know why. But you should see his wife and his four children – *saikhan* [beautiful].'

Selik-Khan walked away from us, casually calling other greetings across the street, confident and relaxed among his own people. I watched him go, as fascinated by people's lack of reaction to him as I was by his half a face of hair. Gansukh's matter of fact statement said it all. There are many places where someone would be feared and ostracised for looking as Selik-Khan does. He spent a lot of time building cabins in the mountains outside Tsengel, and on the handful of other occasions I did see him in the village he always reverted to that sideways stance when he greeted me, and he never once met my eyes. I've told myself again and again that I only felt awkward talking to him because he obviously felt uncertain of himself being next to me, but if I'm completely honest I was never really sure.

I spent that afternoon at school showing my students how to play Hangman, because it was my birthday and I was damned if I was going to spend it teaching adverbs. Later on, while I was having dinner with Gansukh and Sansar-Huu, Amraa turned up with Tuya. They were both immaculately made up and dressed in embroidered *deels* and heeled, polished boots. They looked amazing.

'Louisa, aren't you ready yet? Everyone is waiting for you at the klub. Come on!' exclaimed Amraa, shaking her head in mock anger as I abandoned my half-eaten meal and fled to my dark *ger* to change into – what? All my clothes were grubby or worn by now. My sweaters were snagged, my boots frayed – everything looked a mess, including me. I rummaged and strew garments round the *ger*, finally emerging in a crumpled dress, clutching my lipstick, and feeling something like stage fright. I really didn't want to go to the klub and be a guest of honour – it all felt too much. A show, a performance for my sake. No one else round here celebrated their birthday like this. I would much rather spend the evening here in my *ger* with Gansukh, Sansar-Huu, Amraa and Tuya, drinking vodka and listening to the guitar with an intimate group of friends. I didn't want to deal with the gaze and expectations of the rest of the village. But Amraa had organised the party for me, to make me feel I mattered, and now my absence was being noticed. I tried to straighten my wretchedly creased dress, took a long swig from one of the *arikh* bottles, and blew out the candle.

Hours later yet another man asked me to dance. I tried to plead exhaustion, but he stood with his hand outstretched towards me until I relented and let him lead me on to the 'hillside'. He wished me happy birthday, gently spun me around, and at the end of our waltz, reached under the front of his *deel* for a bunch of plastic flowers and pressed them into my palm. I beamed at him as he led me back to my seat, where the music teacher, Magmyasuren, was now patiently waiting for his dance.

Gansukh and Amraa had obviously plotted with the DJ, a Kazakh woman called Kultii, to empty the 'hillside' and compere an interlude of adult party games. Gansukh glided across the floor alone, clutching the knotted white dancing scarf as everyone started to clap to the rhythm of her gait. She handed the scarf to a young man, and took his seat as he too danced, awkwardly, across the floor on his own, and thrust the scarf at a blushing young woman. He took her seat as she danced over to another teenager, and so one by one dozens of people danced alone, some proud and others cringing in the hot glare of the whole klub. Every dancer got a resounding cheer and warm applause. Then we played other games I didn't quite understand, but Tuya leaned over and gave me a scandalous running commentary and we howled with laughter together until we were both practically weeping, as teams of men and women raced up and down the 'hillside', shrieking, while the crowd heckled, stamped and roared. Then she and I were both grabbed from the audience to join in, and I ran the wrong way, but I didn't care. God, they knew how to enjoy themselves! My head was already light when Abbai clambered on to the stage, and after a mercifully brief speech gestured to me to clamber up alongside him. Abbai was the man who had got me here in the first place by offering me work in the village – and he was the local bigwig, being the head of the Tsengel council. I owed him a debt of gratitude. But I still didn't want to get up on that stage in front of everyone. I shook my head and put my hands together towards him, in a gesture that pleaded, 'No, no. Really. Not a speech. No.'

But Gansukh whispered in my ear, 'You have to say thank you to everyone. Just go up and sing a song.'

I warbled 'It's Been A Hard Day's Night' into the hissing stage microphone, and when I climbed back down the stairs my legs were shaking slightly. Suddenly, on impulse, I jumped back on to the stage and clenched the microphone, which crackled like a bad phone line as I rasped, 'This is the best party I've ever been to. Thank you. Thank you.' When I climbed back down the stairs, Abbai was waiting for me to dance with him.

CHAPTER EIGHT

I didn't even try to go to school. I felt far too frail to teach. In fact, I only ventured outside twice all day. The sky looked as though it was scowling: huge bruised clouds were threatening the mountains, and the air was cold and moist. It was definitely going to rain soon.

Tuya came to see me on her way home. She saw me sitting next to my stove wanly nursing a bowl of tea, and shook her head cheerfully. 'You look terrible! Did you go to school?'

This was why I liked Tuya so much. She blithely said what other people in Tsengel only thought.

I shook my head miserably.

'Menke *bagsh* was looking for you,' she said.

Oh God, I thought. I hope Gerel-Huu didn't tell him she saw me throwing up this morning. Gerel-Huu always passed by our *hasha* on her way to the kitchen, and this morning she'd witnessed me puking outside my *ger*. I hadn't even made it to the toilet.

'Ey! Lou-is-a!' Her raucous laughter rang across the street. 'Did you have a good party?'

I had managed a nod and a wave, wiping my mouth as Gerel-Huu grinned wickedly through the gaps in the fence.

Two days later I was in my *ger* waiting for Gansukh to come in for her lesson. Opia and Yalta were with me, playing with an empty sardine tin and my bottles of shampoo and face cream. The stove was hot. The *ger* felt snug. Suddenly I froze. There was a gentle sound of water pattering on to the canvas roof. Yalta turned

to me and said a word I'd never heard before. He didn't speak
Mongolian yet, just his own Tuvan language. But I nodded because
I knew exactly what he was saying.

Rain.

We ran outside into the dusty yard together. The ground was
already melting into brown puddles as the shower cascaded into
a torrent. I still remember being there, barefoot on the wet earth
with my arms open and face turned to the grey sky. I took my
sweater off, just to feel the rain on more of my skin. It was soft
and cold and I shivered and murmured, 'Mmm' at the same time
because it felt so good. Just as I was getting soaked and Opia and
Yalta were dancing in the puddles, Gansukh came racing through
the gate.

She saw the three of us together and howled with laughter.
'Look at you all!' She scooped up Opia, water streaming down
both their faces. 'Isn't the rain wonderful? This is what we need!
Now Tsengel will be beautiful!' We hugged each other spontaneously
and then scuttled back into my *ger*, to steam and dry off
by the stove.

The rain lashed down the next day and the day after that. You
could see the relief on people's faces as they went about the village
in between these torrid downpours.

'You wait,' said Amraa, as we stood at the gate of her *hasha*,
looking out across the thawing river, 'in a few days, everywhere
will be green. Our valley will change. The river ice will be gone
and all the *mal* will be feeding.'

A fringe of grass had already erupted at the river bank and was
being torn up by herds of starving local animals. For the first time
it really looked as though spring had arrived.

I didn't feel quite as enthusiastic about the rain when my home
started leaking like a cracked cup. The canvas *ger* roof dripped
incessantly in half a dozen places, and a thin stream coursed under
the felt walls and across my floor, ruining a sack of flour. I had
to move everything including my bed into the centre, next to the
stove, and spread all my bowls and buckets on the floor to catch
the constant cold dribbles from the roof. I felt damp all the time,

and craved dry warmth and fresh food: any nugget of respite from this infernal struggle just to keep warm and dry and to survive (there were no more chicken and beer fantasies, they'd degenerated into obsessive cravings for onions, apples and garlic).

Instead, we all watched with dismay as the downpours stopped as suddenly as they'd started, and the sky threw down blizzards of dust and driving snow. My journal at the beginning of May reads:

Today surprised even the hardy people of Tsengel. There was no rain, just screaming dusty wind, and snow, billowing like it was winter again. The school was freezing. I stayed in most of the afternoon, but eventually restlessness drove me outside, into weak, grey sunlight.

All I could see were people shrouded and bent against a world of huge spinning flakes. Even the strays, curled up thin and miserable, couldn't be bothered to harass me. I passed by a horribly emaciated cow, cringing against a rattling *hasha* fence. Just round the corner the rest of the fence had been ripped from its roots like rotten teeth, and telegraph wires were strewn across the street in tangles. It looks like there's been a riot out there.

Rain and snow are a potentially fatal combination, especially if you spend your life herding in the Altai. A young nomad died in the mountains east of Tsengel after being soaked by a downpour and then frozen in a blizzard. He was Gerel-Huu's nephew, and I went to see her when I heard the news.

She was at home, grieving, surrounded by her six sons and one daughter, all of whom hovered around her, seemingly at a loss as to what to do for their heartbroken mother. Gerel-Huu wept quietly the whole time I was there.

'He was my brother's only son,' she told me, her face raw from crying and puckered with grief. 'Who will look after his wife and child now? Who will look after his parents when they get old?'

I could feel her anguish pressing down on her like a tumour. She didn't seem to be mourning just for herself but for her entire family: for the loss of a father, nephew, son and husband. I sat and held her hand and couldn't think of anything to say to console her. My trip into the mountains with Princess had made me realise that these nomads lived in full view of death. The mere fact of their survival here was a triumph of the human spirit. But they walked a delicate, perilous path, at the mercy of the elements, and they were, in the end, as frail as the rest of us. They couldn't afford to relax their guard.

Fear, like death, is an integral part of life. I guess we all need some element of fear in our lives. It's part of living – without it, there would no genuine joy, excitement or triumph. But unless our fear is faced head on at some point, it festers, ultimately binding us in frightened lives.

I'd never yet had any reason to be frightened in Tsengel. I didn't think I'd made any enemies, and I lived in a safe *hasha* surrounded by people I knew and trusted. Initially I'd been afraid of moving to Tsengel, but that fear had been resolved because I'd taken it on. I'd come to the village and made my home here. In that way I'd conquered my fear, and felt as though I was thriving as a result.

But fear is a many-headed beast.

Sansar-Huu and most of the other local men were still out of town when soldiers began to arrive in the village square. These were hordes of teenagers and young men, who drifted unenthusiastically down from the mountains into Tsengel because they'd been called up for a year of compulsory military service. Their arrival caused a ripple of something not entirely tangible; there was a discreet unease, a glint of tension.

I was certainly surprised to see them. Having lived in Ulaanbaatar and worked for the Mongolian press, I knew that city men often dodged the draft, either by bribing the right people or claiming they were sick or mad, or both. But these herders had all complied with their call-up, even though the treatment of soldiers in rural military barracks was a well-documented national scandal. Just the year before, one soldier had died of starvation during his national service in Sukhbaatar province in rural northern

Mongolia, and several of his colleagues had been hospitalised for severe malnutrition at the same time. The press had been banned from entering the Sukhbaatar barracks, even as an Ulaanbaatar doctor had described the surviving soldiers as looking like 'concentration camp survivors'.

The Tsengel conscripts spent days hanging round the village square in appalling weather, waiting for trucks to deliver them to Olgii, where they'd be dispersed to other parts of the country for their training and service. They soon got bored and began to roam round the village, day and night.

I was aware of them as I went about my business, these gangs of strange men, but they didn't bother me and I gave them little thought until Gansukh came to my *ger* with a cord of rope.

'I don't think you should sleep alone here,' she said. 'Not with all these army men around. But if you do want to stay in your *ger* and not my house, use this to keep your door safe.'

I could see she was serious, so I took the rope and hung it by the door. I did sometimes sleep in Gansukh's cabin, and we ate together most evenings. But I also needed my own space. I savoured being in the *ger* on my own late in the evening and was very reluctant to give it up. I did my writing, pottered round and sometimes just sat and watched a sliver of the vast moon and stars cosmos through the canvas skylight. I always felt very at ease, and these conscripts had given me no cause for concern.

Kultii the klub DJ hailed me from across the street a few days later. She had a rich, almost baritone voice, and a strong broad body. She could definitely have been a soldier.

'Ey Louisa! *Sain bainuu?* You must come to the klub on Friday, there will be a big party because the army boys are leaving on Monday. Bring Gansukh, Tuya and Amraa.'

It was strange: I never missed the disco but somehow I didn't like the sound of this. I could imagine the boys getting tanked up and brawling just before they left town, and instinctively didn't want to be there when it happened. Gansukh agreed.

'They are breaking into *hashas* at night now, Louisa,' she said, the small red birthmark on her right cheek flaring as it always did whenever she was anxious or worried. 'Some of the women are frightened because their men are still away. No, no, we shouldn't go.'

Tuya and Amraa pestered us to go to the klub with them, but we both refused and stayed at home that night. Despite Gansukh's protest I returned to my *ger* after dinner. I thought no one would break into it if I was sleeping there.

As usual, it was very quiet outside. Most people seemed to be in the klub. I bound the cord of rope between the door and the latticed *ger* walls, sank into bed early and read. Just as I was floating into sleep I heard the revellers coming home from the disco, men and women hollering and teasing each other as they wandered past on the other side of the high *hasha* fence. They'd all had a good time. I wriggled deep into my blankets and yawned.

When I heard the wooden fence splinter and people crash into the *hasha*, I had no idea what time it was. I couldn't see anything in front of me because the moon had gone and it was a thick, black night. I lay there and did not move at all as they stamped round the yard, urinating and laughing. There were four or five men. Then I reached for my candle and matches, but didn't light the tallow. Instead I crouched, taut, in my bed, and waited for them to leave. But they didn't. They stood together outside my door, striking the wood with steadily louder and heavier knocks.

'Louisa *bagsh*, can we come in? We want to meet you.'

It didn't surprise me that they knew my *ger* and my name. Everyone in the village did. They began to circle the *ger*, kicking the felt walls, closing in on me. My breathing became shallow as one of them tried to clamber up on to the roof and slid noisily down while his friends bellowed. Another one or two shook the bound door until it rattled.

'Come on, open up. Let us in. We want to see you. Now.'

They began to batter at the door with something heavy and solid. Their voices deepened into threats.

'*Odocken*. Now. Open the door. Now.'

I could feel their drunken, blunt intent, and was very, very frightened. I sensed that if they got inside, at least one of them would try to rape me.

I'd known fear like this once before. Many years ago, when I was nineteen and living in Israel. When a man whose face I don't remember any more picked me up and hurled me to the ground like a piece of rotten wood. Then he unzipped his trousers. It was only after several years of ugly dreams and brief, paralysing moments of panic, that I scraped back my confidence. I picked up the shattered fragments and carefully fitted them back together again. I learned to trust my instincts and travel alone once more. I eventually survived intact.

As these images pulsed through my head, I suddenly felt a surge of emotion straight from my guts. It was anger. I'd never been frightened in Tsengel and these drunken bastards outside my door weren't going to break me now. Fuck them. This *ger* was My Home. I knew where the axe was because I'd cut wood that afternoon and had brought it inside for safekeeping. I crouched on the floor and reached around me in a wide dark circle. The axe was next to the stove. Clasping the blade in front of me I stood a few feet behind the door with my arms raised and legs slightly apart, and I swore at them in the filthiest, most vile words I knew in English and Mongolian. I could hear my own voice swelling into a vicious roar. 'I've got an axe and I'll use it. I want to sleep. Go on, fuck off. Bastards. Noisy, drunk, disgusting wankers, cunts. Leave me alone!'

They fell silent, shocked by my onslaught of crude rage. This was not how women spoke to men in Tsengel.

They backed off from the door and walked away. Just like that. I can only guess that it wasn't much of a thrill being confronted by a ferocious woman wielding an axe. I wasn't playing their game. Maybe they'd expected screaming and tears, or an empty *ger* to ransack. But not a foreigner turning nasty and threatening them obscenely in their own language. My mouth was dry and my armpits were dripping cold sweat as I thought I could hear them all walking away, one of them puking as they banged half-heartedly at Gansukh's window. But just as they swung the gate behind them and pushed out into the street, I realised that one of them was still there, at my door, and he suddenly pitched his heavy boot into the wood slowly and deliberately, again and again.

'Come on, Louisa, it's me, Batbayar. Let me in. I want to talk to you.'

I froze, with the axe lying at my feet. For a moment there was something far more menacing about this lone man who'd deliberately stayed behind. And he wasn't Gerele's friend Batbayar. I knew Batbayar's gentle high voice. This voice was different, deep and slurred with drink.

He booted the door again. 'Let me in.'

But his demand was beginning to drone into a whine. He was getting bored and he'd be gone in a few moments. I cleared my throat and calmly ordered him to leave.

'Tomorrow. You can come to see me tomorrow. I'm going to sleep now. Go away. Tomorrow you can come and drink tea.'

He lingered for another couple of minutes, then he too was gone.

I stood and waited for a little while, shivering. Then I slowly sat down on my bed with my head in my hands.

I didn't feel triumphant at all. Just incredibly alone.

CHAPTER NINE

I slept badly, waking with a jerk and a sharp intake of breath every time I heard a noise outside: a scrape at the fence, a whine or a distant shout echoing down the track. I felt exhausted, nervy and irritable.

Of course I told Gansukh and the others about what happened. I had to. I didn't want to keep it to myself.

'*Zowar*!' spat Tuya. 'They're disgusting!'

Gansukh shook her head and berated me for not sleeping in her house. 'You don't know these boys, Louisa. We do and they're like this when they come from the mountains. You ask the other women. It's always this way, them just drinking and fighting and keeping our kids awake. I wish Sansar-Huu would come back.'

She suddenly looked incredibly tired, and I felt for her. It was very honourable for Sansar-Huu to be out in the mountains working with his parents so that they could better survive the spring, but that also left Gansukh struggling on her own with two young children, her full-time teaching work, in addition to studying English and running the *hasha*. And accommodating me. Sure, she and I helped each other out a lot of the time, but as well as her kids, Gansukh also had to attend to her elderly parents just down the street. No wonder she looked worn out.

I slept in Gansukh's house for the few nights before the conscripts left, and then returned to the *ger* because they'd gone and I thought it would be OK after that. But I couldn't relax there. It wasn't only the underlying fear of another man trying to break in, though I knew I was listening for footsteps late at night, and now I slept with the axe right under my bed. It was a mental restlessness, a barrage of anxious thoughts about why I was actually in Tsengel, and whether living here really amounted to anything more than a facile romantic illusion.

I had thought I was doing all right and actually melding into the village, making real friends and learning how to live in this small harsh world. I'd wanted to see if I could adapt to this other life, manage without the things I'd always been used to, the things I'd taken for granted, and maybe even thrive. The challenge and romance of living in Mongolia's furthest west village, surrounded by nomad settlements, had both appealed to me. I'd presumed that because I spoke Mongolian I would be accepted, welcomed into the fold and maybe able to observe the villagers and the nomads in the mountains from within.

I had never wanted to go *native*, just not to feel like an outsider *all* the time. But in truth I knew damn well that was why the soldiers came to my door after the disco: they thought they could try it on with the foreign *bagsh*. Gansukh said it herself, when we were sitting in her house together late at night after the kids were asleep. It didn't sound like an accusation, she was just being honest.

'You know they came here when they were drunk because they wanted to see you, Louisa. Because you're a *gadaad-neen hun*, an outsider.'

Greg, damn him, was right, again.

The bubble had burst, and over the next couple of weeks some of my most carefully constructed illusions about how well I was adjusting were shattered in rapid succession. I was forced to acknowledge that relations between people were as complex, tragic and delicate in Tsengel as they are anywhere else, and that not only was I a *gadaad-neen hun*, but not everyone in the village liked me, or even cared if I stayed around.

I could tell Gansukh was preparing to broach an awkward subject when she sat down in my *ger* and her birthmark flared up like an insect bite. I waited for whatever it was she had to say as she hovered on the stool, fiddling with a stray thread of wool that had unravelled from her sweater.

'One of my relatives has come in from the countryside,' she said finally, gazing into her bowl of tea. 'He's in the clinic and we have to pay for his medicine because he has no money. Can you lend me three thousand Togrog until Sansar-Huu comes back?'

Three thousand Togrog is less than £3. Almost nothing. But I had no salary at all, and wasn't even sure if I had enough cash to fly back to Ulaanbaatar, because foreigners are charged several times more for domestic flights than Mongols and the local exchange rate kept fluctuating. Gansukh earned a full-time salary of about Tg 25,000 a month.

In retrospect I can see how utterly petty it all sounds, brooding over three quid. But as soon as she'd spoken I remembered all those Ulaanbaatar ex-pat voices smugly telling me, 'You wait till you've been there for a few months and they're all borrowing money off you. They'll treat you like a branch of the local bank. They think we're all rich just because we're foreigners.'

Of course with hindsight I can appreciate that while I lent Gansukh and Sansar-Huu money several times during my time in Tsengel, they were incredibly generous in return. During the months I lived with them they gave me milk, butter, yoghurt and meat, and often shared their food with me. I know now that my immediate resentment about Gansukh asking me to lend her money wasn't about the cash itself: it was about setting a precedent whereby the value of our friendship, which was by far the closest relationship I had with anyone in Tsengel, in the end depended on money. It was my insecurities about my relationships in the village that caused my hackles to rise over lending someone a few pounds.

Gansukh and I both knew I couldn't and wouldn't refuse her, so I unzipped my money belt and silently handed over the green Togrog notes.

'Sansar-Huu will come back soon with *yamani-noluur* [cashmere wool],' she said, rising to her feet. 'They are combing the goats in the mountains now, so he'll be back with wool and when he's sold it then I can return your money.'

I nodded and tried to be gracious about it, because after all it was only three quid.

And then there was the situation with my other, absent colleague, Zulmira, who had barely spoken to me for weeks and wouldn't come to the *ger* or even into the *hasha*.

She and I had been skirting around each other at school for weeks and weeks, smiling in an embarrassed sort of way because something had obviously gone wrong between us and neither of us seemed quite sure what it was. Eventually I couldn't stand the delicate tension any longer, and visited her at home, tentatively suggesting we resumed our English lessons.

To my surprise, she agreed. Yes, she said, guardedly. We could meet up after school in one of the empty classrooms and study together. She even offered to teach me Kazakh in return for her English lessons, which seemed like a wonderful idea. We arranged lesson times together and it worked quite well for a week or two, but then either one of us was busy at the time we'd arranged or she had extra lessons because it was getting near to the end of year exams, and, rather predictably, our frail arrangement gradually fell apart. I think we both silently blamed each other for not making enough effort, and it turned into a pathetic stand-off, an undeclared little stalemate. Eventually, after waiting outside school for her several times, I didn't bother any more.

Gansukh never said very much to me about Zulmira and her conspicuous absence from our *hasha*, but just enough for me to realise she and Zulmira had never been friends. Maybe it was simply that Zulmira was Kazakh and Gansukh was Tuvan and they were both very proud. I'm not sure.

Zulmira did eventually come over to the *hasha*. It was a Saturday morning at the tail end of May, and spring was finally surrendering to the sun. Tuya and I were drinking tea in my *ger*. We were happily planning a trip into the mountains to visit her nomad parents now the weather was getting warmer, when Zulmira strode in with a scowl like Armageddon, stood in the middle of my *ger* and told me exactly what she thought of me.

'Why, *bagsh*, do I have to wait for you all the time? Why? We arrange lessons and you never turn up. I wait for you at school, I wait for you at home, and you never arrive. Never. Don't you want to teach me? Don't you like Kazakhs? How can I learn English when you don't care about turning up to teach me? I study all the work you give me and what happens? Nothing. That's what – nothing.'

I opened and shut my mouth again several times before I could find any words. 'Zulmira . . .' was all I managed at first. I was stunned. 'Have some tea,' I offered meekly. She stood glaring in front of me and refused to sit down or accept any tea.

'Zulmira, I've waited for you as well, I'm sorry. We can have lessons together, I promise. We can arrange another time. Of course I like Kazakhs. Please, don't be angry.' I was sounding nervous and probably patronising. She'd taken me completely by surprise. I had no idea how to respond to her abrasive scowl and searing accusations.

'No, I'm not angry, *bagsh*,' she said very loudly, 'not at all. No, I just wanted to know why you never teach me. But I have to go now, and when you have time, you can give me a lesson. Thank you.' She strode back outside and left me sitting there, my jaw agape.

As Zulmira shut the *hasha* gate, Tuya, who'd been silent, exhaled a long breath of disdain and rolled her eyes. 'Kazakhs,' she said.

But Zulmira had a point. I had given up on her without much effort, certainly not as much effort as I'd expended on teaching Gansukh. Zulmira learned English more slowly and was less motiv-ated than Gansukh, so she actually needed *more* tuition. I'd found myself a comfortable little set-up in Tsengel, and so it didn't matter to me very much if Zulmira didn't make it to our lessons. To put it very bluntly, I had enough work and friends to fulfil my life in the village without her.

But I knew that what had actually soured our potential friend-ship was more complex than a series of badly organised English lessons. Princess had also slipped quietly out of my life, stopped visiting me and demanding lessons, didn't now take me on trips out to the mountains. Zulmira's comment about me not liking

Kazakhs touched a nerve close to the surface. I still didn't have any Kazakh friends in Tsengel and spoke no more than a few words of Kazakh. I was living almost exclusively with the Mongols and Tuvans, Gansukh, Sansar-Huu, Amraa, Tuya and their friends. Apart from my students, I had little contact with any of the local Kazakhs beyond greeting them in the street. To Zulmira and Princess — and maybe other local Kazakhs — I'd aligned myself with the Mongols and Tuvans, and had offered the Kazakhs mere lip service — and not even in their own language. The Tuvans all spoke fluent Mongolian, but many of the Kazakhs, from school children to pensioners, spoke little or no Mongolian. As far as I could see, the passion for their own Kazakh identity left no room to embrace any other language or culture. (Most of the Tuvans also spoke fluent Kazakh, but I only ever met one Kazakh in Tsengel who could speak Tuvan properly.) If I really wanted to understand Tsengel, not just survive here but unravel the village's esoteric life, I'd have to make a genuine effort to get to know the Kazakhs. Because the longer I stayed in Tsengel, the more I realised what a divided community the village was.

It was an unspoken and unequal segregation in Tsengel. The Kazakhs and the Tuvans lived side by side but absolutely not together. A mutual apartheid. It began at school, where, from kindergarten to their final year, the classes were divided into Kazakh and Tuvan students and studied separately, in their own languages. They were all taught Mongolian as well, but never shared a class-room between them. The teachers were both Tuvan and Kazakh (plus Amraa and her mother), but the director of the school and the clinic, and the head of the District Government (Abbai), were all men, and they were all Kazakhs. The Tuvans didn't seem to wield much power in the village, which perhaps explained the unspoken but underlying tension, and reactions like Tuya's. I neither knew nor understood the history and animosity between them, but there seemed to be no sphere in Tsengel where the Tuvans and Kazakhs could come together as equals and combine their strength and passions. I'd also noticed that all the shopkeepers were Kazakh. In fact, even the cabins, which looked almost identical, were built in clusters of Kazakh or Tuvan homes. Amraa and her family lived very near Gansukh, in a Tuvan niche.

I spent a lot of time in Gansukh's home, and it was very rare that a Kazakh ever came to the door. I asked her once whether Tuvans ever married Kazakhs, and she raised her eyebrows and thought about it for a few moments before commenting, 'Once or twice, I think. Kazakh men don't ever marry our women, although I know one Tuvan man who married a Kazakh and their children are Tuvan. But their parents never like it, you know, if Kazakhs and Tuvans . . .' She made a circle of her thumb and middle finger on one hand and inserted a finger from the other hand. I nodded my understanding, then we both chuckled.

While I was steeling myself to revisit Zulmira's home to resolve our fracas, Sansar-Huu returned from his parents' camp on the back of a knackered-looking truck and tossed several bulging, greasy sacks to the ground before he clambered down himself. He arrived back in Tsengel just a couple of days after traders from Olgii had driven into the village square to buy up the local cashmere that the nomads had just combed from their goats.

The traders didn't look like rich men. They drove over the mountains in shared, tarnished jeeps and wore the same *deels*, hats and boots as the villagers. But their pockets were crammed with wads of green Togrogs, and these notes lured the Tsengel men back from the mountains like a powerful magnet.

Sansar-Huu took his place in the square amongst the Olgii traders and the other village men. I loitered in the square on my own or with Gansukh, fascinated by the gnarled herders arriving on horseback leading camels bulging with split sacks of cashmere. Tsengel was briefly transformed into a noisy bustling market, with scores of men squatting down together, weighing sacks with cheap portable scales and leisurely bargaining amongst themselves. I saw one of the goat combs sticking out of a sack. It looked like a huge afro comb, with long blunt spikes. The traders paid Tg 7,000 (about US $9) for a kilo of the raw cashmere, which was the colour of straw and felt a little greasy. It left a slight film on your fingers.

Many local families couldn't afford to travel the 80 kilometres to Olgii, where the cashmere price was known to be substantially higher, and the city traders brazenly exploited their advantage. The Tsengel shopkeepers at least were happy, because they did a brief roaring trade in everything they stocked. But even with this sudden flush of money around, there were no marauding drunks. After dark the square was deserted and the village almost silent until the next morning. The teenage nomads had gone to serve their country for a year, and the local men who had come back home, or arrived from the mountains to sell their *yamani-noluur*, seemed to have better things to spend their money on than bottles of *arikh*.

CHAPTER TEN

The villagers were on the move. They'd sold their *yamani-noluur*, bought up the sacks of rice and flour from the stores and now they were packing up their homes and migrating to the mountains for summer. This static community would, for the next three months or so, revert to its ancient nomadic traditions.

Most of the families in Tsengel owned at least a small herd of livestock, which they kept either in and around the village itself, or in the surrounding Altai mountains. Their nomad relatives took care of the animals in the mountains through winter and spring, but in summer almost all the villagers moved into the Altai to graze their animals and live on the glut of milk and dairy foods. Although the weather had been terrible throughout the spring and the local pasture was still brittle yellow, only stained with green near the banks of the Hovd, families were already trundling off. They took everything they owned with them, stripping their houses of furniture, rugs, beds, even the stoves, and stacking the whole lot on top of one of those belching rusty trucks. I saw goats, calves and even a cow hoisted up on to the back of the truck with the furniture, *gers* and excited children. As soon as school was finished, most people would be gone. And it suddenly occurred to me that if my work at the school was almost over then I would also have to leave, because Tsengel would be empty. In the few months I'd been living and teaching here, neither Menke nor Abbai had asked how long I was planning to stay. Nothing had been carved in stone, so I was free to leave in a couple of weeks. If I wanted to.

I was slowly mulling all this over in my unsettled mind, when

Sansar-Huu told me he was reclaiming the *ger*. My house was also his and Gansukh's summer home, and now it too needed to go to the mountains.

'I'm taking Opia and Yalta away with me, to stay with my parents,' he said. 'We'll pack up everything now, and when school is finished Gansukh will come and join us. You can stay with her in our house until school ends.'

'When are you leaving?'

'Tomorrow or the day after.'

I glanced around my small, circular home. I was going to miss it.

'Louisa, what are you going to do when school finishes?' Gansukh asked.

'I really don't know,' I told her. I knew my Mongol residency now needed extending, but felt very reluctant to return to Ulaanbaatar for any longer than a few days. One of the fascinating contradictions about Ulaanbaatar is that although it's the world's coldest capital, it's also a stifling city in the summer. The air is static and the sun beats down in a relentless pulsing wave of dry heat. It wasn't a tempting option.

Gansukh looked at me, glanced at Sansar-Huu and then back at me. 'Do you want to come to the mountains with us, Louisa? You can live with us and Sansar-Huu's parents. We will be,' she opened up her arms, 'far away from here, in a very beautiful place. We'll show you our landscape and how the nomads live in summer.'

I stared at them both, unsure what to make of this outrageously generous offer. I didn't want to leave Tsengel. These last few months had been the hardest and most fascinating time of my life, and it felt as though I was just beginning to delve under the surface of this unique village. If I took a huge deep breath and admitted I actually wanted to be around until Christmas, then I could witness a full cycle of the seasons, a complete year in the life of Tsengel. During my months here I'd gleaned some essence of village life, but Tsengel, this bizarre Tuvan and Kazakh encampment, where the few resident Mongols seemed to placidly accept their ethnic minority status, was still an enigma to me. If I stayed on until the end of the year, my fragmented perception of Tsengel might merge into a whole, offering me some coherent sense of this small, remote world.

I knew summer would be hard work because rural Mongolia was always tough, but in the heat and sunshine, with the luxury of plenty of milk, yoghurt and cream, life would certainly feel a lot easier. I'd also have a chance to live amongst the nomads, which was what I'd dreamt of back in Ulaanbaatar and London.

Oh, life isn't so difficult here, I lied to myself, casually ignoring the dust storms, the haggard women, the stunted kids, starving livestock and awful food. Anyway, I was just getting used to it now: this wasn't the right time to leave. '*Saikhan*, beautiful,' I told Gansukh and Sansar-Huu. 'That would be great. Thank you! I'll have to go to Ulaanbaatar first to extend my residency. But I'll come straight back and meet you in the mountains. *Sain bain!*'

Buoyant with plans for summer and autumn I recklessly approached Menke the next time I saw him at school, and suggested maybe I could continue working at the school for the first term of the next year, and simultaneously train Gansukh and Zulmira to teach my English classes after I'd gone. 'Then you won't have to rely on another foreigner because you'll have two local English teachers here,' I pressed, as he and I sat in the sun on either end of a bench just outside the school front entrance.

'Why can't you stay here all next year, Louisa *bagsh*?' he asked.

I explained that I hadn't been back to England for more than two years, and needed to return home by Christmas to see my family again. Menke nodded slowly and said nothing, his brown face a mask of utter indifference. Then he got up and walked away, without a word. It didn't change my mind about wanting to remain in the village for another six months, but certainly bruised my pride.

School officially finished on 15 June. Most students had already left the week before, and the few that had stayed on celebrated by leaving as early and raucously as they could on the last day. Even as they were clattering out of the front entrance, the teachers started the grim and thankless task of repainting their classrooms with a dribbling silt of chalk and water, the local equivalent of white emulsion. Gerel-Huu, Shinid and Bagit were leaving for the mountains with their large families, and, as soon as the classrooms were decorated, the teachers would also leave. Only a smattering of the richest and poorest villagers would stay in Tsengel all summer. The rich would stay to continue working in one or two stores, the post office or the government building, and the very poorest families couldn't afford *gers*, so they were stranded in the smallest cabins of the near empty village throughout the parched Mongol summer.

On this final day of term, as people scurried to finish tasks and talked about their plans for summer with eager, smiling faces, one young local committed suicide.

Lashun was one of the primary school teachers. A tall slender woman with bloodless-looking skin, she was married to a man called Kalim. They shared a *hasha* with the family of Guul-Naa, the gentle chemistry teacher. Lashun had introduced me to her husband in the disco one evening. He was a short, swarthy man, who told me he was a driver but wasn't working at the moment, because, like most of the men in Tsengel, he didn't own a jeep. The only other time I'd seen Lashun and Kalim together they were laughing as they walked through the village with a couple of friends, and were both quite drunk. Lashun's face bore the first early stains of alcohol: red threads were beginning to rupture her cheeks. She'd leaned her long neck back and yelped with laughter at something Kalim said. Several afternoons later Gansukh and I saw Kalim again. He was coming out of a narrow shop doorway we were entering. We greeted him and he said hello obliquely, reeking of vodka and peering through a black eye swollen as an egg.

'I went to school with him, you know,' Gansukh told me, shaking her head. 'Kalim was in my class. We were the same age.' She and I were inside her empty home that we were now sharing. We'd both just come back from the school, where teachers were sitting on the front steps or amidst classrooms of stacked up desks, murmuring and biting their lower lips as they shook their heads and spoke of Lashun and Kalim.

Gansukh drummed her fingers on the table and lowered her voice, though no one else was in the room. 'He was one of the most clever in the whole year. Maybe that was his problem. He had no car and no work. Nothing. He was always bored, so he drank too much. He should have stayed in Kazakhstan. That's where he used to be, in Alma-Ata, when he was studying – what was it? – oh, engineering. She was in Alma-Ata too, that poor girl, Lashun. Studying primary education. They got married in Kazakhstan, but came back here two years after. His parents are still over there.'

Gansukh spilled out their story in a dull, low voice. It was a small wretched drama that could have been enacted in so many other forgotten rural communities. But it had happened right here in Tsengel, and it laid bare something about life in this village that I'd already witnessed but had never been able to articulate even to myself, maybe because I couldn't bear to.

Lashun and Kalim had come back home to Tsengel. Lashun had easily found work at the village school, where most of the teachers were women, and had settled back into village life, busy with her new baby and her young students. But there were very few other jobs going in Tsengel, and none for men like Kalim, who was clever and qualified but had no local trade to ply. Kalim also had no savings, so he couldn't buy a jeep and work as a driver ferrying people and goods to and from Olgii. There really wasn't much for him or many of the other local men to do. A few of them governed the village, but it was the women who ran the clinic and the school, who stocked the shops, raised the children and cleaned the houses. *They* were constantly busy and usually tired, always on their way somewhere or doing something, while Kalim and some of his old friends spent the days passing sluggish time, loitering around the square when it wasn't too cold, or sharing a bottle of *arikh*.

Kalim and Lashun had always shared a fairly turbulent marriage, but things got worse when Kalim began to drink all day. He got drunk constantly. Tsengel was all he had and perhaps he drank because he couldn't bear to be here any longer. Eventually Lashun packed her bags and moved out with their daughter, protesting she'd had just about enough. This did sober Kalim up, and he finally coaxed his wife back, promising to stay away from the booze.

Instead, it seemed she had taken it up as well.

Their frail reconciliation lasted a year or so, before buckling under the brunt of Kalim slowly drinking himself to death. Then the rows were long and vicious. Guul-Naa and the other teachers stoically ignored Lashun's occasional hangovers and the yellow and purple bruises down her arms. Lashun's rocky marriage was not their affair, and besides, she and Kalim were not the only couple in Tsengel who raged at each other with their voices and fists. It wasn't their battle to fight. On 14 June, the night before our end of term, Kalim and Lashun fought bitterly once more. Guul-Naa said she could hear them screaming threats and abuse at each other all night. Kalim drank *arikh* from dusk through till dawn, and apparently carried on drinking when his wife left for school in the morning. He could have gone to bed and nursed a hangover. He and Lashun could have made it up once more. But Kalim unnotched the wire clothes line that straddled the *hasha* and hung himself from the rafters of their cabin. Guul-Naa's husband Balakh Khan was crossing the *hasha* when he saw him flailing. By the time he got into the cabin, moments later, he was too late to cut him down. Kalim had garrotted himself.

'He was twenty-six, Louisa. I don't understand it. This does not happen here.' There was a very long silence between us. 'This does not happen here,' Gansukh said again a while later. She stood up and began to sweep the floor with her head bent. I stood up and went outside.

Early the next morning Gansukh and I were wringing out our washing in the *hasha* when she stood up and motioned me to my feet. 'Look.'

A small convoy of jeeps were scaling the hill ahead of us to the cemetery. We shielded our eyes against the sun, squinting as the mourners picked their way through the adobe tombs until they came to a fresh grave.

'His father hasn't returned from Kazakhstan yet,' said Gansükh quietly, 'and Lashun's parents are still in the countryside. But the Kazakhs always bury their dead the next day. That's their way.'

CHAPTER ELEVEN

It was strange, the thought of leaving. Even though I knew I was only going away for a couple of weeks at the most, it felt odd . . . unsettling. I instinctively wanted to stall for time and delay the departure, because now that I'd decided to stay on in Tsengel there was no real value attached to my visit to Ulaanbaatar. Oh, the food and beer would be great, a welcome indulgence. I'd dabble in gluttony and take lots of very slow, hot baths. But I didn't want to be in the city for very long. In fact I wasn't even sure I'd get there at all, because unless I could swing a Mongol-priced ticket, I didn't have enough money for the flight back.

Those last few days in the village before I left for urbanity were memorable, not least because Tsengel finally seemed to bloom. The weather got hotter, the pasture got thicker, and even though there was no more rain, the river water level rose as the distant mountain glaciers began to melt.

A dozen or so families moved out of their homes and literally went just around the corner, to a wide sweep of the river about quarter of a mile from the southern end of the village. They pitched their *gers* and grazed their small herds on the bank of the Hovd, and in the now longer evenings you could see the women and children milking rows of tethered goats. They waved cheerfully as trucks trundled out of Tsengel to embark on longer journeys, but seemed perfectly happy where they were. I gazed across the warm, comparatively lush landscape and wished I didn't have to go: after all, the grass is always greener when you're leaving . . .

Tsengel had just buried one of its sons in quietly horrific

circumstances, but life was carrying on, and in the end that is the way of it: the only way we all survive.

I rang Greg to see if he'd be in Olgii when I arrived back in town.

'Sure,' he said down the phone line, sounding like he was communicating from a distant planet, instead of only 80 kilometres away. 'How are you getting on, Louisa?'

The line was so bad I gave up trying to tell him, and simply yelled down the mouthpiece that I'd see him very soon. Greg and I had known each other most of the time I'd been in Mongolia, and we seemed to understand each other very well. I was grateful he'd left me to my own devices in Tsengel, and was now looking forward to staying with him and sharing our months of news.

Abbai, whom I'd barely seen since our New Year day out, came round to Gansukh's home and offered to escort me to Olgii to catch my flight to Ulaanbaatar. I didn't ask him how he knew when I was going. By now I'd accepted that local news travelled at the speed of gossip. I told Abbai I was hoping to secure a Mongol-priced ticket because I didn't have the equivalent of $160 left, and his face fell into an almost comic expression of dismay.

'Very difficult, *bagsh*. Very, very difficult. Maybe you will have to go in a truck.'

'To Ulaanbaatar?' Gansukh shook her head.

I pictured myself spending four or five days in the back of a truck bashing its way east over the mountains and through the Gobi desert. It didn't really bear thinking about. If it came to it I knew I could endure 1,700 kilometres to Ulaanbaatar, mostly by unpaved road, but desperately hoped I didn't have to. It sounded awful.

'When are you coming back here, *bagsh*?' asked Abbai, who also obviously knew I was returning.

'Very soon. Maybe in two weeks. I'm, er, going to the countryside with Gansukh and Sansar-Huu for the summer, to work with their family.'

Somehow I'd thought Abbai would be pleased with this obvious enthusiasm for learning more about the nomads, but Gansukh blushed as he frowned intently and hunched his slender neck into his narrow shoulders. 'You need to learn about Kazakhs also,' he said quietly. 'We are also nomads, *bagsh*. After summer why don't you live with a Kazakh family? You can stay in my *hasha*, where we have a room.' You can live with us and choose to learn about the rest of the village, about our people, he seemed to be saying. It was an irresistible offer. I thanked him and assured him I would love to live in his *hasha* with his family, but that I would have to return to England in time for Christmas. I also explained the school situation, as it was Abbai who'd employed me at the school in the first place.

Abbai listened carefully and then waved his hand across his face, as though swatting a lethargic fly. 'Do not worry about Menke *bagsh*. You can stay and teach at the school and train Gansukh and Zulmira. I know this, because I am the *Hural Darakh*. The boss.'

And that, it seemed, was that.

The word *Hural* means Government or Council. Abbai was chief of the Tsengel *Hural*, which decided how the village and the outlying district of Tsengel were administered. He was the local chief councillor. However, the Tuvans also had their own smaller Tuvan *Hural*, where they made decisions about their local Tuvan community. It was attended only by Tuvans and usually just by men, but Gansukh told me she wanted to take me to one just before I left for Ulaanbaatar.

The village was quiet as we walked down the track, through the square and arrived at a huge wooden gate opposite the clinic. It was taller than any of the cabins, and there was a padlock large as a man's clenched fist dangling half open on a wooden bar that slid across the front, protecting it as surely as a ferocious guard dog. There must be something very precious inside.

'Push, push,' Gansukh urged me, 'we have to get through here.'

We shoved our combined weight against the gate and it yielded, grinding open. We stepped into a small courtyard.

In front of us was a shattered shell of a building, with a broken pagoda roof that sloped downwards, casting rich black shadows on the ground even at this time of day. I could smell damp in the ancient, rotten wood. A small crowd of men were sitting inside the shell, leaning against the thick pillars, or crouched on the pitted wooden floor. One or two were smoking. Occasional sunbeams strayed through the half-collapsed roof, casting dusty shards of light amongst them, as breaths of their smoke hovered around their heads. A gaunt man with scooped out cheeks was standing in front of the crowd, talking to them in a low, angry, passionate voice. They ignored us.

Gansukh and I stood silently on the threshold. Everyone was listening attentively to the gaunt speaker, their eyes flicking to and from his thin face with its feverishly bright eyes. They didn't say a word to each other, or fidget or yawn. They just listened.

Gansukh put her hand on my shoulder. 'He is Amer-Huu, the head of our Tuvan *Hural*,' she whispered. 'He is saying our Tsengel village has more Tuvans than any other village, so we need to rebuild this temple and have a place to pray together. This place, you know, was destroyed by that Choybalsan, and we haven't had a temple for the last sixty years.' She listened again before smiling and adding, 'He says they need to stop buying alcohol and give the money to rebuild this temple, because it has to be finished before winter. He says they should brew *arikh* from the mare's milk instead.'

Every nation has had its despots or dictators, its times of fear, or what a Mongolian friend of mine once described to me as 'many long days of no light or hope'. She was referring to the regime of Horloogiyn Choybalsan, who was Prime Minister of Mongolia 1939–52. He personally instigated the notorious purges that swept across Mongolia from the end of the 1930s. Inspired by Choybalsan's close relationship with Josef Stalin, these purges set in motion the imprisonment and extermination of Mongol counter-revolutionaries for more than a decade. It has been conservatively estimated that during the first eighteen months of the purges, more than 20,000 Mongols were sentenced to death. Thousands of academics and Buddhist monks were targeted in the bloody suppression of any perceived dissent or opposition to the communist state.

Mongol families had long traditionally encouraged their eldest sons to take the vows of a *lama* and don the familiar burgundy robes. By 1945 more than 18,000 *lamas* had been executed, and all but three of Mongolia's 800 monasteries had been looted or razed or both. Only Ulaanbaatar's Gandan monastery, where I'd been teaching, was spared. It was preserved as a state showpiece.

Mongol Buddhists continued their worship and rituals in fearful defiant secrecy, holding on to their faith with a clenched determination no dictator could ever break. Icons and Sutras were hidden or buried, *lamas* disguised and prayers chanted under Buddhist breath. Buddhism survived Choybalsan, who died in Moscow in 1952. But this small ruin of a temple was a poignant reminder of how bad things had been, even in this remote corner of the country.

It wasn't until the 1990 Peaceful Revolution that the tide really turned and a fragile Buddhist revival was gradually encouraged by the same state that had for years done its utmost to obliterate it. I have no idea why it had taken the Tsengel Tuvans eight years to start reconstructing their temple. And to be honest, after watching the solemn local men crouched inside their decrepit shrine, I felt I had no right to ask.

I left Tsengel two days later. I had a hangover that morning, because Gansukh and Sansar-Huu and I had knocked back a bottle of vodka together as a farewell gesture, and then Amraa and Tuya had arrived with another one, and of course we drank that too. Abbai amazed me by arriving at exactly the time we had arranged, which no one in Mongolia ever did, so I hadn't finished packing when the beep of his jeep squawked through the wooden walls.

'I told you!' Gansukh scolded me as I scrabbled round the cabin frantically stuffing grubby clothes into my rucksack and searching for painkillers at the same time. 'Oh, Louisa, Abbai says your plane ticket is going to be a big problem. I hope he is wrong.'

I assured her it would be fine, and I'd see them all very soon, and could she please say goodbye to everyone but remind them I was coming back. And then I limped outside into the dusty street, where Abbai and, of all people, Menke were waiting for me.

But Abbai was so, so right about the damned plane ticket. Despite his best efforts, and the generous help of both Greg and Greg's boss, a baronial-looking Kazakh called Attai, there were no local-priced tickets to be had for me. Eventually both Abbai and Greg had to leave town.

I was completely stranded in Olgii for more than a week, miserable and defeated: my visa had almost expired and I had no one else to blame but myself. The irony was that I actually had the money for a full-priced ticket, but it was held in an Ulaanbaatar bank account and I couldn't get access to it from Olgii. I was seriously considering returning to Tsengel visa-less and illegal and just taking my chance, when Attai, bless him, offered me a way out of the hole I'd dug for myself. He had managed to organise a lift for me in a jeep that was just about to set off on the long journey east to Ulaanbaatar, via the Gobi desert. The driver was Attai's elder brother, Orulsen, and Orulsen's wife, Alma, was going as well.

We left just before dawn the next morning, drove across the mountains to Hovd, and then down towards the Gobi.

CHAPTER TWELVE

I never told anyone very much about the 1,700-kilometre drive from Tsengel to Ulaanbaatar. There wasn't much to say. It was just a very long and gruelling journey. For four days and three nights, Orulsen, his wife Alma and I drove relentlessly across arid steppe, parched by unflinching 90C heat as we flanked the Gobi desert. For the first two days there wasn't even a track across this orange and brown moonscape, which was devoid of trees or foliage and offered only occasional fleeting glimpses of anything that was alive. For hours at a time nothing disrupted our flat, glaring horizon and the earth's crust we were jolting over. The western Gobi was so barren it was beautiful, but it was also quite frightening because it seemed so dead. I couldn't imagine how any nomad could survive here, because I couldn't see anything to survive on. Nothing grew and nothing seemed to breathe. But, eventually, we spied a distant loping camel and then a hunched thorny bush defiantly casting a thin shadow over the cracked ground. So there was a pulse beating here after all. Much later that day we passed a camp of several *gers*, with a woman standing alone outside, and I just shook my head and wondered how and why she survived here. It seemed a self-inflicted cruelty, to immerse yourself in wilderness where there was no water or pasture to be seen, no respite from the heat and the huge, searing, empty space. The indifference of the nomads here to any notion of comfort or ease is something I knew I'd never understand. For me Gobi-Altai province made Tsengel village live up to its name.

I remember at one point leaning forward in my seat with my

hand on Orulsen's shoulder, asking him could we please stop even for just a little while at the edge of the white lake shimmering in the distance.

He chuckled and shook his head as he gripped the steering wheel. 'No, *bagsh*, we can't stop. Because there is no lake, you see, there's nothing here but rock.'

It was the first mirage I'd ever seen.

We drove on north-east and ate in solitary shacks which stood on vast, naked plains recoiling in the sun. A handful of wind-burned, male drivers on other interminable journeys sometimes joined us and smoked, drank tea and ate plates of steaming, greasy meat. We slept in the jeep the first night, and rested in *gers* with nomadic friends of friends during the rest of our journey. After dusk the temperature plunged like a heavy stone and we pulled our sweaters back on and zipped up our jackets. We drove more than eighteen hours a day and gave rides to silent nomads with skin like old leather as we crossed half a dozen provinces. When the jeep engine overheated, as it did several times, Alma and I sat on the bank of a placid river somewhere greener than Gobi-Altai, and dangled our ankles in the cold water. By the second day my feet had swollen up like mounds of sausage meat.

When we finally saw Ulaanbaatar's infamous Power Station Number 4 belching out dark fumes beyond the last hillside, we all cheered hoarsely.

'Louisa – is London as big as our capital?' asked Orulsen, nego-tiating craters in the road, which was now tarmacked.

'London's got ten million people,' I replied without thinking.

The jeep veered on to the stony verge, as his head swivelled round and he gaped at this astounding figure.

It was wonderful, but strangely harrowing to be back in Ulaanbaatar. At first I felt incredibly nervous about even going outside on to the streets. I must have had some sort of culture shock because I didn't want to see anyone or go anywhere, and began to wish I'd never even come back at all. I just felt overwhelmed.

When I did finally venture out, the city looked crammed.

Blockades of flimsy shops, kiosks, nightclubs and bars had been erected along central Enkh Taivan (Peace Avenue), and were full of shiny new stuff. Huge glitzy adverts were posted up around the city square. The air tasted of metallic fumes. The street urchins begged in English now.

Before I moved to Tsengel I had always lived in one city or another, and assumed I belonged in urbanity. But during my week or so in Ulaanbaatar, I was thrown completely off balance by my reaction to being back in my old home. I had expected to love every moment of it. But instead of enjoying a social whirl with my friends, I collected my new visa and then fled straight to the MIAT Mongolian Airline building to book myself on to the next available flight back to Bayan-Olgii. It was the end of June, and a lot of people wanted plane tickets. The weary clerk told me to come back and try again two weeks later. But I knew the score in Ulaanbaatar, and I returned to MIAT very early the next morning with a wad of dollars in my purse, and emerged clutching a ticket stamped for the weekend flight. I was so thrilled I did a little dance on the building steps. Even the thought of six more months of eating boiled sheep couldn't deflate me.

I bought as much food and as many presents as I could carry, and five days later flew back west. As the small plane droned over the capital I gazed down, and knew that I would still pine a little for Ulaanbaatar from afar. I'd spent two years living there, and it still felt like a sprawling friendly town rather than an impersonal capital city. But it was a relief to leave. Tsengel had worked some strange magic on me, and more than anything in the world I wanted to be back in the mountains with my friends, celebrating the Naadam festival and toasting Tuya's wedding.

PART THREE

Our Mountains

CHAPTER THIRTEEN

Sansar-Huu's mother, Deri-Huu, never learned to pronounce my name. She spent the summer calling me Elizaa, and I eventually called her *Eej*, which means mother, because everyone else did and in the end it was just easier. Deri-Huu was a statuesque matriarch of fifty-six, with cheeks the colour of oak and a bosom like an overhanging cliff top. She was a large woman who laughed deeply and moved lightly, with a thick black plait coiled into the nape of her brown neck. I never saw her get agitated or angry. Everything about her was comfortable, and serene.

Her husband, Bash-Balbar, looked like an old man. He was gaunt and frail, prone to bouts of trembling ill health. His skin was as white as Deri-Huu's was sunburned. Bash, as he was known, often rasped when he breathed, so he was forced to depend on his son, Sansar-Huu and his robust elder brother, Bayan-Saikhan.

Bash and Bayan-Saikhan had always herded their flocks side by side. They dismantled their *gers*, loaded up their camels and drove the animals to fresh pasture four or five times a year. With Sansar-Huu's help they'd built two wooden cabins plus a sturdy stone coral for their animals on a wide natural ledge, high in the mountains. This was where they sheltered for the coldest months of winter. At the beginning of spring they started herding again, and every year they chose a new site for their summer camp, where the air would be cool and the grazing good. They were quite wealthy by now. Between them they owned more than 450 sheep and goats, plus herds of horses and yaks. Bayan-Saikhan's name means 'Rich and Beautiful' in Mongolian. It had served them all well.

I arrived at the summer camp on the back of a truck, which had belched out of Tsengel and down the river gorge trail like a bloated drunk. I was excited, because I hadn't seen Gansukh and Sansar-Huu for what felt like ages, and I'd never met Deri-Huu and Bash. I didn't really know what to expect at the camp. When the truck eventually rumbled to a halt, we were in a wide, boulder-strewn valley, where three *gers* stood near a river the colour of lapis lazuli. Gansukh was walking towards her *ger* with a pail of milk, and when she put it down to hug me, we both burst out laughing.

'*Saino*! How are you?'

'And how are you, Louisa? We heard you were coming, we've been waiting for you!'

The news had travelled faster than I had. I'd spent several days in Tsengel waiting for a truck going this far west. We perched on stools in Gansukh's *ger*, where I'd also be staying, and drank tea. The winter rugs had been rolled up and the carpet was cool, flattened grass.

Sansar-Huu came in and nodded at me casually. '*Saino*, Louisa.'

There was no fuss to be made and that felt nice. I was just welcome back. Deri-Huu and Bash were next door with three of their five daughters. Bayan-Saikhan, his wife Manike and their two sons were in the other *ger*. The final member of camp was a cowed dog, who barked at me ferociously for the whole of the first week, and was regularly booted in the head and backside by everyone except Opia, Yalta and me. When I asked her what its name was, Gansukh shrugged and said it was Dog.

'How was Ulaanbaatar?' she asked me that evening. 'Was it exciting being back in the city?'

'It was OK,' I said, shrugging. 'Yes, it was fine. But I wanted to come back here, to the countryside. The city's just hot and dusty, but it's beautiful here.'

'It might be beautiful,' she retorted, 'but it's very hard work. You'll see. Every day it's the same – from early morning till late at night, all we do is work.'

It only took me to the next morning to find out this was no exaggeration. Deri-Huu rose at five in the morning, and everyone else was up by 6.30. I opened my eyes as Gansukh was pulling on a soiled *deel* and a pair of tatty old boots.

'Louisa, you stay in bed and sleep, it's still very early,' she urged me. 'You can get up after we've done the milking.'

But I didn't want to stay in bed when she and Sansar-Huu were already getting ready for work. When I stumbled outside, the dawn was cool and delicate, the valley rinsed in pale early light and the short grass drenched in glistening dew. We brewed and drank tea, then I followed them outside to help tether and milk the goats.

'That one, the black and white one over there!' Deri-Huu's teenage daughter, Shilgee, screeched at me. 'No! Not that one – *that one!*'

I glanced around me, thinking, And which bloody one would that be? They all looked exactly the same to me. I eventually grabbed one of the damn things by the scruff of its neck, and after a couple of minutes' tug-of-war, dragged it to the other goats tethered between two short posts, with a long coil of rope binding them together by their necks.

Shilgee, who had the face of a fourteen-year-old and the hands of a middle-aged manual labourer, rolled her eyes and shook her head, letting the goat go and giving it a good kick up the bum as she said, 'We can't milk that. It's a male.'

I closed my eyes and almost laughed.

Instead, I offered to help Deri-Huu with the milking, which was an even worse idea. As Deri-Huu milked goat after goat (there were forty-six to get through) I knelt behind my first, and cautiously tugged at its teat. A thin white drizzle dripped into the pail. Deri-Huu had already filled her pail while I was still grimly tugging at my second goat. The third one kicked my pail over, and Shilgee scowled at me as she snatched it away.

'You can't do that again,' she said. 'We need the milk, you can't just waste it. I'll have to do it.' She knelt down and drained the swollen teats as I skulked back to our *ger*.

I'd just wanted to join in and help, to feel as though I was working with everyone. But I didn't have a clue about milking, or any of the other tasks. So I was more of a nuisance than anything else. For the next few days I kept asking Gansukh what could I do to help, because everyone was so busy all the time: tending to the animals, collecting water or dung, cooking and cleaning.

Gansukh shrugged. 'Louisa, don't worry. You can read your book, or go for a walk. You like walking. You don't need to milk goats, you will never live like this again. It's no use to you.' She seemed uneasy about me working, which puzzled me, because we'd already worked together so much. When she and Sansar-Huu were outside I'd scurry round the *ger* covertly, and tidy up, fetch buckets of water from the river or sacks of dry flammable cow pats for the stove. Just to do something.

So when Deri-Huu suggested I helped Shilgee herd the goats and sheep for a day, I jumped at the chance, and as soon as the next morning's milking was over, she and I set off. We crossed the rugged valley, then, guiding the passive herd between us, began to climb the escarpment as the sun rose higher. Eventually, while the animals were gorging themselves on stubby bushes of tiny glossy leaves, like tea plants, we perched on high, flat rocks. Now the valley was splayed below us. We could see a few other summer camps at either end, and a herd moving across the green floor like a silent swarm. My rock was already warm to touch, but just as I was settling, comfortable and drowsy, Shilgee bounded to her feet. 'Let's go! The herd needs to move!' Though she was only fourteen she had already left school to help her parents, and took her work very seriously. She marched me relentlessly up and down and around our end of the valley, to the best patches of grazing. I was determined not to complain, but after just a couple of hours I was knackered and already lagging behind.

'Come on!' Shilgee yelled at me from over her shoulder. 'Can't you walk any faster? We need to keep the *mal* together!'

'Shilgee, wait a minute!' I had to jog to keep up with her, swearing under my breath and panting like a dog as the temperature soared. Mongolia can be searingly hot in summer, and though our camp was in a valley, it was much higher than Tsengel. I'd spent the last few weeks looking forward to being reunited with Gansukh, Sansar-Huu and their family, and learning how the nomads lived in summer. But I'd had no idea there was so much work to be done all the time. And herding with Shilgee, who was less than half my age, incredibly fit and utterly tireless, was like being suddenly drafted into the Foreign Legion.

We finally got back to the *ger* camp late that afternoon. Parched with thirst and rancid with sweat, I limped to the river, stripped off everything but my grotty, damp underwear, and plunged in, gasping out loud as my burned skin hit the clear, freezing water.

CHAPTER FOURTEEN

Every day started and ended with those uncooperative goats. At dawn and then dusk they were all rounded up, and the females tethered and milked. Gansukh, Deri-Huu and Manike spent part of each day making *tsagaan idee*, 'white food', or dairy produce. All the nomads were making masses of yoghurt, cream and cheese. They eat and drink dairy throughout the summer and autumn, literally fattening themselves up for the lean winter ahead. Best of all they love mare's milk, which is frothy, rich and creamy. The mare milking season only lasts about a month, and that's when the nomads make gallons of their famous *airag* – fermented mare's milk.

Early one morning I watched Deri-Huu and Manike milking half a dozen placid mares. They often worked together and always looked like a good team: unhurried and thorough. When they'd finished, the mares were left to graze and the pails of milk poured into a huge, stiff leather sack, which could hold up to 60 litres of *airag*. It was stored inside the *ger* on a home-made splint that was nearly as tall as me. Deri-Huu churned this fresh mare's milk into the *airag* using a wooden mallet the size of a small oar. As the milk fat slowly solidified and floated to the surface, she scooped it up in handfuls and squeezed it into pats of butter. 'Hey, you can do this for me, Elizaa,' she said, thrusting the mallet over to me.

My arrival at the camp hadn't phased Deri-Huu at all. Whenever she saw me hanging round looking lost, she set me a task, and slowly I began to feel I was taking part in the life of the camp.

Gansukh started to relax about me wanting to work, and as she also started asking me to help her with cooking or cleaning or collecting dry dung, our old camaraderie drifted back, which was a real relief. Maybe she'd needed reassurance that I wanted to get stuck in and not just sit around watching everyone else graft.

That morning with Deri-Huu I churned the *airag* until I thought both my arms were about to drop off. Meanwhile she and Manike lashed several brown cloth sacks to the latticed *ger* walls, simmered that morning's goat milk, and poured it into the sacks. As the milk slowly separated, clear yellow whey trickled into pails they'd put underneath the sacks.

'By tomorrow morning this will be fresh yoghurt, Elizaa,' Manike told me. 'Now come and have a rest. *Tsai oh.*'

We sat and drank several bowls of Deri-Huu's incredibly salty tea as I rubbed my throbbing arms.

Manike must have been about the same age as Deri-Huu. But compared to her sister-in-law's dark skin and hair, Manike's complexion was very pale, even soft. She had a headful of white curls and her eyes were somewhere between hazel and green. Together they looked like shadow and light.

'I'm going to distil *shimin-arikh* tomorrow morning,' Deri-Huu told me as she spooned a knob of butter into my tea. 'Maybe you can help me. But you always look very tired, Elizaa! And if you want to be there, you'll have to get up very early because we always distil before dawn.'

'Oh, I'll be there,' I promised her. I knew the nomads brewed *shimin-arikh* vodka from their mare's milk, but I'd never actually seen the distillation. And even though I was indeed tired a lot of the time, because the camp was high and the work was hard, this would be worth getting up for. It sounded like alchemy.

Deri-Huu called me before anyone else was awake. In the silent half darkness she placed a deep cauldron on to her stove, and poured litres of freshly skimmed *airag* into it. Then we hoisted a four-foot aluminium sleeve into the cauldron, standing it upright in the *airag*. This was our cooling tower, to distil the *airag* steam into vodka. Deri-Huu secured an empty pail with two lengths of rope, tying a large stone on to the end of each length. She handed me one of the ropes. We suspended the pail inside the tower, counter-balancing its weight with the stones. Finally she sealed the tower with a wide dish of cold water.

'I will keep the stove very hot and the pot full of *airag*, Elizaa. You have to remember to keep refilling the dish. The water must stay cold.'

The flimsy tin stove heated quickly. As the *airag* boiled, the steam rose up the tower, condensed on the surface of the cold dish, and splashed into the suspended pail. Within a couple of hours, just as everyone else was going out to round up the goats, our first brimming pail of *shimin-arikh* was ready.

'Drink, Elizaa.' Deri-Huu passed me a bowlful of pure vodka. I gulped down a mouthful and shuddered. It was so warm, but it tasted better than the toxic stuff in the village.

Of course the *airag* was completely undrinkable after distillation, but even then it wasn't thrown away. After we'd milked the goats Deri-Huu poured the thick sediment into a couple of brown cloth sacks. She and I dragged the damp sacks outside, and crushed them under nearby rocks to extract every last drop of moisture. Several hot, dry days later the sediment had desiccated into slabs of white curd, which looked something like mozzarella and tasted as tangy as sweet cheese. This is *aaruul*.

We sat out in the sun, leaning our backs against her *ger* as Deri-Huu showed me how to break up these slabs of curd, lay them evenly on one of her home-made wooden trays, then wedge the trays under the sloping *ger* roof ropes.

'After another three or four days they will be hard *aaruul*, dried by the sun. Look, Elizaa!' She suddenly bared her large white teeth, startling me for a moment and laughing out loud as I jumped. 'Don't be frightened! You see this is why we use *aaruul* – it keeps our teeth strong because it's so hard. If you chew *aaruul* every day, you won't need a toothbrush.'

We sat there, munching as we worked. Fortified by the sun, the small chunks of *aaruul* were soon the texture and colour of bones.

*   *   *

While I was helping the women inside the *gers*, Sansar-Huu and the men were outside, repairing the temporary summer coral, which was made of wire and wood, branding horses, and tagging or shearing the sheep.

They sheared more than 150 sheep between them, using only a couple of tiny pairs of scissors, like nail clippers. Those sheep were harder to catch than the goats. They kicked and struggled and ran and we all took turns to chase them, or to stand and call laughing encouragement as one of the others tried to wrestle a fleeing ewe or ram to the ground. When the shearing was finally done, Sansar-Huu, Bash, Bayan-Saikhan and his boys stripped to their waists, waded into the river together and dunked the wool again and again, scrubbing it with their bare hands until it was rinsed clean. They wrung the wool out and stretched it between them, separating the clumpy layers until each was as fine as dandelion seed fluff, then draped it all over the grass hassocks. When I stepped outside at dawn the next morning, it looked as though an army of immense spiders had been secreting their silvery webs all night.

The part of my Tsengel journal that I wrote at the camp is crammed with details about work: how men and women did separate but complementary tasks, how we made the different dairy foods, the endless herding, milking, fetching and carrying . . . I shared several adventures with Gansukh and Sansar-Huu over the summer, but most of our days were spent working, and my world became even smaller than in the village. In this wild rocky valley there was no time or space for philosophical reflection on the nature of summer nomadic life because I was in the midst of it. Like Gansukh, Deri-Huu and Manike, I rarely left the camp, and found myself caught up in the tasks to be done each day. The very few hours I had to myself I spent either scribbling my journal, or bathing in a secluded corner of the river and dozing in the sun afterwards. I can't remember ever analysing what I was doing here, or pondering whether this ancient way of life would survive beyond the end of the millennium. I just got on with it like everyone else. The only conclusion I did come to was that the nomads work harder in summer than any other time of the year.

'Summer is always very much work in our mountains, Elizaa,' Deri-Huu told me more than once, 'because you know even now we have to prepare for our long winter.'

The people I saw from Tsengel during the summer, like Tuya and Gerel-Huu, echoed that sentiment. They were out in the mountains to provide for themselves, and they never ceased working, because that's why they were here. The fleeting summer was their food harvest, their glimpse of plenty. It was no languid holiday.

However, our camp did have a couple of days out together over the summer. The first was to visit the local Naadam festival, which was held in mid-July over in the next valley. (I don't know the exact date because I didn't write it down; occasionally I wasn't even sure what month it was.)

Naadam is Mongolia's national sports festival. Best known for its displays of the 'three manly sports' – horse racing, wrestling and archery – the major Naadam festival takes place every 11–13 July in Ulaanbaatar. But hundreds of smaller-scale Naadams are held all over the countryside throughout mid-July. These local Naadams are usually one-day events, because no one can spare any more time from their animals. And for some reason they never seem to include archery.

'Sansar-Huu is going to wrestle today, you know,' said Gansukh as we were getting ready to head off to the Naadam. 'And Tuya and Gerel-Huu will both be there. It's going to be a wonderful day out!'

We all got dressed up for the occasion. Deri-Huu looked magnificent in a burgundy *deel*, with her raven hair woven into a crown on top of her head. We trooped boisterously over a high rocky pass with dramatic overhanging rocks, and down into the next valley where a crowd had already gathered at the open-air site. Only Shilgee and Bayan-Saikhan's boys stayed behind, to do the herding.

At first sight the Naadam looked something like an ancient rustic summer fête. Long white sheets had been spread over the ground and laden with mounds of *buurtzug* and *aaruul,* wagon wheels of cheese and bowls of thick, crusted cream. Huge kettles of milk tea were being served by dozens of younger women. All the men and women sat apart, their barefoot kids running between them, excited and squealing.

I lost Gansukh in the crowd, and just stood looking round me, smiling. I could see Deri-Huu and Manike sitting comfortably with a group of other older women. Their ornate earrings were glinting in the sun as they nodded and shook their heads and laughed easily together. Everyone, including the children, was dressed in *deels* embroidered with gold, silver or scarlet thread, and some of the men wore the traditional Mongolian peaked hats. I was in a baggy black and white summer dress, and felt like a real scruff.

'*Saino!*' Gansukh had found Tuya and then we all found each other. It was lovely to see Tuya again. She was glowing with health, but cheerfully complained about everything.

'I hate it here! It's too much work getting up at half-past six every morning.' She pulled a face. 'Milking the yaks and making all that food! Urgh! I can't wait to get back to Tsengel and see Gerele. How was it in Ulaanbaatar?'

As I told her about my trip, a posse of rheumy-eyed grand-fathers settled themselves in front of us, on half a dozen felt rugs. These wizened old gentlemen were the local VIPs because they were the wrestling judges.

Wrestling is the highlight of Naadam. Mongols consider it a performance art, and the ancient performance rituals have been fiercely preserved. Each wrestler dons a skimpy, eye-catching outfit of crimson briefs and a turquoise and crimson cropped jerkin with short tight sleeves. They also wear the traditional leather *gutals* with the upturned toes. Even at as small a Naadam as this, there was a real selection of wrestlers: short, tall, gaunt and occasionally podgy. There were swaggering, spotty teenagers and broad-shouldered, muscular men in their forties. The best of them are awarded titles according to how many opponents they manage to topple. They become a Naadam eagle, elephant or a bull. It's very ritualised and grand. Each bout begins with the two opponents imitating 'the eagle dance' to bless their sport. There's something beautiful about watching muscular, grown men fluttering their arms as though they've suddenly sprouted wings, circling the grass arena as the crowd cheer them on.

Several pairs wrestled simultaneously, and we clapped and groaned dramatically whenever anything looked likely to happen, but if two men were well matched, they could stand with their arms interlocked for a very long time. This championship lasted for several hours, so people also wandered round greeting each other, eating and drinking and toasting the Naadam with plenty of *shimin-arikh*. Gansukh, Tuya and I wandered off, and came back again just in time to see Sansar-Huu wrestling Tuya's brother, Altan-Hudag. When Sansar-Huu finally forced Altan-Hudag backwards until he lost his balance and keeled over, Tuya burst out laughing, and Gansukh nudged me and beamed with pride.

Later on I went looking for Gerel-Huu's *ger*, which I knew was somewhere nearby. When I found her she was with her whole family: six sons, one daughter and her husband Dorj, whose eyes often twinkled and whose hands often wandered. He was a shameless rascal. They were all eating a sheep and I joined them for lunch. More and more people crowded inside as we ate, including a couple of the teachers from school. We were just settling down to a *shimin-arikh* toast, when Gansukh ducked through the door. 'The horse race is just about to start – come on!'

Squeezing on to the back of a very crowded open truck, we jarred to the other side of the wide valley, a hot, dry wind bristling our faces. Scores of others had walked or ridden over, and soon we could see the beginning of a dust cloud drifting towards us at ground level. As it moved steadily closer, the Tuvans stood up, and everyone began to clap, cheer and roar. It was a cloud of children racing bareback horses, clutching the tangled manes as they thundered towards us. We hollered and waved as the children whooped, and the pounding, wide-eyed horses looked as though they'd never stop.

I always loved watching horse racing in Mongolia, though I

never really understood who came first. There was no actual finishing line drawn up, and two or three slathering mounts always seemed to arrive at exactly the same moment. But judgement was pronounced, and we all crowded round the winning horses as they were draped in blue *khadags*: folded silk scarves, presented as a symbol of respect. They are usually white or pale blue, and can also be seen fluttering around cairns to bless journeys, and adorning temples. The draped horses were then solemnly anointed with *airag* and *shimin-arikh*. Their young riders were given crowns but didn't get half as much attention as the horses themselves.

While we were lingering, Deri-Huu suddenly appeared at my side. '*Yamar bain*, Elizaa, how was our Naadam?'

'*Saikhan.*'

As we waited for the others, she and I sat down together on the warm ground and enthused about Sansar-Huu's wrestling. We decided that next year he was definitely going to become an elephant.

CHAPTER FIFTEEN

We were sitting round Deri-Huu's stove late one evening, some days after the Naadam. The evening goat and yak milking had been done, the animals were settled for the night near the *gers*. We could rest. This was always my favourite time of the day. Deri-Huu would simmer the yak milk, dipping her ladle into the cauldron just as it began to boil. She'd raise her arm high and cascade the milk again and again until it foamed like beer. Then it was hauled off the stove and we'd drink as much as we wanted as we sat by that cracked stove in candlelight, sipping frothy yak's milk and talking sleepily, or maybe saying nothing at all.

This particular evening I sat listening to the men making plans. They were going to leave the camp very soon. They'd be riding more than 60 kilometers south, to a renowned fertile plain, where they would join dozens of other herders, all camping in makeshift tents and roasting meat on open fires. Together they'd cut tons of grass, using hand-held scythes, which would be tossed on to open trucks by hand, taken to the winter cabins and stored in the corrals for feed.

But before they could go off to scythe hay, Sansar-Huu and Bayan-Saikhan were going marmot hunting. Marmots are large, stupid-looking steppe rodents, about the size of a hare, with buck teeth and a long bushy tail. They are hunted for their thick, dark pelts, which are sold to traders in Olgii in the autumn because they make elegant hats and coats.

Sansar-Huu and Bayan-Saikhan began to ride into the mountains every afternoon with their guns, returning at dusk with half a dozen carcasses hanging from each of their saddles. Bash didn't go with them, but stayed near his *ger*, pallid and sweating. He was sick again.

After the morning milking Gansukh would kneel outside our *ger*, squinting in the sunlight as she flayed the marmot flesh from its fur. The clean skins were staked out in the sunshine to dry, and then strung upside down from the *ger* rafters, like large headless bats.

'If I can shoot one hundred healthy marmot,' Sansar-Huu told me, 'our family will make five hundred thousand Togrog.' This was the equivalent of almost £400 – more than Gansukh's annual teaching salary.

All this hunting meant there was usually a vat of oily marmot meat simmering on one of the *ger* stoves. It actually smelt quite good but the marmot is also the only edible carrier of the bubonic plague, which still lurks in remote central Asia. Every year there's a local outbreak somewhere in western Mongolia, so I was reluctant to tuck in at first. I knew that if I ever got really sick in Tsengel, then I was in deep trouble. I couldn't afford health insurance, and to be honest, I didn't fancy my chances in the village clinic.

'Elizaa, don't worry,' Deri-Huu assured me, seeing me hesitate as everyone else started chewing on chunks of marmot. 'Sansar-Huu and Bayan-Saikhan, they know these marmots very well. When they're sick, they are very slow and nearly blind, so the men do not shoot them. This meat is fine. You just have to remember never to eat marmot and drink milk tea straight afterwards. That will make you vomit, because it's very strong, oily meat.'

I took her word for it.

When our *ger* rafters were festooned with marmot skins, all the men and boys, including a now slightly healthier-looking Bash, rode off to scythe the hay. They cantered away at dawn without a backward glance, leaving four of us women at the camp, plus Shilgee, Yalta, Opia and Deri-Huu's other two young daughters.

When I blearily joined the women and girls for tea that morning, a sliver of transparent new moon was poised in the early sky. I was surprised to see Deri-Huu had arranged tea and food outside on her low table, because Mongols and Tuvans always eat and drink inside their homes. Apart from a celebration like the Naadam, you'd never see a nomad consuming food outdoors. It's considered rather vulgar.

Deri-Huu lit incense, which wafted around us as we breakfasted, and I asked Gansukh what was going on. 'Why is today so special? Is this a religious occasion to bless something?'

Gansukh blushed and giggled. She leaned over and said to me in English so no one else would understand, 'Sex, Louisa. The yaks need sex. We are outside to ask Buddha for baby yaks.'

I glanced over to the placid herd, which already had several young calves. 'Erm, Gansukh,' I said, 'don't you think they need a bull?'

That had already been arranged. He arrived that afternoon, and was the ugliest, most terrifying beast I'd ever seen. He weighed more than a ton, with a neck as thick as a truck tyre, a swollen hulk of a body and a murderer's glower. I couldn't stay far enough away from him. Even the children were less intimidated than I was.

As the bull's owners turned round to go back home, Deri-Huu, who could no doubt see the fear in my face, calmly told me he was extremely dangerous. 'He could charge, Elizaa. I'll look after him.' I told her that was absolutely fine.

Deri-Huu had a staff like an elongated shepherd's crook, which she used to control the bull, rapping him on his huge rump when he came too close to the *gers*. But within a couple of days he was unmanageable. He trampled the camp with his thick neck lowered, ruined the milking by intimidating the yaks, and terrified Opia and Yalta. And me. When another mammoth bull gate-crashed the camp to stake his claim on the female yaks, the two of them roared and fought for control of the harem, swaggering towards each other like punch-drunk brawlers. Their skulls collided, and the usurper eventually slunk off, cowered into

Inside my *ger* before the felt is wrapped around the lattice walls.

My front doorstep. A most embarrassing pair of sunglasses.

The Kazakh cemetery above the Hovd river.

Kazakh boys hauling water.
The boy on the left is one of Zulmira's brothers.

Kazakh mosque.

Gansukh and I sawing a log in the *hasha*.

The road to Ulaanbaatar.

Khadags (prayer scarves) and a cairn en route across the Gobi desert.

submission. Deri-Huu and Manike said that was quite enough: conception or not, the bull had to go.

The bull's owners, Enkhbat and Nanselmaa, returned on horseback to drive him back home. Enkhbat had a rifle, Nanselmaa brought her own wooden staff. Gansukh, Deri-Huu and Manike warned the rest of us to stay in the *ger* as they herded the yaks and the bull into camp, and tried to separate him from the females. He was enraged, and charged round the camp roaring, as Enkhbat and his horse side-stepped and goaded him again. I stood at the *ger* door, my mouth wide open. It was wild out there. But the women stood their ground and were absolutely fearless. Deri-Huu raised her staff and battered the bull ferociously, and when he careered straight towards our *ger*, Manike stood in his path and hurled rocks in his dark face. He swerved heavily and changed direction, towards the hills adjacent to our camp. The women screeched and raced after him, as Enkhbat and his horse galloped off in pursuit.

I suddenly felt sorry for the bull. His chest had been heaving, snatching lungfuls of hot air as he slathered past, relentlessly pelted. But for the women, it was a sweet victory. They'd expelled this bully, and when he dared to veer back once more towards our camp, they stoned him with rocks and hurled abuse. Enkhbat and Nanselmaa finally drove their beast back across the valley, and Deri-Huu, Manike and Gansukh wandered slowly back to camp, red-faced and grinning wickedly. They'd all had a great time. We celebrated with pots of tea and a toast of *shimin-arikh*, and when I asked them had they really not been at all frightened, they laughed so much that Gansukh almost lost her balance and fell off her stool.

CHAPTER SIXTEEN

Although I had been in the valley for several weeks now, I'd only visited one or two of the other nearby camps, because there just didn't seem to be enough time. But while the men were still away we were all invited to a wedding reception about half a mile down the valley.

Deri-Huu was especially pleased with our invitation. 'These are rich *malchin*,' she told me as we were all getting dressed up, again. 'They will have a big wedding *khurim* [party], with horse meat and lots of guests.'

I desperately tried to smarten myself up, marvelling at the new *deels* and silk sashes Deri-Huu and Gansukh were pulling out of battered wooden trunks, then pressing smooth with an ancient iron scorched over the stove. I had only clean-ish jeans and a shirt to wear. I hadn't expected to be attending elegant Naadams and wedding receptions throughout the summer.

When Deri-Huu had finished dressing in an emerald *deel* she'd just stitched herself, she looked like an Amazon. She took one glance at my shoddy outfit and shook her head gently. 'I think maybe you could wear this instead.' She handed me a burgundy *deel*, embroidered with silver round the high collar and the sleeves. It fitted me well and when I was ready she nodded her approval. 'Yes, yes, *mini okhin*, this is much better.'

I smiled my thanks because she'd just called me 'daughter'.

Deri-Huu, Gansukh and I arrived at the camp early. People were already milling around outside the main *ger*, waiting for the *khurim* to begin. A tin summer stove had been kindled outside, trailing reams of forlorn white smoke into the air as it simmered a cauldron of milk tea. Vats of meat were bubbling on smouldering circles of stones near the *gers*, and I could hear the sound of horses' hooves cantering towards us.

Tuvan and Mongolian weddings are, in essence, identical. In both cultures marriages are traditionally negotiated by the groom's father, a respected male elder and the bride's parents, although the bride and groom do choose each other. When it's all finally been agreed, the groom's family is expected to provide the couple with their own *ger*, which is an expensive item costing the equivalent of at least £100.

On the wedding day itself the groom rides off to the home of his in-laws, and escorts the bride and her parents back to his own family *ger*. Both bride and groom dress in brand new *deels* and boots, and the bride always wears blue. From the moment they arrive at the groom's *ger* the couple are considered wed. The exchange of rings, with their distinctive male and female symbols, isn't important. Although relatives and close friends do visit the newly-weds on the wedding day itself, Tuvans celebrate the *khurim* a few days after the actual wedding. If they're rich, his parents will slaughter a horse. If they can't afford that, several sheep are slain instead.

As more people began to arrive at the *khurim*, Deri-Huu led Gansukh and I into the main *ger*. We were just settling down on the rugs when hordes of guests all arrived at once. More and more people crowded inside: toddlers, children, teenagers, pregnant woman, weather-beaten herders and crumpled old men with faces like raisins, all noisily squeezed or pushed their way in, kneeling or crouching on every inch of bed, rug and grass. The frailest-looking men clambered over everyone else to the rear of the *ger*, opposite the door, which is traditionally where guests of honour sit. I was surprised to see a young woman sitting among them there. Even the oldest women usually sit at the sides.

Several low tables were stacked high with food, and the *shimin-arikh* was already doing the rounds. It's deceptive stuff, *shimin-arikh* – a stallion masquerading as a gelding – and before long one of the elderly men had passed out, smiling inanely to himself as he was cheerfully hauled into the fresh air, and everyone carried on celebrating. Only Gansukh shook her head and tutted. 'He's always *sogtuu* [drunk],' she muttered. I nodded happily. I'd already knocked back three bowls of *shimin-arikh*, and was starting to feel a bit *sogtuu* myself. Every time the silver bowl is passed back from guest to host, it's refilled before the next person drinks. If you're handed the bowl and your host doesn't think you've drunk enough, she can refuse to accept it back until you've swallowed half. It is a lethal tradition. The woman serving our side of the *ger* laughingly insisted we all drink deeply, and by the time Gerel-Huu arrived and squeezed herself in next to me, most of us were plastered. I certainly was.

Gerel-Huu took one look at me and roared her wonderful blast of laughter. 'Louisa! You are red and drunk!'

Gansukh, who was being far more decorous than I was, suddenly nudged me as one of the elderly Tuvans at the back struggled to his feet and pointed at me. I also got up unsteadily and we stumbled towards each other through the mêlée. He embraced me, sniffed my neck (which is a genuine sign of affection from an elder), and then, with a great theatrical flourish, offered me a brimming tumbler of *shimin-arikh* topped with a thick wedge of cheese. I smiled and wondered what on earth to do next. Mongolia is a land steeped in rituals, and it can be horribly easy to offend someone, especially if everyone presumes you already know local etiquette.

'Taste the *arikh* and the cheese, then give him back the *arikh* and keep the cheese,' hissed Gansukh, who always knew when I was stymied. I did so, and sat down feeling even more sloshed.

There were so many people crammed in the *ger* that I had no idea who the bride and groom were until Gerel-Huu introduced me. They were a very young couple, called Tseverlee and Bat-Tsengel, and both seemed overwhelmed by the whole event. Tseverlee was flushed and silent; her new husband frowned sternly and didn't look at his wife. When they'd finally greeted all their guests, which took a long time, everyone in the *ger* suddenly rose to their feet and surged towards a fringe of white *khadags* hanging from the rafters. Gerel-Huu and I were swept forward with them as people tied Togrog notes on to the *khadags* as a gift to the newly-weds. I was glad Gansukh had reminded me to bring some money. As soon as we'd made our offering, we squeezed outside for a breath of fresh air and a pee.

'Ah, it's very hot inside, this is much better,' she sighed as we slumped on the grass. 'How is your head, Louisa?' I told her it was clearing now we were outside. 'You need to eat meat!' she said, grinning. 'You need to fill your stomach. We think meat is good for everything! Hey – do you see that woman over there?' Her voice dropped. 'Do you know who she is?'

I shook my head. The woman Gerel-Huu had nodded towards was young, though her age was somehow indefinable. I watched her for a moment as she walked past us, back towards the crowd at the *ger* door. She had the gait of someone much older and more weary than her apparent years. When she turned round to greet a friend or acquaintance, I saw that her eyes were inflamed and bloodshot, and she wore heavy, square-framed glasses as if to shield them from the light. She was the woman who'd been sitting at the back of the *ger* with the eldest men.

'Who is she?' I asked Gerel-Huu.

Gerel-Huu pursed her lips as though she wasn't quite sure what to tell me. 'She is our Enkhtuya, our Shaman,' she said after a moment. 'This family are very happy she is here. It is very good for them to have our Shaman at their wedding.'

I wanted to ask her more, but it was time for us to go back inside and eat. The guests were crouched in circles around platters of dripping horse meat and mutton. A man wielding a dagger rapidly sliced the meat and innards while the rest of us ate with our fingers. The *ger* was quiet for a few minutes while everyone tucked in. But as soon as the meat was finished, the *shimin-arikh* toasts carried on, and now the old men stood up one after another, and began to offer rambling eulogies, poetry and even marital advice to the newly-weds – who began to look as though they desperately wanted to escape.

The old men droned on and on, and could no doubt have

eulogised all night. But the women knew how to revive the *khurim* and when they'd heard enough of the men and their warbling advice they began to sing. I felt a lop-sided grin spread across my face, like a palsy, and leaned my head against Gerel-Huu's shoulder as she sang with the women. As soon as they'd finished, the men took up the mantel and they sang too. I knew a few of the songs by now, but was always too entranced to join in. I just wanted to listen and drift into pleasantly drunken dreams.

The Tuvans lamented their homeland over the Altai, heralded their mothers, grieved over love and honoured their horses. Cracked with emotion and wrung with such fierce passion, these are the most beautiful and tragic songs in the world. They rang from the *khurim ger* across the rocky valley and the clear river, where they were surely absorbed into the spirit of the mountains herself.

We staggered home in time to milk the goats and yaks, and I wanted nothing more than to go to bed very early. But Shilgee asked and then begged me to go out with her that night.

'Louisa, they're all playing the Game tonight and I have to be there. But *Eej* [Mother] won't let me go on my own and no one else will come with me, so you have to.'

I'd already heard something about this 'Game'. This is not a Mongol tradition, but strictly a Tuvan rite of passage, and only ever played after a wedding *khurim*, to celebrate the marriage. Only young adults play: no children or older people are allowed. It starts late at night and usually lasts until dawn. And it can be bloody. Of course I had to go.

It was already late when we set off. 'See you in the morning, Elizaa,' Deri-Huu said beaming gleefully. Gansukh, ever vigilant, warned me not to walk home alone as all the men were bound to be drunk. Shilgee was to be my escort all night. I began to wonder what I was letting myself in for as Shilgee marched me back across the dark valley. She'd never learned to stroll.

'Come on! Hurry up!' she harangued, grabbing my arm and dragging me towards the *khurim* camp.

We squeezed into the *ger* – and Shilgee promptly vanished. I turned round and she'd gone. Cursing her under my breath, I waded forward, suddenly feeling very out of place. Everyone I'd met that afternoon had obviously left, and I didn't recognise any of the young men and women who were now staring at me without saying a word. I panicked and wondered if my being here was an indiscretion, or a real taboo. Maybe I wasn't welcome here, but I'd never find my way back to our camp in this darkness . . . where the hell was Shilgee?

Glancing round for somewhere to sit and hide myself, I was waved over to the rear of the *ger* by someone I did recognise, a young woman who'd visited our camp a few times because she lived nearby. I smiled and gratefully crouched by her side. She was sitting next to Enkhtuya the Shaman, who looked drunk, her inflamed eyes glinting bloodily in the candlelight.

Enkhtuya was friendly and boisterous, ordering tea and sweets to be passed to me and demanding I sat with them both. She seemed very much in control of the whole event. I took a gulp of *shimin-arikh*, relaxed, and asked them about the Game. Sarantuya and Enkhtuya threw their heads back and chortled.

'You wait and see!' Enkhtuya cried. 'We are the only people in the world who have this Game! It belongs to us! It's Tuvan!'

There must have been about forty women and men sitting opposite each other in the *ger*, and before the Game could begin we were all matched into pairs. The smoke from the men's cigarettes hung thick in the air. The candles cast ominous shadows over the players' burned faces and the women's bright headscarves. One of the men stood up, and the voices hushed as he unwound a narrow leather strap, about an inch wide and half a metre long. The crowd murmured and chuckled. I gulped.

Then Enkhtuya rose to her feet. For a moment she displayed a wide silver wedding ring in the open palm of her hand, and then she bent in turn over every woman in the *ger*, as though passing the ring into their waiting cupped hands. Each of the women then meshed their fingers together, and she moved on to the next. The men watched, impassively smoking and nodding. There was a short pause as they conferred as to which girl had the ring. Then one young herder confidently pointed and called to one of the women, who shrugged and held out the ring. Out of three attempts to conceal the ring from them, the men found it twice. We lost.

Enkhtuya nudged me. 'Stand up and raise your left arm, you're first!' My heart started beating ridiculously fast as I stood up and timidly held out my arm towards my partner, Tumur. Everyone hollered, 'Roll the sleeve back and lift it higher!' I pulled a face, which made the women laugh even more than the men. What am I doing here? I thought as Tumur raised his hand. I flinched, though he flicked the strap so softly over my arm I scarcely felt the impact. The men, and especially the women, mocked him loudly. But I beamed at him, pathetically grateful. I have a low pain threshold.

This is the esoteric Tuvan wedding game. If one sex can guess the whereabouts of the hidden wedding ring, they get to thrash the other. I winced as the men happily strapped the women, who stood up one by one in the candlelight, and did not flinch. Many tossed their heads after the strap cracked across their arms, deriding the blow as weak or badly aimed. You could hear the leather whistle through the night.

When the men first hid the ring, we also found it easily. 'Hit him hard,' I was urged. I didn't really want to inflict pain on my friendly partner, for my own sake, but purely in the spirit of the game, I tried to give him a stinging strap. He laughed at my attempt, and the women groaned. They were far more vicious than the men, raising the strap higher and cheering when several of the men winced. The next time we won I really went for it, and Tumur bit his lip, which earned me a round of applause from the women, and a playful, but vengeful look of reproach from him. I almost apologised.

Considering how much pain was being inflicted, the atmosphere was both light-hearted and jovial. I soon found myself cheering and heckling with the other women. 'Go on. Get him! Yes – *sain bain*!'

When we all paused for a while to drink tea and *shimin-arikh*,

Enkhtuya showed me her bruised wrist. 'What are *khurims* like in England, *bagsh*?' she wanted to know.

'Oh, very dull compared to this,' I told her.

We resumed playing and my luck ran out. I was matched with a new partner, the bridegroom Bat-Tsengel, who was still frowning and didn't return my appeasing smile. In the next round, the men found the ring easily – I had it. I stood up, raised my other arm and reluctantly rolled back my shirt sleeve. I turned my back to Bat-Tsengel, expecting the worst – and howled when the strap burned into my wrist. The *ger* rocked with laughter, which I joined in because it was one of those times where you literally either had to laugh or cry. This was the Tuvans' idea of a good night out, and I wouldn't have missed it for anything. It was bizarre in the extreme.

As dawn washed over the *ger*, I was suddenly exhausted. Most people had finally had enough of the game, and were ducking or dodging the strap. Enkhtuya and her friend said they were ready to go home. I finally cornered Shilgee, who, like a true teenager, had ignored me all night, and she said she was coming too. We said our farewells and staggered out of the *ger* as the sun began to rise.

'So, how was our Game, *bagsh*?' asked Enkhtuya as we walked slowly back towards our respective *gers*.

I turned to her. 'It was the strangest night out I've ever had,' I said, 'but also one of the best.'

Enkhtuya laughed quietly. She looked tired, but I sensed hers was a life-long weariness that came from somewhere deep inside. She was a woman who seemed to carry a burden from within, the weight of other people's grief, anxiety, sadness and yearning.

CHAPTER SEVENTEEN

Gansukh and I were on the endless search for dung when the sky above us rumbled and bruising clouds began to roll. The rains, which had started months ago in spring but released nothing more than a few days' downpour, finally seemed imminent. The air began to feel hot and thick. Deri-Huu and Manike called me to help them gather the nets of sheep's wool that were still lying on the riverside hassocks, and were now dry and stiff. Some of it we bundled into sacks, the rest we spread evenly across a large mat woven from reeds, and then we all knelt around the rug and beat the wool soft with sticks.

This was harder than it sounds. Deri-Huu gave me two sticks and showed me how to cross one on top of the other, so the wood didn't splinter on impact. It was one of the few times we all worked together, and we sang out loud as we whacked the wool. Webs of fluff floated above and around us, until we were enveloped in a hairy cloud. It was several hours before the lanolin had been beaten soft and the wool was fluffy. We rested inside the cool *ger* and drank tea for a while.

But Deri-Huu was soon back on her feet. 'Come on, Elizaa – I'm going to show you how to make *esgii* with this fresh fleece before it rains.'

Making *esgii*, or felt, in Mongolia is like harvesting a diverse crop, and it is work that only women do. Felt provides walls for the *gers*, it's used as mattresses and blankets for the narrow beds, is dyed and stitched into elegant rugs, or moulded into huge stiff, knee-high winter boots for the men. Felt boots are perfect for wading through the snow – your feet don't get wet at all.

Deri-Huu and Manike spread the fleece evenly across the tightly woven reed mat. Then Gansukh appeared with two large pails of warm water.

'Now, watch.' Deri-Huu poured a thin stream of water into her dark palm, her fingers splayed open. Drops trickled on to the dry fleece. 'We have to soak the fleece before we can roll it into *esgii*,' she said. 'If the wool isn't wet, it won't bind.'

When the whole fleece was damp, the four of us rolled the mat and fleece slowly and tightly into a long, thick sausage. Deri-Huu swaddled it with lengths of grey rope, binding it fast. When she'd finished, we knelt down again on the dry grass and rolled it backwards and forwards, backwards and forwards, until our singing was parched and even Deri-Huu admitted she was weary. We had a rest, drank tea and then started rolling all over again. We worked until Shilgee herded the flock back to camp for the evening and we had to milk the goats and the yaks. Gansukh and I were shattered, and spent the late evening comparing our throbbing arms and backache.

The next morning we slowly unfurled the rigid mat. 'If the fleece hasn't bound properly, we'll have to roll it again this afternoon,' said Manike casually, as she released the ropes. I couldn't even bear to think about that prospect.

The emerging fleece was pale as a newborn, the wool fibres meshed and inseparable. Gansukh nudged me and grinned. 'It's OK,' she said in English. 'It is good *esgii*. Look.'

Together we'd rolled a stiff white wall of felt.

The rest of the wool was either stitched into the lining of winter *deels* or blankets. Gansukh had a decrepit manual sewing machine, which whirred in the afternoons. She also made clothes for Opia and Yalta, pillow cases and curtains from bolts of pale coarse cotton.

'There's always work to do in the countryside,' she said, hunched over the machine and rubbing her stiff fingers. It was the nearest I'd ever come to hearing her complain.

After days of brooding, the clouds suddenly ruptured. Our *gers* were battered by driving, freezing rain. Thunder bellowed, while the lightning ricocheted spasms of white light across the valley. I've always relished a dramatic storm, but the Tuvans were scared. Everyone, including Deri-Huu, frowned and bit their lips when the elements collided overhead. She even pitied cowered old Dog and let him into the *ger* while the lightning was crackling. When Gansukh and I clambered into bed that night, we could hear streams trickling across the grass *ger* floor. We bailed out by candle-light and went back to bed miserable and shivering.

'This happens every year,' she said. 'Now you know how diffi-cult it can be for *malchin* in our mountains. The village is so much easier, Louisa.'

In the morning our *ger* floor had been transformed into a horrible, sticky, thick mud paste. The rain threw down its worst every afternoon. As soon as we heard the drops splatter against the *ger*, we all had to dash around stacking stuff on the beds and snatching up clothes we were trying to dry outside. Trays of *aaruul* had to be pulled off the roof, the canvas *ger* skylight had to be closed, the mounds of dried dung covered with shreds of old felt. Meanwhile the young goat kids would flee into our *gers* from the lashing rain, and dive for cover under the beds, before they were dragged or kicked outside.

In the midst of one sodden storm, I thought I could hear sea-gulls, and listened in disbelief: but the squalling continued. There were gulls screeching outside. I didn't know the Mongolian word for sea bird because I never had to use it – Mongolia is as land-locked as a nation can be. But when I tried to ask Gansukh about the gulls, she nodded as she sat cuddling Opia and Yalta on their beds. There was nothing else to do until the rain had stopped.

'Yes,' she said, 'it's very strange, Louisa, because I have never seen the sea, but I've often heard these birds! I think they are the young ones who aren't strong enough to fly to their destination without resting, so they spend the summer here. Do you know what kind they are?'

When the rain finally abated, I stepped outside into the watery valley, and there they were, with their familiar blanched white beaks and oily, white feathers.

There was no mistaking them. They were gulls all right. It was a poignant little reminder that, even out here, the world was still a surprisingly small place.

A few nights later a screaming gale ripped across the valley, making the *ger* walls beat like a pounding heart. In the midst of this rampage little Opia had a screaming fit. She was usually a happy and boisterous infant, but was suddenly terrified by something, and woke the entire camp with her shrieking. Deri-Huu came quickly to our *ger*. She lit several candles and sprinkled incense on to a smouldering ring of dung, which she passed over and under and around the frightened little girl, until, swathed in a cloud, her cries subsided. Then Deri-Huu poured hot candle wax into a bowl of cold water to determine the cause of Opia's fear. When she shook her head, her plait swung gently. 'It was a dream of demons,' she said.

The following morning we received bad news. A herder arrived early and, over tea in Deri-Huu's *ger*, told us Gerele's father had died. He had been swept away while trying to ford the swollen Hovd river on his horse. His body had been dragged out of the water by nomads several kilometres downriver. Gansukh and I were silent as we listened to his story. We both knew Tuya's wedding would have to be postponed.

Gansukh and I worked all morning, and left for Tuya's *ger* on horseback early in the afternoon. It took us less than an hour to canter to the valley where we'd all attended the Naadam the month before. Tuya was sitting near her *ger*, on a flat rock at the river's edge.

'Gerele's brother also died in the river, three years ago,' she told me later. 'He came out of the disco in Tsengel and had a fight with someone. He fell into the Hovd and drowned.' Lightning had struck twice.

Tuya knew there was now no way she'd marry Gerele by the end of summer. She shook her head in resignation. 'I don't know what we'll do – Gerele and his mother will have to decide. He'll have to stay at home anyway – he's the oldest, you know. He can't leave, he's got four younger brothers and sisters.'

'Have you told your parents about Gerele?' I asked her. Tuya had always laughingly claimed her romance with Gerele was a well-kept secret, and had even hinted they might elope together.

She shook her head again. 'No, they still don't know. But anyway, after this, everything is going to be different. Now that his father is dead.'

CHAPTER EIGHTEEN

The men returned from scything hay. Their skin was darker and their bodies were leaner. It was mid-August now, and our summer together was coming to an end. In just a few days I'd be leaving for the village with Gansukh and Sansar-Huu, and I would move into a new *hasha* with Abbai and his Kazakh family. I had spent two years in Ulaanbaatar with Halkh Mongols, and this spring and summer with the Tsengel Mongols and Tuvans. It felt a good time to move in with a Kazakh family for a while. Gansukh and Sansar-Huu had known about this move for a couple of months now, we'd all discussed it, and had even joked that I'd be part of their family even though I wouldn't be living with them any more. But there was a sudden awkwardness between Gansukh and I about my leaving. We both said nothing about it, but for the last week or so of camp it was there in the air between us.

During these, our last days in the Altai, the rains ended as abruptly as they'd started. There would be no more downpours for another nine or ten months now. But though we all dried out, the temperature cooled overnight, and a smattering of fresh snow dusted the valley escarpment. Herders began to pack up and prepare to move off to more secluded camps for autumn. This change in weather was their compass. I went herding with Shilgee one last time, and we saw a train of Bactrian camels loping across the valley below us. We could make out tables and chairs strapped to the back of one, and red *ger* poles bound to another as they headed slowly, timelessly west.

'We will move in that direction too,' Shilgee said. 'We always spend autumn at the edge of the White River, you know. Sansar-Huu will fetch our three camels and then, when you've gone, we will move our *ger* and all the *mal.*'

I wished I could go with them, for the sheer epic romance of moving house by camel. Village life suddenly seemed tame by comparison.

On one of our last evenings together, Deri-Huu asked me to herd the yaks back to camp from their grazing ground with her. As we walked slowly towards them, I asked her what winter was like.

My question made her laugh. 'Ah, Elizaa! I know this has been very difficult for you – you are always tired and you've worked hard this summer. But for me this work is easy now. I've been doing it all my life, always in the mountains with my animals. You know now that summer is our busiest season; in winter it gets a little easier. Bash, Bayan-Saikhan and my son Sansar-Huu have stored the hay, and our cabins will be warm. But the snow is deep in winter, and some days Shilgee can't herd the sheep, and then even our yaks give us very little milk.'

Deri-Huu summoned her yaks home by emitting a shrill, piercing whistle. They raised their shaggy heads in response and lumbered towards camp. We strolled behind them, filling a sack with dry dung we found on the way.

'I'm sorry to be leaving,' I told her.

Deri-Huu smiled. 'But you can come and visit us at the White River, Elizaa. You don't have to say *bayartai* now.'

It was our last day. I was sitting on my favourite rock near the *gers* when Sansar-Huu strode over with a twitching sheep. He trussed up its scrawny legs and cut its throat with one slash of his knife. It bled to death in less than a minute, crimson blood pumping into the bucket beneath its throat. Afterwards the women rinsed the internal organs clean, the lungs, intestines and bladder, and hacked up the carcass. They emptied and boiled the stinking stomach, but waved me away when I asked if I could help. My assistance wasn't needed, or wanted, for this. There are

some things only family do together. Gansukh had also cleaned
the sheep bladder, which she hung to dry from the *ger* rafters.
It looked like a large, transparent balloon, and would soon be
stuffed with butter or cream. It made a sturdy container. The
rest of the sheep, including its head, was simmered for hours in
salty water. It smelt fine, although I wasn't keen on the intestines or head, which I'd eaten too many times before. Mongols
consider it a real honour to slaughter a sheep or goat for a guest,
and in keeping with their life-long austerity, they eat just about
the whole thing.

As we were sitting down to eat, Deri-Huu sliced a small chunk
of blood-clotted intestine, a slither of meat, a slice of the heart
and a small section of bone, and tossed them all into the stove
flames. 'There is a spirit in our fire,' she said. She always knew
when I was watching her. 'Now the spirit has been offered its food,
we can eat. We do this before we eat anything, even marmot. And
we have to keep the fire clean, Elizaa. You can only burn clean
paper in here – and no onion skins.'

Blood-stained rags were discreetly buried outside, along with
onion skins, which sting people's eyes if they're burnt and so would
also offend the fire deity.

This, our final supper together, was also a ritual. The men sat
at the table in Gansukh's *ger* and ate first. We sat on the floor with
the children, or leaned against the beds. Compared to our former
casual gatherings around Deri-Huu's stove there was a strange,
stilted formality about the meal, and everyone ate quietly and
quickly. A little later Manike called me into her *ger* with Gansukh
and Deri-Huu and we ate again. Sated with meat soup, we toasted
our summer together with bowls of *shimin-arikh*. Bayan-Saikhan
wandered outside, and we carried on drinking.

Manike offered me a final chunk of meat. 'This is from the
breastbone, the part of a sheep that is traditionally the best for a
woman – try to eat it.' Her eyes were glinting slightly from the
drink.

'What is the best part for men?' I asked.

They were engulfed with laughter. Deri-Huu's bosom heaved

as she set down the bowl of *shimin-arikh*, and wiped her eyes.
'Aiye, Elizaa! It's the rump!'

The next morning we rose as always at dawn. It was a cool morning
of clouds. When a scarred truck arrived early to take us back to
Tsengel, we were still in the middle of dismantling the *ger*, which
is quite a feat.

First you unwrap the outside canvas and then the felt walls,
until there's just the sturdy wooden frame. Then the poles that
hold up the trellis have to be pulled out until, with just a few left
in place, the crown itself can be taken down. Meanwhile the beds
are taken apart, clothes and utensils stuffed into wooden chests,
sacks and split suitcases. All in all, it took us about two hours to
take our house down. It felt very strange when all that was left of
our *ger* was an indent and a small pile of ash where the stove had
been.

We were almost ready to leave, except of course that we had
to drink tea first. In Mongolia you drink tea before any departure, and so you always leave much later than you thought you
would. It was early afternoon when we finally started clambering
aboard the truck. I sat on top with Sansar-Huu, Yalta and a sheep
trussed up in a sack, because I wanted to savour the view. Even
after all these weeks together, our farewells were almost casual, and
anyway, we'd all insisted we'd be meeting up together at the White
River in the autumn. But I spontaneously threw my arms round
Deri-Huu's neck and thanked her for everything. She'd made the
summer very special for me. She pressed an enormous bag of *aaruul*
and cheese into my hands. We all waved as the engine was cranked,
the ignition sparked and the truck clumsily trundled out of the
camp to begin its slow grind east.

Seven hours and one puncture later we reached Abbai's large
hasha, and I swung down into the dusty, quiet street. Tsengel
looked deserted. Gansukh climbed out of the cabin, and there was
a moment of static tension between us. We both looked away.

'Come and stay with us tonight, Louisa,' she brokered. 'You
can go to Abbai's tomorrow. They might not even be there.'

But I knew they were – and if I wanted to know anything about the Kazakhs, I had to move in with this new family. I shook my head. 'No, it's OK. They'll be waiting for me.'

We hugged and I thanked her, suddenly anxious that now I was living with a Kazakh family, I wouldn't see her any more.

'If Abbai's not there – come back to my father's house,' she called after me, 'we'll be staying there tonight.' There was no chance of finding my bags amidst the truck cargo, so I walked into Abbai's *hasha* with just the clothes I had on. The rest I could collect later.

PART FOUR

The Life of Death

Chapter Nineteen

Summer was almost over. The weather was still hot, but the Tsengel valley was drying out, colour draining from the pasture as autumn poised to throw her flames and herald what the Mongols affectionately call 'the short golden season'. After the intimacy of the summer camp I felt as though I'd crash-landed in the village, and felt unsettled in my new home. In the mountains Sansar-Huu's family had treated me as one of them, but now I felt cast out on a limb once more. I was in a new *hasha*, living with a family I'd hardly met and whose language I barely understood. Abbai, his wife Guul-Jan and their five children made a great effort to welcome me, but at first treated me like a visiting dignitary. Everyone spoke to me in polite, careful Mongolian, the complete antithesis of the casual, friendly banter I'd drifted into with Gansukh and Sansar-Huu. This new formal rhythm of Mongolian made me feel estranged and suddenly very lonely. It was literally a different language and constantly reminded me of who I really was – the outsider, the temporary guest, the English teacher who would leave in winter. And I didn't even know if I would be working at school the next term: school director Menke was nowhere to be seen.

I'd spent the last six months binding myself into the fibres of Tsengel, carving my niche in and beyond the classroom. Now I saw my efforts unravelling in front of me, like a reformed alcoholic waking up back in the bar. My crude Kazakh faltered as I also tried too hard to be friendly, jovial and grateful. From the very beginning of my time with Gansukh and Sansar-Huu there'd been an implicit understanding between us that I would fend for myself, and they would help me only if I needed them. We'd lived together as equals. Then, in the mountains, Deri-Huu had been affectionate, but she'd expected me to help out, and that was exactly what I'd wanted. Now Guul-Jan cooked all my meals and refused to let me assist her, and her daughters cleaned the house around me, hauled all the wood and water, and milked their small herd of cows. This bustling *hasha* within the village, which was already my home, felt like a foreign place. I missed Gansukh, Sansar-Huu and Tuya, who all seemed reluctant to visit me at Abbai's, and withdrew from my hosts, head bent over my journal and notes as I wrote in the chaotic dining-living-everything room of Abbai and Guul-Jan's house.

The room Abbai had promised me wasn't ready. When I asked about it he calmly showed me a ramshackle outhouse next to his garage, at the far end of the *hasha* from his own cabin. It was filthy and empty, with panes of glass splintered or missing from the window frame. I was a bit stuck for words when I saw it. It didn't look very habitable.

'Soon, soon. We will fix it soon,' Abbai assured me. He was delighted to have me living in his home and was already arranging for me to teach his kids English, while he constantly gave his overworked, harassed wife a barrage of instructions on how to make my life easier.

Guul-Jan usually obeyed her husband without retort. Like all the other Kazakh women in the village, she always wore a headscarf. Her hair fell almost to her waist in a thick plait like a length of rope, and she cut her nails brutally short. She was the senior midwife at the clinic, and usually looked too weary even to speak to me. Her two daughters, Amina and Azina, helped her by scrubbing, chopping, dusting and hauling throughout the day. The three boys did nothing as far as I could see.

Abbai's brother Addai, who ruled the post office, also lived in the *hasha* with his wife Szandrash and their three children. Their house was directly opposite Abbai's. Addai was large and laconic; his wife was talkative and cheerful. I thought Szandrash was beautiful, though her skin wasn't so much prematurely aged as ravaged by the combined onslaught of the climate and her own poor health. She was only six years older than me, but when I first saw her I'd assumed she was probably fifty. Szandrash's eldest child was her daughter Nuur-Guul. She also had a shy teenage son, Macanbet, and a docile year-old baby called Umit. Her and Addai's home was dark and spartan, with very little furniture, but they owned one supreme luxury – a chipped red telephone, the only phone in the village apart from the temperamental post office instrument. Most evenings there was a small queue of people waiting to make hissing calls to Olgii or our neighbouring provinces. The first time I heard the phone ring I paused mid-step across the *hasha* with my mouth open and brow furrowed, and spent several puzzled moments wondering what the hell the shrilling was.

Abbai and Addai had both worked all summer, so their families had stayed in the village. They'd erected two Kazakh *gers* at the back of the long *hasha* – tall regal domes, which could each sleep tens of people. During the day the two families lived in their wooden cabins, at night they each retired to their own *ger*, where the air was cool because there was no stove. Inside Abbai's *ger* I padded barefoot across cool wooden boards. Half a dozen cots were arranged round the walls in a semi-circle. The bed linen was pristine: starched embroidered pillow cases stacked on smooth white sheets and draped with heavy blankets. The walls were adorned with brilliant hangings. The whole interior was as luxurious and immaculate as an arabesque, dim and cool as a shrine.

At night I shared this *ger* with Abbai's family. I was used to sleeping in a family *ger* by now, but was beginning to crave my own alcove where I could write, or just think alone. When I crossed the *hasha*, I looked over at my dilapidated room with something like longing.

Outside, on the track, a trickle of people was gradually arriving back from their summer camps. But the streets were still mostly deserted, the cabins boarded up and silent. It was eerie walking past rows of shuttered windows and meeting hardly anyone, just the odd roaming pack of mangy strays.

Szandrash's brother, who lived just a few *hashas* away, owned a psychotic mongrel called Actuz. He was a feared and hated beast, this scraggy mutt. He terrorised his neighbourhood all day, and howled like a werewolf at night. Actuz sometimes appeared in our *hasha*, where he was left to roam, instead of being chained up like many of the other dogs. He loved nothing more than charging at unsuspecting *hasha* visitors, baring his rancid yellow teeth and sending the heftiest men scurrying for cover. I slyly fed Actuz scraps of food, because it looked like no one ever did – and he blindly loved me for it. Soon he was permanently in the *hasha*, begging, and I earned great respect from neighbours and guests alike when I grabbed the tatty knot of rope round his neck, and stopped him from taking a chunk out of them.

'Is he yours now?' they'd ask, edging across the *hasha*.

'Oh yes,' I'd tell them, hanging on to his dry scruff as he snarled.

Tuya hated Actuz and threw handfuls of stones at him when she did occasionally visit. I just wanted him on my side. I knew that when I moved into my own room, on the far side of the *hasha*, Actuz would keep any drunk in the village from my door.

'The man down the street, Menee, he has a wolf in his *hasha* instead of a dog,' Guul-Jan's eldest daughter, Amina, told me casually one afternoon.

'A wolf?' I started and stared at her. I had occasionally heard people talk of keeping wolves in Tsengel, but had never seen one.

Amina was just fifteen but already had fine lines etched across her forehead. She was bolshy too, just like Shilgee. I liked that. 'Yes, a wolf. Menee took it when it was just a cub. They will keep it for a few more months and kill it before the end of winter. Do you want to see it?'

We walked down the street together. Menee was one of the wealthier men in Tsengel and his *hasha* was long and wide, surrounded by a sturdy wooden fence. When we pushed through the gate there was no one around, just a parked-up jeep, an immense stack of logs in one corner, and, in front of the logs, the wolf chained to a stake in the ground.

Amina wouldn't go any nearer. She shook her head, backed away nervously and stood next to the fence. I walked slowly towards the wolf. At first he looked just like a young Alsatian, all fluffy fur, bright eyes and pricked-up eager ears. But as I got closer it was his paws that gave him away: they were the huge raised paws of a much larger animal, and kicked up a curtain of dust as he circled the stake, jarring against his short chain. Feral energy radiated from him like sparks from a plug. He was a wild creature, manacled and restless. The wolf would be kept in the *hasha* and well fed until mid-winter, when his fur would be at its thickest and warmest. Then his throat would be cut and his pelt sold to one of the Olgii fur traders. But I didn't feel sorry for him. I had got used to the way animals were treated here, without either cruelty or sentiment. He'll keep someone cosy this winter, I thought, as he grinned at me, oblivious to his fate.

Every morning Abbai and his sons would leave the *hasha* to scythe hay in a valley of tall grass a few kilometres south of the village. I didn't really have anything to do, because there was hardly anyone around to visit. But when I asked Abbai if I could go scything with him and the boys one day, he shook his small dark head intently.

'No, no! It's very difficult for you, *bagsh* – very dirty, too many insects!' He waved his hands in front of him, as though swatting biblically proportioned plagues of flies.

'Abbai, it's fine,' I tried to assure him. 'I was just in the mountains for a month! I don't care about dirt.'

But he wasn't having it. This was the start of a quiet, undeclared battle of wills between Abbai and I that lasted right up until I left the village. Like an over-zealous parent, he shrank from anything he saw as a risk to my frail physical or moral welfare. After they'd gone I wandered to the post office, and easily found a lift on a truck going out to the fields from the father of one of my students.

Streaked in shadows cast by the surrounding mountains, the valley was clustered with scores of men and a few women, all wielding long curved scythes and slicing waist-high green and yellow grass in perfect semi-circles around themselves. So this was where everyone had gone. The grass was left to dry in thick furrows and then pitched loose by hand into trucks or carts. Some people had brought their camels with them and were strapping enormous wispy bundles on to their backs. The scythers spent days here together working almost without rest: some camped out in tents flung together from sheets of sodden canvas framed with branches. This stretch of land was owned by the district government and leased out in plots by Abbai and his acolytes. It was the only private land ownership I ever saw in Tsengel. The herders knew and respected each other's grazing areas, but this part actually had a fenced perimeter. I recognised Kultii the DJ among the workers. She was stoically razing the grass around her to its stubs.

'*Sain bainuu*! How was the countryside? You like living with the *malchin*, eh? Well then, you can try this!' Grinning, she handed me her scythe.

I grasped the curved handle with both hands and swung the lethal-looking blade in front of me, grunting as the grass tore. The tufts looked like a cheap, terrible haircut when I'd finished. Kultii put her hand over her mouth and the people working alongside her laughed so much they had to stop scything. I had to laugh with them. Incidents like this (and that first time I'd milked Deri-Huu's goats) made me realise how much I still had to learn about rural Mongol life.

'I'm really sorry,' I apologised to Kultii, 'I've never done it before.'

'I can see that!' she grinned, shaking her head at my butchery. 'Ah – don't worry! Don't listen to them! Come on – *tsai oh*.'

CHAPTER TWENTY

Each day a few more people arrived back in the village to repair their homes for winter. I saw Dorj and Gerel-Huu's truck tottering into Tsengel and went to visit them. Dorj and the boys were busy outside, but Gerele was in the house, sitting with Gerel-Huu and drinking. His hair was longer and thicker than I remembered, and his skin had been stained dark by the sun. For the first time I realised how good-looking Tuya's lover was. It took me a minute or two to realise that he was quite drunk. His companion, a red-haired Tuvan I'd never seen before, produced a bottle of local industrial *arikh*, and we all toasted each other. Compared to home-made *shimin-arikh* it tasted sour and metallic. Gerele's fixed smile and glinting eyes made me slightly uneasy – I suddenly couldn't ever recall seeing him sober.

'My father, he died on the thirteenth of August, the thirteenth of August.' He leaned towards me, wafting his cigarette in my face. 'Four brothers and sisters I have, four to look after. Very difficult, very, very difficult, you don't know, because now I am head of the house alone. Did you meet my brother? My dead brother. He died three years ago in that same Hovd river, and now I cannot find any work and . . .' I stopped listening. The half-full bowl of *arikh* lapped in Gerele's right hand as he passed it back to Gerel-Huu. His voice rose. 'I want to move to Ulaanbaatar this year! My wedding, ach! That'll have to wait.' He began to slur.

As he lit another cigarette from the smouldering butt of the last one, I rose silently from the table, startled by how angry I felt. I was actually clenching my fists. The sadness I'd harboured for

Gerele, for the loss of his brother and then his young father to the treacherous Hovd, was withered by my disgust at his self-pitying drunkenness. I wanted to shake him by the shoulders and shout into his bleary face, 'And what about your family, Gerele? What about Tuya? What are they all supposed to do while you're getting smashed? How are you going to help them? You can't work like this.'

But I couldn't. Alcoholism is widely accepted as the national malaise of Mongol men, and the Mongols tolerate their drunks. They pat them on the shoulder and smile at them till they pass out or go home. No one was going to berate Gerele, or demand he sober up and take responsibility for his family, and it absolutely wasn't my place to remonstrate with him. I doubted if even Tuya was prepared to fight that battle. The irony was that Gerele, as a talented furniture painter, was one of the few local men who could find work fairly easily, and it galled me. His Buddhist icons and swirling illustrations graced many tables and tea chests across the village. But he wasn't working now, because he was sodden with *arikh*, so there was no money for his widowed mother and school-age sisters and brother. I couldn't bear to watch what he was doing to them, and to himself. Smiling tightly and shrugging my shoulders at Gerel-Huu, I left the two men draining the bottle.

When I arrived back in the *hasha*, Abbai, Guul-Jan and the children were salvaging my room. Nuur-Guul was whitewashing the grimy outside walls with the local chalk and water silt, and I helped Guul-Jan clean the room. We dragged furniture inside, and beat rugs against the *hasha* fence till we were plastered in dust. Abbai found half a dozen broken panes of glass and taped them together – and I moved in. The room was set apart from the other two cabins, near the *hasha* gate, and for the first time in almost two months I slept and woke on my own. It was solitary bliss.

The curtain Guul-Jan and I strung across my window was a square of violent fuchsia material from the Olgii black market. It was comically Caribbean, with palm trees, yachts and the odd demented parrot daubed across the thin fabric. The curtain glowed in the morning as the sun shone through the cracked panes, drenching my awakening in lurid, cheerful pink. I also had a stove, a large, solid desk from the school, and a tin bath that leaked everywhere when I bathed or washed my clothes. But nothing compared to the toilet. A tilting, flimsy cubicle with floorboards that sagged every time I stepped on them, it had, for some inexplicable reason, been built a few yards outside the *hasha*. Every time I squatted down to pee, I was painfully aware of the gaps between the slats, and the people and animals wandering past. I always felt as though I was peeing or shitting in the middle of the street – which I was. The toilet was also the favourite haunt of the *hasha* cows, who hunkered in its sliver of shade. Several times one of the cows pressed her wet nostrils against the door, and bellowed so loudly that I staggered backwards with my knickers round my ankles, and almost fell through the hole.

As I collected my daily buckets of water from the Hovd, I passed by the *hasha* next door: a pitifully small yard marked by a low, unfinished wall of mud bricks, containing one of the smallest cabins in the village. Aimak and her husband Merim-Kahn lived here with their six children. Two of the boys had severe squints, another limped badly, and Merim-Kahn, whose clothes were faded and slightly tattered, seemed to spend a lot of his time laid out on one of the small beds, looking gaunt and hunched, unable to stretch out his long folded limbs within the confines of his cramped room. Except for Aimak they were not a healthy-looking family. But she was incredibly robust, and would shout extremely loudly through her broken teeth whenever I strolled or lurched past, with my empty or brimming pails.

'Hey, *bagsh*! Oi! *Tsai oh, tsai oh*!'

And so I would, crouched in their home that was smaller than my room, as Aimak loudly bossed her family round, scolding her husband and the children and gabbling at me non-stop in the fastest Mongolian I'd ever heard. 'You! What do you think you're doing? Go on – get out! Out! And you, you're as bad. Can't you

see the *bagsh* is here? You – go and get some more milk for the
tea, go on quickly, and tell your sister to get inside and make some
buurtzug. My children are all terrible and look at my husband,
lying there without work.'

I couldn't always understand what Aimak said, and she talked
(and yelled) far too much, but she had real spirit, and we laughed
together. I liked her a lot.

For a while time passed easily in the *hasha*, as I resumed my routine
of chopping wood and fetching water, cooking and cleaning.
Though I always hated hauling water, because it hurt my back
and the buckets slopped unless I was careful, which I usually wasn't,
I relished chopping wood: staking the blade into the logs, splintering the grain and inhaling the perfumed sap. My arms were
strong and muscular now, and I could kindle a fire quick and hot.
I spent part of each day just at these tasks, then writing and
walking, chatting with the two families in the *hasha* and nearby
Aimak and family, teaching the older children English and greeting
the stream of people who came and left. By then, dusk would be
falling. I would read or write a letter in the candlclit evening, and
another day would have slipped carelessly by. I'd be weary and
seem to have done little but take care of myself. But I felt quietly
satisfied by the stack of wood, pot of cooked food and the full
water bucket, and glad that I'd learned how to live in the village,
although, compared to spring and summer, the 'short golden
season' was a lonesome time for me. I greeted plenty of people
every day, but began to feel starved of real company, especially in
the evenings. My Tuvan friends usually stayed away, and even the
disco in the lovely, shoddy klub seemed to have packed in.

I spent a lot of time in and around the *hasha*, and it didn't take
me very long to realise that there were more similarities than differ-
ences between the Mongols, Kazakhs and Tuvans. They were all
traditionally nomadic herders, moulded by equally conservative
cultures. But of the three nations, the Kazakhs were the true patriarchs. If I was sitting with a group of women in Szandrash or
Guul-Jan's house and a man entered, the women would rise swiftly

from their stools like a flock of disturbed birds, and all but the woman of the house would usually leave the room.

The men never helped out at home, they just gave orders to their wives and daughters, and, just like the Mongol and Tuvan women, the Kazakhs always served their men tea or food first. Though I was always very aware of this, it never became a burning personal issue, far from it. I'd already conformed and offered male guests the first bowls of food or drink in my own home. Once or twice I had mulled over the idea of deliberately serving women first, but was sure it would embarrass my male and female guests, and leave them feeling awkward about coming to see me, which I didn't want. It would serve no purpose except making me look arrogant, or weird. Most importantly, it would make no difference at all to what the men did or didn't do at home. And in the end that wasn't my business either, no matter how I felt about it. I wasn't here to convert anyone to anything.

Instead, I asked Guul-Jan if I could help her, Szandrash and their daughters to milk the cows in the evenings, in the street just outside the *hasha*. The women always milked their cows in the street and I wanted their company. Guul-Jan nodded reluctantly, but agreed. So at dusk we squatted or balanced on rickety stools, squirting warm milk into pails and letting the calves suckle mid-milking to stimulate the flow from the swollen teats. After dragging the calf away and tethering it howling to a post, my hands would slip off the drooling teat, and my fingers stank of sour milk and warm hay afterwards. I milked the same placid cow every evening, and nuzzled my head against her warm, wide flank. As we milked the shadows stretched around us, and locals wandered past calling to us or each other as they strolled home. Every day now there were a few more people around. But one young woman strode by with no greeting, her head covered, an air of guarded silence about her.

'Who was that?' I called to Guul-Jan, as she dissolved into the dusk.

'It's Lashun, *bagsh*,' she replied softly.

The young widow was on her way home. I crouched in the

thickening shadows, and wondered how she and her young daughter were coping without Kalim.

After a couple of weeks Abbai and his boys finished the scything. They tottered home on a truck stacked high with hay, the boys grinning and waving triumphantly from the top. Together we spread the hay around the *gers* and the back of the *hasha* to dry, where it danced in the wind like a fettered green sea.

Autumn is usually a brief interlude in Mongolia: the swift burnished prelude to winter. A fire before the long tunnel of cold. But this year was different. This year, the villagers told me, the seasons were contrary. 'This spring was too long, and then our summer was late. Now look at this autumn. Hot and cold and then hot again. It's not right. This is a very difficult year, *bagsh*.'

The autumn blazed and cooled, and then defiantly blazed again. The valley shrivelled and dried up in yellow, brown and orange. On the warmer afternoons I bathed in the freezing Hovd, searching out hidden inlets amongst the sparse trees, or wading over to tiny islands where I could strip naked. I spent hours splashing round in the water, and would lie on the warm rocks afterwards until my hair and skin were dry. While I was roaming by the river I never felt lonely at all. I always enjoyed my own company there. What is it they say: loneliness is a crowded room? But Amina and Nuur-Guul were curious about where I disappeared to in the afternoons, and when I told them, they wanted to come too. So we strolled over to the river together, and as we scrubbed ourselves and washed our hair, they taught me new words in Kazakh.

'I'm feeling very happy today,' Amina said to me on one of our riverside afternoons, 'because my mother is coming home soon.'

I frowned at her. 'But . . . Guul-Jan's already at home,' I said. We'd all been in the *hasha* that morning.

'No, not Guul-Jan. My real mother!' she retorted in Kazakh. 'She's coming over from the mountains.'

I wondered if I'd understood her properly and later, couldn't resist asking Guul-Jan about Amina's mountain mother. She smiled and paused from wringing out one of Abbai's shirts. 'Oh, she means Abbai's mother, Apam. It is our Kazakh tradition, you know, to give our first child to our husband's parents. So Amina's mother is Apam.'

'But . . . Amina lives here with you and Abbai,' I persisted, trying to make sense of it all. 'She's your daughter – isn't she?'

'Mmm, yes. But when Apam comes to live with us in winter, Amina will share her room. Because we gave Amina to Apam, so now she's her daughter. It's just what we do.'

'How many children does Apam have now?'

'Fourteen.'

'Fourteen! So, are they all Amina's brothers and sisters as well?'

'Yes. You don't do this in England, do you?' said Guul-Jan.

Intrigued, I quietly asked Amina if her uncle, Addai, was now also her brother.

'Yes, he is,' she said calmly.

Knowing I was probably about to blunder, but unable to resist, I cleared my throat and cautiously queried whether Abbai was therefore her brother, even though he was already her father.

She shook her head, appalled at the suggestion. 'No, of course he's not! How can he be – he's my dad!'

I smiled at her and then shook my head, completely fascinated by the answer to my question.

CHAPTER TWENTY-ONE

'So, how is life with the Kazakhs?' Gansukh asked me pointedly the next time I visited her.

We lived less than ten minutes apart. I still saw her a lot. But she was pensive and seemed uneasy about me living with Abbai and his family.

'Why don't you come back and stay here, Louisa?' she suggested. 'Sansar-Huu's gone back to the countryside, and I'm on my own here with Opia and Yalta. There's plenty of room.'

'Because I want to learn about the Kazakhs,' I said feebly. I knew I was making my life difficult. It would be much easier to live with Gansukh again. But I also knew Abbai and his family would be mortally offended if I moved out. It would be a real insult to their hospitality, and they were being very generous to me. I'd resolved to stay with Abbai and his family for the autumn and winter, because I wanted to unravel the story of the Kazakhs for myself, and this was the only way I knew how.

I could sense Gansukh's resentment towards my new relationship with the local Kazakhs. Every now and again I was reminded of this animosity, this fear of the potency of their Muslim culture. I was beginning to understand that this was why most of the Kazakhs were here, on the edge of Mongolia, and hadn't ventured further east, why they were so fiercely self-contained. As I gradually settled into life with the Kazakhs, my friendship with Gansukh suffered. She'd ask me stilted questions about what I was doing 'over there with them' and, for the first time since I'd met her, we sometimes had little to say to each other. I'd leave, smiling awkwardly, and return home alone.

The village was still quiet when school started again. Many families hadn't returned from the mountains. As a thin stream of pupils dribbled towards school, Menke ordered Gansukh to take an English language exam in Olgii.

She was delighted and nervous. 'I need to pass this exam,' she told me earnestly. 'Menke has cut my hours teaching Tuvan, because he says the students need to learn Mongolian and English now. So I need this qualification.'

I gave her some swift conversation practice before she left. My own students now had no English teacher and I had no work, but Menke hadn't asked me to teach, and I didn't want to approach him after his previous response. Abbai hadn't mentioned work. He seemed content for me to live in the *hasha*, teach his children for an hour a day, and write my journal.

'Yes, soon, soon,' he said when I asked about the other teaching we'd tentatively planned. 'The students will all return to school soon and then you will teach.'

I'd enjoyed the end of summer free time, but now term had started I longed to go back to the school and be caught up in the noisy, friendly chaos of the classroom.

I realised how much teaching had helped me take part in the local community.

During the spring I'd been engrossed with it and learning to fend for myself. But now I felt restless and aimless as the two *hasha* families went about their business, and only Szandrash and I and the younger children stayed at home. We talked and drank pots of tea together, and I still walked and wrote, but a delicate lethargy began to set in. Everyone needs their niche and purpose within a community, and teaching had provided me with mine. I'd never wanted to merely observe Tsengel, but to be involved in the fibre of its daily life. Now, for the first time, I felt as though I was on the outside gazing in, minus any role to play.

I didn't harbour many illusions about the value of teaching English in Tsengel. The villagers already spoke three languages between them (four if you include Russian), and I knew damn well most people would never get to visit Ulaanbaatar, and even less would enrol in a university where speaking English would be an asset. It did offer advantages in urban Mongolia, but did nothing to improve the quality of life in the countryside. The only mitigating factors were that a few of the students might use their English language skills at university, and that Gansukh really needed the work.

The school was still more than half empty when the first and then the second week of term ended. Finally a posse of teachers took the absences into their own hands and rumbled towards the river gorge on the back of an open truck. They were cheerful child catchers and said they didn't mind bashing their way through the gorge collecting nomadic truants until the truck was full. They did it every year.

'Mongols,' Abbai told me, tutting and shaking his dark head sorrowfully. 'Mongols do not know time, Louisa. They do not understand this word!'

'Most of my students haven't even arrived yet,' Tuya complained more pragmatically, with a grin and a shrug. 'You know what, every year it's the same. They stay in the countryside until we go and fetch 'em back.'

The teachers soon returned with a truck load of bundled-up children clutching rolls of bedding and small sacks of clothes. Two shy young girls and one little boy moved into our *hasha* to live with Addai and Szandrash. Many families took in their relatives' children for the school year, because there were always too many pupils from the mountains sharing the cramped, overcrowded boarding rooms above the school kitchen. The Gang of Three, as I affectionately nicknamed Gerel-Huu, Shinid and Bagit, had their work cut out now.

Abbai also drove through the river gorge to reproach parents and collect their skiving children, and Tuya asked me to go into the nearby Hairkhan mountains south of the village with her, to find some of her missing boys.

'The girls usually turn up on time,' she said. 'But the parents keep the boys behind to do the herding, and sometimes almost half of them are absent from school. They need an education too, you know. They might be *malchin* but they have to learn to read and write.'

She found us a lift with a local driver called Simotei, who accelerated across the steppe chain-smoking and spinning the steering wheel with hands protected by dainty, nicotine-stained white driving gloves. Simotei had a small transistor radio, which blasted static Kazakh music at full volume as the jeep bounced through the shorn valley of the haymakers.

'How long have you lived here?' he yelled above the horrible din.

'Seven months!' I yelled back.

'Why don't you stay and marry a Kazakh – I can find a nice *malchin* for you!'

Tuya giggled and goaded Simotei to find me a suitable boy. Now that I'd been in the village for more than half a year, local families had begun to offer me their sons or relatives as a husband with worrying frequency. There were regular, flippant and light-hearted but occasionally deadly earnest attempts to inveigle me into a local marriage. I felt flattered but sorely untempted by these proposals. Almost all the men my age were already wed; if they weren't, there was usually a very good reason, and rural marriage was viewed as a functional long-term arrangement, not a declaration of eternal romantic love. Tuya, with her brazen passion for the rogue Gerele, was a rare and frequently gossiped about exception to the rule.

We swerved and bantered beyond Tsengel, and into a valley, which lay beneath the Hairkhan mountain range south of the village. *Gers* were clustered across billowing pasture now pale as hay, a wide dark river coursed towards the Hovd, and white peaks glinted in a sky without cloud. It was a tranquil setting. There were moments when nomadic life still seemed utterly romantic to me, despite what I'd learned of life and death in these mountains.

Before Tuya and I visited the parents of her absent pupils, we
stopped to visit a family of her local relatives.

'This is the family who lost their son in spring.' She didn't
repeat the name of Gerel-Huu's nephew who'd frozen to death
months earlier, and who had also been one of her distant cousins.
Mongols rarely invoke the names of the dead. 'They are still very
sad, you know. This might be difficult, but I have to visit them
while we're here.'

Even as we stepped into their *ger*, the unshed grief bore down
on us with a silent roar. The man and woman inside barely moved
from their stools for several minutes. It was as though they were
immersed in a deep and disturbing slumber. Catatonic with grief.
I said, '*Sain bainuu*,' quietly, but they did not reply. The man,
Ganbaatar, sat still and erect on his stool, his arms folded across
his stomach. When his wife, Bolormaa, passed me a bowl of tea,
her hands began to tremble, and the tea almost spilt.

It's easy to assume that people from poor or developing countries are more used to death than we are, to believe they don't
hurt so much when someone is killed, and that our culture
somehow has a monopoly on anguish. I've never felt grief like I
did there, in Ganbaatar and Bolormaa's *ger*. They had lost their
only son and heir. He'd been raised right here in the *ger*, and
after he had married he'd moved into his own, just metres away,
where his young wife sat listening to her child scream. When we
visited her she didn't say anything either. The photo of her dead
husband was framed and suspended at the rear of the *ger*, draped
in *khadags*. But it was possible to believe this young woman
would eventually move on. There was a future for her somewhere later, with a new husband and maybe more children. In
the battered face and shattered nerves of her mother-in-law there
was just defeat.

When Tuya nodded to me, we left them preparing food for our
lunch, as they'd insisted they would, and we walked silently towards
a derelict quadrangle that stood in the centre of the valley, as
though it had been flung down from the sky. This had once been

a fine *hasha* of half a dozen cabins surrounded by a sturdy mud-brick wall. But the bricks had long crumbled and the ground was strewn with rock and earth debris, dry cattle shit and a half-starved dog that growled as we approached.

'Oh, people live here.' Tuya finally spoke, guessing my thoughts as she bent down for a stone to aim at the dog. 'There are maybe five families. All women, you know. All without husbands. Divorced or widowed. They live here with their kids, my students, who need to go to school. Look at this place.'

She stepped inside a shack in the corner. The splintered door was open and she beckoned me over the wasted step. A woman stood by her stove and glanced over at us, but didn't move. She must only have been in her late twenties, but everything about her was hollow. Her face was hungry and her eyes flinched. When Tuya moved past her to sit down, the woman stepped nervously out of the way, and I saw that her boots were so ground down she walked on the leather above the erased heel. She stumbled as she crossed the room. The floor was bare, uneven stone and the one small window was half-covered by a sheet of fluttering plastic.

'You must bring him to school. I'll give him a notebook and pen, but he must come in every day.'

We were drinking salty brown tea, and I hadn't even noticed the woman's son, who was crouched on the second bed stroking a kitten. When he stood up to greet his teacher, he was tall and rakishly thin. His mother passively nodded at Tuya. Yes, he would go to school if she would give him the book and pen, because she, his mother, couldn't. Yes, he would go in next week.

We didn't stay long. Stepping outside where it was warmer I felt glad autumn was lingering.

'There are plenty of Tuvan women like her,' said Tuya, as we crossed over to the next shack. 'Her husband died and they've got a few animals, but no other family and no money at all. So they live here with the other women. But if her son doesn't go to school, his life will be as miserable as his mother's. Come on. We'll go back for lunch after this.'

I reluctantly followed her into the next ruin of a house, though I didn't want to go inside at all. Tuya was offering pragmatic advice and support. But I was just looking at lives made wretched through circumstance.

CHAPTER TWENTY-TWO

The visit to Hairkhan left me quiet and sombre. I still met up with my friends, though mostly in their homes, but the days seemed long and my spirits were low. I didn't always know what to do with myself. Gansukh flung open my door one morning, flushed and eager to share her triumph.

'I passed the exam! They rang from Olgii! Menke *bagsh* says I can teach the second and third years for twelve hours a week! Can you help me with this?'

She produced a copy of her English language text book – the bizarre and dislocated *Blue Sky*. Over the next three months we slowly and painfully studied the text together, sentence by sentence, until we both understood the entire jumbled contents. I taught Gansukh several times a week, and we soon referred to *Blue Sky* as 'that strange book'. I often had to read the exercises two or three times before I understood enough to explain them to Gansukh.

I sat in Gansukh's home after one of our *Blue Sky* lessons, brooding and preoccupied, while she, Tuya and several other local women spoke and laughed together for a long time in Tuvan. I'd learned some Tuvan in the mountains, but made no effort to join their conversation. Instead I uttered a sudden excuse and left, fleeing to the edge of the river, in floods of sudden tears that I couldn't understand or control. A sense of utter loneliness and bewilderment tightened round my throat like a tourniquet until I was choked and sobbing. I'd been feeling unhappy for weeks now and had been waiting for this sense of aimlessness and lethargy to pass. But it hadn't and I quite frightened myself with this outburst. My self-confidence suddenly collapsed, and I felt more alone than I ever had in my life.

For days my Mongolian was monosyllabic, because I couldn't think of anything to say to anyone. I just sat, mute, with Gansukh, Tuya, or Abbai and his family, resentfully wondering why, if an anecdote or scenario was so damn funny, no one actually bothered to explain the joke to me. In Abbai's home, people who had seen and talked with me before and who knew I spoke good Mongolian, still referred to me in the third person while I was in the room, as though I wasn't even there. What does She do? Where is She from? Is She married? Suddenly it was too much. Panic reared up in me, and I fled again, burning up with anger and self-pity.

I avoided the *hasha* as much as possible, and trawled the parched river bank scowling at mountains and longing to abandon it all. I wanted to sit down and talk English instead of spending every waking moment talking a foreign language; for someone to reassure me that I was panicking because things weren't going too well but it would all be OK, and I would look back on it, and maybe even laugh. Because right now I couldn't do that for myself, and I felt as though I'd become a real mess.

Up until now I had loved the smallness and remoteness of Tsengel. I'd found it reassuring to know so many of the villagers and feel welcome in their homes. But for several long, heavy days all that turned on its head, and instead Tsengel felt like a claustrophobic, suffocating village. It was that paradox of feeling lonely but having to be on my own because I just couldn't be around other people. Loneliness really is a crowded room.

I bit the flesh on the inside of my lip till it bled and retreated into my room and my few unread books, sprawled on my bed with the door sullenly latched. I wondered why I was still here: I wasn't enjoying it. I was just proving some sort of brutal point to myself with this determination to see the year through. It was a useless exercise that did no one any good, including me. I didn't belong in the village. I had no job and nothing to do any more. I suddenly didn't feel so much a foreigner as a trespasser.

*   *   *

While I lurked in my room, scowling and absorbed in my own self-pity, the school finally filled with students, and Altangerel, one of the recent graduates, packed his bags for university.

Tuya appeared at my door, cheerfully oblivious to my crisis. 'Come on,' she said, 'let's go to Altangerel's farewell party.'

'But I thought he was leaving today.'

'He went an hour ago. The party couldn't start till he left.'

I laughed in staccato. 'Why?'

'To bless his journey. So he arrives safely. Come on, you look like you need to go to a party!'

I protested in vain but Tuya wouldn't leave unless I went with her.

Altangerel was the brother of a woman who lived in a small *ger* next to Gerel-Huu. Most people preferred the wooden cabins but a few families were in *gers* all year round. Altangerel had just left Tsengel for Hovd city, about fifteen hours away. Everyone was talking about how expensive the fees were – Tg 160,000 (about £120) a year. His parents and relatives had stoically handed over their savings, and had sold livestock, skins and their summer dairy surplus. Now that he had gone, we could have a party for him.

When we reached the *ger*, more than a dozen people were already crammed inside. I liked these parties, which always started with the ubiquitous platter of mutton and bowls of tea – but swiftly moved on to the hard stuff. As Altangerel's parents sniffled over their son leaving home, the guests one by one raised toasts to his intellectual brilliance, and more people arrived to join in the vodka and singing. A bizarre, final shower of summer rain drummed a brief evocative crescendo on the *ger* roof, startling us all. The rains were supposed to be over. Two of the men stepped outside to check the skies, and came back in shaking their dripping heads, which made everyone laugh. This year the seasons were very strange. I sat back on my stool and finally smiled, inhaling the scent of meat, cigarette smoke and drenched earth.

But suddenly everyone began to weep. Altangerel's parents had already cried, blotted their tears, then wept again amid shoulder patting and soothing words, then the charismatic Gerel *bagsh* took over, bursting dramatically into tears as he toasted his father who had died earlier that year. The Gang of Three were all there, and first it was Shinid whose face crumpled as she began to cry for a relative who was desperately ill. Then Bagit put her head in her hands for a close relative who had expired a couple of years earlier, while her plump daughter sitting beside her snivelled, her lower lip quivering dangerously, and finally Gerel-Huu bawled on my shoulder for her long-dead parents.

Tuya was blithely chatting as though she hadn't even noticed this incredible outpouring of communal grief. Some people carried on singing; others concentrated on weeping alone or propped up in pairs. The *arikh* was still being passed round. I looked around me and wondered what I should do, and consciously thought about joining the weepers. But I suddenly, utterly, did not want to cry. In the midst of all this grief, I managed to smile inside for the first time in days. I realised that things really weren't so bad for me. My mother and twin sister were very healthy, and my father had left us so long ago I didn't think he was worth weeping for. With this small crucial moment of realisation my mood swung like a pendulum, and I throatily joined the singers.

I tried to beg out of one toast, fearing not for my emotions, just my hangover. But Tuya was having none of it. 'This is my vodka, and you've got to taste it,' she warned me, looking admirably drunk and defiantly dry-eyed.

I surrendered. I was going to arrive home late and reeling, and no doubt wake up to a headache that would wreck the entire next day. I shrugged my shoulders and raised the cup. Mongols get terribly offended if you refuse to share a toast with them. Vodka-soaked hospitality has been the downfall of many a foreigner here.

Still drinking, crying and singing we eventually left the *ger* and careered out of the village in a jeep driven by someone who squinted hard as he swerved round a camel being led across the street. The camel owner skidded out of danger and shook his fist as we all roared with glee. When we arrived wherever we went, I drunkenly milked a few goats for some reason, beaming at one of my former pupils who said carefully, 'It's OK, teacher – I can do that for you,' and led me by the hand to a *ger*. Inside, the Tuvans were chorusing and vodka toasting with a jubilant vengeance, as extreme in their joy as they had been in grief. Tuya and I drank a little more, then lay down together on one of the beds. The *ger* tipped and spun as I closed my eyes. It felt like moments later when I was shaken awake by someone wafting a glass in my face and yelling that we were leaving. '*Yavi!*' Let's go! Oh God. It was obviously late when we lurched outside: the sky was onyx and swarms of stars shimmered in a more sober galaxy. This time the jeep braked viciously outside a Tsengel cabin, and in we all rolled. A local woman I knew vaguely produced a fresh pail of *shimin-arikh*, which everyone happily quaffed. I began to feel extremely ill and knew I had to go home. I was fading like a flat car battery. I realised Tuya had vanished.

As the revellers chorused on, I begged Gerel *bagsh* to take me home, knowing I'd weave across the unlit streets until I keeled over, but would never find Abbai's *hasha* alone. We tried to rouse the driver, but he looked as though he was just about to pass out. So Gerel and I staggered obliquely towards my room, and I prayed very hard that Abbai and his family were asleep and Actuz wouldn't howl with his usual rancour, and promised I would never ever get drunk in the village again. Please.

At my mercifully empty gate Gerel kissed me on the throat and suggested 'we get to know each other better'. I untangled myself from his arms and staggered to my room, knowing that if I stayed any longer I would take him up on his offer.

The next morning I threw up, Menke summoned me to school – and Tsengel was quarantined.

CHAPTER TWENTY-THREE

It was while I was cleaning my teeth and scouring my room for paracetamol that Abbai arrived and told me about my new job. 'Menke *bagsh* wants to see you at the school today. He wants you to help Gansukh teaching.'

I nodded dully, my shrunken brain bouncing off the walls of my skull. I felt far too ill to care, never mind be pleased, that I was being offered work back at the school.

Abbai lingered, frowning. 'On the radio this morning they say our province is under quarantine till Monday. In Olgii two teachers are sick from *tarvag takal* [bubonic plague]. They are from Buyant village, and ate sick marmot, and now they have the plague. So they are in the Olgii hospital and everyone has to stay in their village now, because it's very dangerous.'

'But no one here is sick, are they?'

'No, no, but they can catch this plague very quickly. So the soldiers are outside Olgii and at the border with Hovd, Uvs and Gobi-Altai provinces, to stop people driving in or out.'

Before I came to Tsengel, if any mystic had predicted I would live in a village temporarily quarantined because the bubonic plague had struck, I would probably have laughed. I had known about the traces of it in Mongolia long before I came to Tsengel. Bubonic plague is just one of those eventualities, like being struck by lightning, that you assume will never happen to you. Deri-Huu had assured me there was no risk when we'd all tucked into the rich, pungent meat for days on end, and I'd thought no more of it. Now I felt unsettled, but not frightened. There were several times during my year in Tsengel when life took on an almost surreal quality, and this was definitely the most significant episode. I felt emotionally stumped, and couldn't decide exactly how I should be reacting to this amorphous crisis. There wasn't anything I or anyone else in the village could actually do about it, except stop eating marmot. I couldn't leave the village, and now I didn't really want or need to. Where would I go? Tsengel, I realised that morning, was definitely my home at the moment.

Somewhere in my bags I had several lethal-looking tablets, large as horse pills and wrapped in a clear plastic sachet marked 'Plague'. An American volunteer teacher on his way home had given them to me while I was first packing for the mountains.

'Just in case,' he'd said, casually. 'They'll give you an extra twenty-four hours to reach a hospital and get an antidote – in Ulaanbaatar.'

When I finally dragged my wretched hungover body to the school, Menke and I talked in his office.

'Louisa *bagsh*,' he scowled, as I sat down heavily, 'our teachers and I are all very happy you will be working with Gansukh *bagsh*. The school directors in Olgii are also very happy and want to thank you. They know Gansukh *bagsh* needs your help. But we can't pay you because we have no money. We will give you coal and wood as a salary.'

Abbai's *hasha* was laden with wood, and I already knew the school had no coal because the truck had broken down, and there had been no fuel in the village for the last three weeks. I had very little money left apart from my aeroplane fare back to Ulaanbaatar, but when I asked Menke if I could earn half of a teacher's £20 a month salary, he shook his head purposefully. 'We have no money for you.'

I asked Tuya and Gansukh what they thought I should do.

'Tell him to get lost!' said Tuya. 'He is paid so much money his wife runs that big store in the village, and she goes to China to buy flour and shoes!'

'They should pay you something,' said Gansukh, 'because I will be able to work as a teacher when you leave. I need to study that strange book with you before you go.'

But it was very simple. I could refuse to work without a salary, and stay at home in the *hasha*, or I could accept that I was leaving halfway through the school year, which was very unprofessional, and that I taught at the school in the meantime because it gave me a purpose to stay in the village. I needed to be 'Louisa *bagsh*' more than I needed the money. So I drew up a schedule with Menke and returned to school.

I never heard the quarantine mentioned at school, although after three days it was extended, because one of the Buyant teachers had died. Buyant was 100 kilometres from Tsengel, and no one was eating marmot, so we still weren't in any great danger. There was no sense of panic in the village at all, and I felt calm and even complacent about the quarantine after a few days. Any fear I held inside myself had nowhere to go. It couldn't fester in this calm world around me, where people referred to the plague but mostly talked of other matters as our confined lives drifted on.

A week later, however, the audible hum of bad news was buzzing across Tsengel. The post office was crammed the following Wednesday as people shared newspapers and discussed another bubonic outbreak, shaking their heads and exhaling in calm dismay.

'Look, it's true,' hands slapped the front pages, 'all the planes have been stopped from Ulaanbaatar and the radio last night was right, about those five small children from Hovd going to hospital. Now Hovd is closed as well.'

There was resignation in these voices, pity for the children and sorrow for their parents. But even after this tragic news, local anxiety was quiet and rarely expressed. The villagers were stoic about life and fatalistic about death.

Despite the risk of contracting the bubonic plague, almost everyone in Tsengel ate marmot during summer and autumn, and I knew they'd do this again next year. The marmots were only hunted in these seasons, while they were plump and their pelts glossy, and they were usually safe to eat. Most people were obviously prepared to take the chance.

While our quarantine was monitored, the jeeps remained parked in the *hashas*, and people continued working, whitewashing and repairing their homes for winter. Several days later the whole Bayan-Olgii province quarantine was quietly lifted, and still no one had mentioned the second Buyant village teacher. Maybe she survived. Doctors had arrived from Ulaanbaatar with antidotes. But the Hovd borders were closed by the military for a month. Because the five young children were all dead.

CHAPTER TWENTY-FOUR

'Louisa, come here after your lessons,' Gerel-Huu called through a half-open steamed-up window, as I walked past the school kitchen on my way to class. 'We've got vegetables for lunch!'

As soon as traffic had resumed between Tsengel and Olgii, vegetables had been brought in. Once a year for several weeks the village had sacks of potatoes, turnips, cabbage and onions. Cheap fresh vegetables from China. We had to rely on these seasonal imports because Bayan-Olgii is too arid to grow most vegetables, and no one seemed very interested in trying anyway. But when the Chinese vegetables were sold, people resolutely ate potatoes with every single meal for more than a month. At Abbai's we shared the bounty between us, savouring stews with chunks of *nogotta hol*, literally 'green food'. We talked rather a lot about how delicious these fresh vegetables tasted.

Aimak and her family also had vegetables, and the next time I visited we ate mutton and potatoes together. 'From his brother.' She nodded towards Merim-Khan crouched wearily on his stool like a long, drooping plant. 'He's very good to us. You know we have very little money and he's always giving us things. Who would have thought he had such an important brother! He speaks four languages, you know. Yes. Very well – and he wants to meet you. "Oh, the English teacher," he said. "Yes, I want to meet her."' Our conversations were often like this, requiring some deciphering.

'His brother is the Imam Sanak Sailik.'

'Does he live near here?'

'Yes . . . just round the corner. That big house next to the river, with his two wives and ten children. He wants to see you and practise his English. He speaks very very good English . . .'

When Aimak finally paused for breath I arranged to visit the Imam with her the next afternoon and pay my respects. I left their cabin feeling intrigued and vaguely excited.

'Yes, yes,' enthused Abbai when I told him I was going to see Sanak Sailik. 'This is very important. He is a good man this Imam – not like her, that woman in the mountains who is *hortlaa* [a liar].'

'Who?'

'That young woman . . . Enkhtuya.' He leaned forward over his bowl. 'The old Shamans were true Shamans, you know. They knew what they were doing. But after Choybalsan, when they stopped all the practices and destroyed the temples and our Kazakh mosques, then there were no more Shamans. She is not a real Shaman. They have all died.'

I ingested Abbai's words uneasily, knowing it would be fruitless to discuss the subject with the local Tuvans. It would merely breed the already active local resentment, and I wanted no part in that. Instead I thought of the Imam, and wondered if he could possibly speak a little English as Aimak had proudly insisted he did. That would make talking religion with him much easier. Sanak Sailik lived a couple of minutes from Abbai's *hasha*, in a wide quadrangle alongside the Hovd. His was a large and sturdy house, boldly drenched in terracotta coloured paint. It was brazenly the most colourful *hasha* in the village: every other building was either unpainted or chalked white. It was bizarre that after eight months in the village and weeks of walking past his *hasha* daily to haul water, I'd never yet met the Imam. Now Aimak escorted me to his door, chattering as though her life depended on it.

'Oh, he's so happy about meeting you, so he can practise his English. I've told him all about you and your family and he speaks six languages you know, and he's always travelling!' Aimak was a great exaggerator. At first she'd told me the Imam spoke four languages. So now it was six. It would probably be eight by the time I actually met him.

I felt a tinge of cynical scepticism wash over me as we beat the dust off our boots and stepped over the wooden threshold. Abbai's tirade against Enkhtuya had already soured my enthusiasm for this meeting. Inside the house a large, florid man was comfortably perched on a tall stool beside a woman hunched over the stove, cooking. For the moment before Aimak introduced us, I presumed he was a relative or guest and wondered where Sanak Sailik was. This could not be the Imam: to me the word suggested images of pallid skin starved of fresh air, funereal black robes, straggling beards and pious silence. Not this. A beaming, plump and hand-some man with rosy cheeks, dressed in breeches and a chunky sweater, who immediately took my hand and invited me to sit next to him by the stove.

He had the obligatory beard. But it was not wisps of thin grey that crept down past narrow shoulders. Sanak Sailik's beard grew thick and coarse, black carelessly flecked with white, arrested at his collarbones. His fingers were thick and warm as he held my hand for a moment. 'Ah, the English *bagsh*!' he beamed. '*Tsai oh*! Then we will talk!'

After tea he led me into a side room with thick woven carpets on the walls and handsome wooden furniture, and closed the door behind us.

'I don't know English, but you, I think, know Mongolian. So I will talk slowly, and you will listen well!' Somehow this sounded more like an invitation than a command.

We sat at opposite sides of a wide and empty desk. I wanted to unravel the Imam's biography, his vocation in the village – and his fascinating domestic arrangements. But the Imam certainly knew what he wanted.

'I will tell you my story. But first you need to listen to this.' He waved his clean fingers in my face. 'This is important. Islam. You know this word? Islam – surrendering to the will of God. Our Kazakh Islam first came from Persia, from a conqueror called The Abbasid, who swept across our land in the sixth century. Yes. But our Muslim religion was also influenced by Arabia, Pakistan, Turkey and Kazan. Do you know Kazan? The land of the Tatars. Tataristan. Kazan is now the capital, and there in that place, east of Moscow, I don't know how far, the Muslims established their religion there before the Christians. But . . . it doesn't matter who was first. It is only important that these Kazakhs know about Islam. I speak Arabic and I know the Koran very well. I have read the Koran from Tataristan and from Turkey and Persia. I have studied my religion for twenty-five years and now I know it well. We have this book – Kitab-Al-Jafr – our secret teachings. It has verses from the Koran, and other very important thoughts for us to realise. We call it The Book of Hidden Things. I know this book. I studied it in Turkey.'

He didn't reveal anything about the contents, but suddenly stood up and vanished into a back room screened by a curtain of scarlet beads. I'd never seen such a big house in Tsengel. He emerged clutching a small stack of artefacts: scrolls hand-scribed in Arabic, small books bound in heavy serious leather, prayer beads, and a small black plastic camera, which he pressed into my hands.

'Look, look at this. These pictures. They are all Mecca. Do you see the rock? Ka'bah – the rock at the centre, next to the Great Mosque. This is the most important place, in the centre of the city. Do you see this cloth covering it? Kiswah, it is called. Every year after the haj is finished this Kiswah is taken off and cut,' he mimed the tearing of the cloth, 'cut, and given to pilgrims, piece by piece. Every Muslim should visit Mecca once in their life. I have been once. Five miles before the gates you have to take off your shoes, and wear only clothes . . . how to tell you, clothes . . . without stitches. Not sewn. Look.'

The camera rotated ten photos of Mecca, revealing an ocean of worship around the Ka'bah: men in cascading white robes prostrating en masse like a rolling wave, the women concealed behind chadors and billowing black. I went through the sequence several times. The photos were clear and sharp. The final snap was of a fountain spouting from a wall.

'What is this?'

He glanced at the photograph before handing it back, beaming. 'Ah, this is Juupa. Our most holy water. Here.' He produced a bottle as if on cue, and dabbed me liberally about the face and shoulders with a soaked handkerchief. His every movement was intimate but never lecherous as he stood close but not over me. I could see why he had two wives.

Just before I tried to steer the conversation round to his marriages, the Imam changed the subject. 'I am from here, you know. From this village. What is your profession? Ah, journalist. I trained as a radio technician, in Olgii, and I lived and worked there for more than ten years. But my parents were very religious, and they encouraged me to go away and study, and then return to live here as Imam. I went to Turkey to study, where many Kazakhs go – so I speak that language, and Russian, Mongolian and Arabic. I think you have been to the mosque? You know it is very new.' His voice was calm as he explained decades of religious turbulence with utter brevity. 'It was only in 1991 that we could build our mosque here. Before then politics in Mongolia was very different for a long time, and we had no mosque and no place to pray together. Before this democracy our religion was hard.'

The Imam called through to the other room, asking his wife if lunch was ready. I could sense he didn't want to discuss religious repression, although I did. But I changed the topic, and instead asked about his family.

'She is my first wife,' he said evenly. 'You know I have two wives and ten children. She and I, my first wife, we were together for ten years before I took a second wife. I talked to her and she agreed to this other marriage. She knows it makes our life easier. My second wife now lives in the Altai with our *mal*, and from the animals I can make money to travel and continue to study. I could have four spouses, you know. This is our tradition. But it is important that when one comes from the city another is from the mountain: for,' he imitated tilting scales with his large hands, 'for balance, *bagsh*. Balance! My children do not know which is their mother. Because it doesn't matter. We are one family.'

I wondered if the Imam's wives and children would agree with this blissful sentiment. It was the only thing he'd said to me that sounded slightly hollow. We moved next door for the shared lunch platter, and chewed on chunks of tender red meat, which looked and tasted oddly reminiscent of bacon. A couple of visitors arrived and joined us and four of the children. The Imam hosted us all, answering and asking questions as we ate, and roaring with deep and easy belly laughter from his seat at the head of the table. 'Did you understand that, *bagsh*?' he demanded, still beaming. I hadn't and shook my head. 'This man,' he gestured towards one of the guests, who were all hanging on to the Imam's every word as they tore shreds of meat from the platter of bones, 'he asked where you come from, where is your home. I told him you come from *tenger* – from the sky!'

I laughed and blushed like a girl. I was delighted I'd finally met this extraordinary man, who was everything I thought he wouldn't be. His wife sat opposite me, a drained-looking woman of indefinable age, who spoke quietly and moved economically. 'We've had many children together, he and I,' she told me. 'We had triplets once, but two of them died.' The constant struggle that was her daily life was etched into her desiccated skin. The Imam was courteous with his wife, but she toiled wearily, and trudged outside to fetch more buckets of Hovd water.

I lingered a little after lunch, relishing the company of the Imam and his family and friends. As I finally rose to leave, Sanak Sailik grasped my hand once more. 'Thank you, Louisa. I am happy you came, *bagsh*.' He pressed a string of pale-blue prayer beads into my palm. 'For you,' he said. 'From our Mecca.'

They have hung from the wall of every room I have lived in ever since.

CHAPTER TWENTY-FIVE

One hundred and thirty kilometres north-west of Tsengel lies a frontier with both Russia and China, the only point in western Mongolia where the three nations meet. A range of barbed mountains and a wide, permanent glacier preside over this impassable border. The five highest peaks of this fortress range are known as 'Tavan Bogd' – the Five Kings. The mountains belong to Mongolia, but the summit is shared with Russia and China. Occasional parties of mountaineers have stood astride all three nations simultaneously. The simple geography of Mongolia is a high plateau with chains of low mountains. Nayramdal, 'friendship', the nation's ultimate peak, is less than 5,000 metres, but lies amidst a breathtaking wilderness where the snow leopard still stalks at night, and the nomads kindle fires outside their *gers* to thwart marauding wolves.

In the summer Tavan Bogd erupts with wild flowers, and the pasture is rich and moist, irrigated by the melted mountain snow. The nomads and their large herds thrive for three or four months. But the autumn is brief, and winter long and brutal. The pasture freezes solid, the livestock cannot forage, and snow falls in drifts deep enough to drown the yaks. So, as the 'short golden season' is eclipsed by winter, the nomads and their animals abandon the throne of the kings, and retreat to cabins built against high and sheer rock a day or two's ride away. They return at the beginning of spring.

Tavan Bogd has its own civil servant. The district is administered by a man called Erdenebaatar, a wise Tuvan who drinks too much. His brother is Gerel, the Mongolian teacher with whom I'd recently drunk too much. Gerel and I had, at a more sober time, compared our summers in the mountains. He'd spent his herding at the base of Tavan Bogd.

'Ah, *saikhan!*' he recalled, as we walked home from school together. 'They are all there, my mother, brothers and sisters. My family has always herded there, and everyone at Tavan Bogd has plenty of *mal,* because the pasture is so good. This year was a terrible spring, but a good summer, and now winter is going to be late, so they're still there, at the bottom of the mountain. But they will all leave soon. Look.'

He gestured towards the tallest mountains surrounding our valley, which began north-west of Tsengel and stretched beyond the Sino–Russian frontier. The peaks and ridges were now crowned in fresh snow.

'There. That first snow fell a few days ago. They will all move to the cabins just before winter starts, and then no one will herd at Tavan Bogd till spring. My family are the last people there. My brother Erdenebaatar is riding out there to help them move.'

It was the end of September. The autumn was finally cooling. We were beginning to kindle fires in the evenings to keep warm. I assumed it was too late to visit the mountain, but grimaced, remembering that Deri-Huu and Bash spent their winters in the Altai en route to Tavan Bogd. I was longing to visit them. Abbai and Addai had dismantled their Kazakh *gers* and the two families were back in their cabins. I had abandoned my river bathing and resorted to the tin bath, scrubbing myself and then my clothes, and spreading the steaming wool and cotton on the communal *hasha* clothes rack, an old gate propped up against the cow shed. When my wet hair stiffened into spikes as I draped sweaters one morning, and then my laundry froze, arms and legs outstretched as though in surrender, I knew winter was finally looming.

I'd thought little more of Tavan Bogd and had resigned myself to not seeing the range, except that Abbai surprised me. We were having a private English lesson; Abbai still desperately wanted to learn English. He was usually very busy with meetings or trips to Olgii or the mountains, but sometimes, in the late evening, he would suddenly arrive at my door, present me with lists of unrelated words from an archaic Kazak–English pamphlet, and while I pronounced them slowly in English, he would scribble the phonetics in Kazakh. I never doubted that Abbai was a clever man. He was a qualified economist and a respected local government chief. He could also read English surprisingly well. But words literally failed him. Abbai and I never spoke in English because he couldn't. We painfully waded through these rare ad hoc lessons, but with his work and my other classes, we couldn't usually, thank God, find the time.

Impatience. Happiness. Confused. Laziness. Abbai was scribbling as I pronounced the words slowly. He nodded gravely and repeated them back to me with great difficulty.

'Zaa [OK]. Good. Thank you.' He closed his thin notebook and frowned at me, rolling his pen between his thumb and index finger. 'It is going to get cold very soon. Winter is coming now. If you want to go to the countryside, you need to go now. Afterwards it will be too cold and dangerous for you. Where do you want to go?'

I was startled. Abbai hadn't suggested a trip to the countryside since our New Year outing the day after I arrived in Tsengel, and had always encouraged me to stay in the village. This, I knew, was probably my final opportunity to travel to the mountains before winter.

'Tavan Bogd?' I said hopefully.

Abbai frowned unhappily. 'Very far, and now very cold. Too difficult.'

'I would like to go there and see it for myself,' I persisted. 'Gerel *bagsh*'s brother Erdenebaatar is going to Tavan Bogd soon. We could stay with his family.'

'You have to ride for hours to see Tavan Bogd – and there is nothing there but this mountain. What about Tsergal?'

'Please, Abbai – I will pay for the fuel,' I brokered, ignoring the fact that I had hardly any spare money left, and that jeeps had been parked beside the fuel pump for weeks, because all the petrol had run out, again. If anyone could get hold of fuel, it was Abbai.

He nodded glumly. 'Zaa. On Saturday morning. For one night. Just to see the mountain.'

I thanked him warmly, and went to bed, quietly thrilled.

* * *

We left late Saturday afternoon. Abbai had spent the morning underneath his cantankerous jeep while I tried not to hover. I had vainly hoped that eight months in Tsengel would anaesthetise me to this ritual waiting for a journey to begin, and the inevitable departure hours later than planned. But the delays still drove me crazy.

Gansukh, her two children and Erdenebaatar all came with us. Gansukh was going to stay with Sansar-Huu and the family; Erdenebaatar was accompanying Abbai and I to Tavan Bogd. I had packed a small bundle of my warmest clothes, as Abbai had spent days warning me how cold the frontier would be. No one else brought anything for the journey except handfuls of sweets for their relatives. Mongols travel unladen.

Abbai calmly passed the small, hopeful crowd at the petrol pump, drove to the home of the attendant and escorted her back to work. There was petrol at the pump, but only for those with the money and power to buy it. After he'd filled the tank we left the attendant shrugging her shoulders at the other, stranded drivers, and we forded the shallowest waters of the Hovd.

It was more than 60 kilometres to Deri-Huu and Bash's *ger*. The light waned as herds of Bactrian camels loped away from the droning jeep. Erdenebaatar paused from addressing Abbai in Kazakh rapid as gunfire and nudged me. 'Up there. See. In the rock. That's where the *malchin* live in winter. Their cabins are high up there. There are many *malchin* here, because of the good pasture.'

There were no lakes and the cabins were far from the river we were trailing. 'How do they find water?' I asked him, wondering how they even managed to scale the valley walls.

Erdenebaatar stared at me, frowning. He was an unusually pale and fair-skinned Tuvan, with almost translucent blue eyes. 'Snow,' he said slowly, as though fascinated by my ignorance. 'They don't need rivers or lakes. They melt snow.'

At sunset we stopped at a small settlement known as Zagas Nuur – 'Fish Lake'. Deri-Huu's *ger* had been erected near half a dozen others, all close to the edge of the lake. The valley had narrowed around us, its walls glowing like sandstone and ochre. Silhouettes of camels drank from the dark water.

'Elizaa!' Deri-Huu stood up and embraced me in her strong, thick arms. It was wonderful to see her again. The *ger* was crammed with her and Manike's families, plus a dozen people I recognised from either Tsengel or the summer camp. There'd been a *khurim* the day before. We squeezed down and said *sain bainuu* to everyone as bowls of tea were ladled.

These are some of the most precious memories I brought home with me from Tsengel: crouching in a dim and noisy *ger* some- where in the mountains, blowing on a bowl of tea and immersed in a crowd of local friends, briefly forgetting that I came from another place.

'Hey, why are you still here, Louisa *bagsh*?' asked one young woman I'd met in summer. 'Don't you like your own country?'

I leaned my head back and laughed. My self-confidence and humour had returned since I'd started teaching at the school again, and now I could appreciate that this was a good question. 'Yes, I do! I do like my own country. I will go home in winter. I just want to stay here till the end of the year, until the river freezes again. Then I'll go home.'

She nodded and then shook her head. 'I still don't understand why you want to stay here alone,' she said.

Why did I? What was it all about, I asked myself as we crouched en masse in the cosy *ger*. Why this need to move about as far from my own country and culture as possible? And why did I have to do it alone – was it somehow not valid if I had a friend beside me? I found these questions really tough to answer, and gave the young woman no response, except to smile and shrug my shoul- ders. But when she had turned back to her own friends, I crouched for minutes in deep thought about what she had just said.

I did find it hard being alone in Tsengel. I also found it wondrous, exciting and unique, but hard. However, I honestly believed that the only way I could genuinely experience living in the village was to be here on my own. Having another foreigner with me would have diluted things, made it too easy, if you like.

Maybe I needed it to be tough to feel like I'd had the real experience, which, in light of how hard life was in Tsengel for everyone I had met, suddenly seemed a very misguided principle. After all, I could leave here whenever I liked and go back to my easy life, but for everyone else life here would continue just as it was. And it was hard.

It was late evening when Erdenebaatar, Abbai and I said goodbye and clambered back into the jeep. Tavan Bogd lay another four hours to the west. It was the road to hell.

The jeep lurched like a drunk and bucked like a horse as the track straggled into the mountains, the headlights occasionally snaring a stray yak or horse, which snorted and glided away. Their glistening eyes reflected the full moon above us, which shed pale lustre on the uninhabited landscape. I felt as though I was looking at the world from under clear water. The Altai peaks rose immense and laden with snow as the valleys narrowed into jagged mazes.

Erdenebaatar knew the trail intimately, where it disappeared and then re-emerged, where to drive slowly or veer from hidden rocks or water. Suddenly he made Abbai stop near the centre of a small, smooth plateau. 'Come on.'

We climbed out of the jeep and walked, shivering, towards two figures poised before us as though calmly waiting for guests. We stood and knelt before them. Erdenebaatar struck match after match, revealing flares of detail: the contours of a man and a woman carved from rock, each around four feet high, with faded but intact features, and ingrained with whorls and crude characters gouged across their pocked and shrouded lower limbs.

'See these lines? Twenty-one people are buried here, under this monument,' he told me with the conviction of an eminent archaeologist on a well-sifted site.

'Who are they?'

Erdenebaatar smiled across at me. I had noticed he didn't smile much, and that he'd left Deri-Huu's *ger* wafting and swaying with *arikh*. 'These are the stones from the Turks who lived here before us.' He spread his arms around him. 'Here. This was their land long ago, before we were here. Maybe a thousand years before we came. The Turkic Uigher people. These stones are where they buried their dead. There are so many other stones around here, where their families lie together. You will see them if you look carefully.'

These desolate ancestral graves have lain neglected and barely visited since the Mongols forged their Empire in the thirteenth century, under the brutally efficient regime of Temujin the Unflinching Emperor – Genghis Khan. Now the Uighers were across the frontier, in China's Xinjiang province, but had left two lasting remnants of their history in Mongolia: the classic, vertical Mongol script, which was adopted by Genghis Khan and is still used today by Mongol scholars and artists, and the Hun Cholloe, the Stone People.

It was strange I thought. When Genghis Khan died in China in 1227, the hordes escorted his body home to Mongolia in a vast cavalcade of mourning – and slaughtered every single person they met en route. This was their bloody, barbaric tradition, to avenge his death in carnage. But the dead here, however they died, had always been accepted as the original keepers of the land. The Mongols had conquered the Uighers, but had not desecrated their graves. I felt a shudder of tremendous respect for them. The wind blew around us as we turned back to the jeep. I wondered how much further we had to go.

Erdenebaatar's sister Narantuya and her husband Enkhsaikhan were sleeping when we arrived in the early hours of the morning. Their small *ger*, erected in a hollow against a granite mountain side, looked as though it was the last home on earth. A huge and silent herd of yaks, sheep and goats stared unblinking as we stumbled through the doorway. Our hosts instantly rose, greeted and kindly fed us, before we sank to sleep swaddled in blankets and layers of felt.

At dawn the next morning I stood shivering in front of the *ger*, and cheered out loud at the immense sierra of dark rock and crusted dazzling snow. The cobalt sky was deep and brilliant as an ocean. I felt almost glad the journey had been so rough. This panorama did not belong at a road well-travelled.

Nara was already milking her yaks. She smiled at my outburst and gestured towards the final peak in our horizon. 'That last mountain is the first of the Tavan Bogd range. That is where you will ride.'

She and her husband were young and had one small baby. They were moving back to their winter cabin in a few days, with the herders from the other four *gers* also tucked into the nearby rock. 'Everyone else has left, there's only the five *gers* here now,' she said, 'and we are all from the same family. Next time it snows we'll move back to the cabins together. In a few days.'

Tavan Bogd lies on high terrain. We were now 3,000 metres above sea level. My head felt light, as though I'd been drinking. When Erdenebaatar emerged from the *ger*, he obviously had. His eyes glinted as he, Abbai and I saddled our horses. He was an intriguing man. Born and raised in Tsengel, he'd spent half a dozen years in Moscow training as an economist, and had been director of a large Ulaanbaatar meat company for fifteen years, before returning home to the mountains and this most remote of civil servant posts. Abbai was his boss.

I swung into my saddle cloaked in the padded winter *deel* the men had insisted I wear on top of my thermals, sweaters and jacket. I had protested lamely: it felt warm outside the *ger* that morning and we rode without gloves. But they were right. As our horses climbed into the mountains, the sun blazed but the air cooled. Erdenebaatar sobered up as there were no *gers* to visit for *shimin-arikh* and rode ahead on his white mount. I trailed slightly behind him and Abbai, turning in my saddle to gawp at the sheer white cliffs rising around us.

We saw one person during our ride – Enkhsaikhan herding his sheep and goats on the snow-streaked slopes below.

It was a long ride. We climbed high into the mountains and then wove down again to the floor of a frozen valley, where a herd of stocky horses streamed towards us. They looked wild and beautiful. Erdenebaatar and Abbai hollered commands in a language the herd understood, and guided me away from them, around a small solid lake as our own horses skidded on the snow and ice. My calves were cramped and my cheeks numb, but when

Erdenebaatar waved his arm to indicate the way, I cantered boldly ahead, gleeful and excited. Our horses jumped frozen tributaries and waded through drifts, their nostrils flaring and pouring steam. The peaks ahead grew huge and resolute.

Erdenebaatar and Abbai changed direction, and I followed as they clambered up a huge and steep ridge, the horses matted in freezing sweat. We were suddenly directly in front of the Five Kings, which towered above us, colossal, jagged and white. Thousands of tons of snow had compressed into edifices and gorgeous bizarre sculptures folded between the mass of peaks and crevasses. A breath of flakes was rising from one summit into the rich, almost dark sky, like incense from an offering. We were all silent.

This was one of those long rare moments you know will inspire you beyond the thrill of its beauty and sustain you through difficult times. It's true, I thought, as we stood there, this is it, right here and right now, the mountains and this silence. It's what I wanted to see and write about. This is all that matters right now, nothing else. That I'm here. I'm glad I stayed. This makes everything worthwhile.

Abbai was beaming. 'Now you have seen the best of Mongolia!' he told me triumphantly. 'Where is your camera?'

We gaily snapped all the combinations possible with three people. The photos of our bundled-up figures in front of the Kings still make me smile. I'd never seen Abbai so relaxed. With his rifle slung across his shoulder in case we spied wolves, his bulky black Kazakh *deel* and stiff fur hat, he looked like a film extra for a Russian epic.

We didn't tarry; it was too windswept up there. Erdenebaatar led the three horses down the sheer brae. We scrabbled down after him and an hour later stood together near the glacier, which encased the base of the range like a huge oyster pearl. We turned our horses south, and the men sang with abandon as we rode back to camp. I just beamed.

Abbai and I were planning to leave early in the evening, but Erdenebaatar refused to let us go. 'No! You must stay tonight and visit all my family. They will cook for you and we will go to my mother's house together tomorrow.'

Abbai agreed passively to this demand. '*Zaa*. Maybe this is better,' he told me. 'I will be able to see the way back this time.'

By dusk I felt as though we were being held hostage by an insane captor, who dragged us round the other four *gers*, bellowing at his placid siblings for more *shimin-arikh* and demanding we drink as much as he. No one could keep up with him.

'Louisa, try to drink a little more,' Abbai murmured, as I reluctantly raised my bowl to another weary toast. 'He will fall over and sleep soon.'

Erdenebaatar's alcoholism was patiently, stoically tolerated by his family and his boss. No one reprimanded or berated him as he ranted, cried, drank himself senseless and finally passed out on the floor. The Mongols claim they learned to love alcohol from the Russians, which is probably true. But regardless of where their passion for drink evolved, the nation is full of men who celebrate, mourn and socialise with vodka. It's cheap and in the countryside there are very few other luxuries or distractions.

In this respect, Tsengel was an exception. The Kazakhs rarely drank (though some did indulge in *shimin-arikh*, insisting it wasn't really booze), and most of the Tuvans (bar Gerele) were fairly sober most of the time. After my trip to Tavan Bogd I learned that Erdenebaatar was a notorious local drunk. It seemed very sad to me: to be the guardian of this fragment of heaven, but drowning in your own alcoholic hell.

In the morning I said goodbye to Narantuya and Enkhsaikhan, as Abbai and a pitifully hungover Erdenebaatar coaxed the jeep engine back to life. Erdenebaatar cringed in the back seat as we tilted and jarred towards the winter settlement where another of his many brothers and his ancient, shrunken mother welcomed us. Her name was Tseverlee. Her shoulders and back were so crippled she almost resembled the letter C. By the time we departed Erdenebaatar was drunk again. We left him with his sober, forgiving family.

The homeward trail was much easier in the sunshine. We followed the sweep of the river back towards Deri-Huu's *ger*, and, almost within sight of Zagas Nuur, swung past a large and ornate

Kazakh cemetery, even larger than the one in our village. Abbai braked. I glanced at him, wondering why we had stopped so suddenly, and then stared out of the window, speechless.

A huge family of Kazakhs, from infants to great-grandparents, were at the edge of the cemetery, digging their own communal tomb, while several women were cooking lunch next to them, on a close circle of smouldering stones. Everyone was bantering cheerfully as the women began to ladle out bowls of food next to their graves, and they started to eat with relish. It was wonderful to see this almost joyful preparation for their own funerals, this gracious acceptance of all their deaths. The whole family was spending a day out together building an ornate adobe tomb in which they would each eventually lie. It was a glimpse of fearless mortality. I'd never seen anything like it. Looking over at them I felt as though maybe I could finally understand how people lived with death in these mountains, how they dealt with its potency and its constant tangible presence: they looked it in the face.

Abbai slammed the jeep door and strode towards the family, calling greetings. I watched him through the window, kneeling, accepting a bowl and eating. Then I looked away. I wanted to be there too, but I didn't quite have the confidence to join them. I remembered being in Deri-Huu's *ger* two evenings before, laughing and joking easily, and stared through the windscreen, feeling conspicuous, awkward and stymied by my sudden shyness. I remained unsure of myself amongst the Kazakhs. I still didn't feel I knew them very well. It was like standing outside a party you really want to attend, but haven't actually been invited to.

'Louisa! *It jey, it jey!*' Eat meat!

They called me from my seat, beckoning me with hands and smiles. Grinning uncontrollably I walked to the family, knelt with them in the dust amidst the living and the dead, and was given a bowl of steaming meat soup. We exchanged greetings and news slowly in Kazakh, as I gulped my soup and Abbai related our journey to the Five Kings. I caught someone's eye, laughed out loud with them and suddenly couldn't ever remember feeling happier.

PART FIVE

In the Rich Cradle

CHAPTER TWENTY-SIX

'Louisa, wait.' Gansukh came out of her gate just as I was passing by on my way to school. I turned round, smiling, but when she walked towards me her expression was intent, pale and fraught. We walked on together in silence for a moment. 'Did you hear about Zorig?' she demanded. 'Did you? Did Abbai tell you?'

'Yes, we heard something on the radio last night. It was an accident?'

'*Yanaa*!' She restrained me with her hand and we both stopped dead on the track and turned to face each other. 'No! He was killed by someone. Why didn't Abbai tell you? They waited for him for hours before he came back from the *Ikh Khural* [the Parliament]. In his home! These men asked his wife for something and she opened the front door, and they took her and tied her to the chair and put something over her mouth. And then they waited, and when Minister Zorig came home they killed him with an axe and she saw it all.

'They had only been married for one year. Now everyone is on the streets in Ulaanbaatar. They are angry and very, very frightened. Because he was one of our "swallows of freedom" you know. Yes. He was one of the leaders of the Democrats when they went to the *Ikh Khural* in 1989, and they told the communists, "We want democracy, we need democracy now." And when those huge crowds stayed in the Sukhbaatar Square for days and said they wouldn't leave until the communists left, Zorig stayed with them in the square until the communists said, "*Zaa*, we will go, the *Ikh Khural* belongs to the Democrats now." When the Democrats won the election they made him a minister, and his name was even on that list for Prime Minister. Why do they want to kill the man who will be our Prime Minister?

'I tell you, the radio says so many people are in Sukhbaatar Square right now, shouting at the *Ikh Khural*. What is happening in Mongolia? This is not Russia with the Mafia. We don't understand who is doing this terrible thing. We always think our politicians are safe to do their work. You know nothing like this ever happened since *Choybalsan*. Nothing. Even during the Democratic Revolution nobody died, nobody even went to prison. This is our free country. Look, look at this: the newspaper has no other story, just photos and stories of Zorig. And everybody here can only talk about him, and we have no electricity so we can't even watch the funeral on television.

'Something has changed now this has happened, and I tell you, you should be worried too, Louisa. Because we don't know who this was or how many people are involved. There might even be a civil war because of this. I am serious. Sansar-Huu says whoever did it, whoever these men are, they will be very frightened now, because they didn't expect our people to feel so violent. He says nothing else will happen now, no one will be killed because our people are so angry, even here in the village they are so angry. He says it will be OK now. But I don't know, I just don't know.'

Tsengel talked about little else but Zorig for the next couple of weeks. The whole village seemed stunned by his murder, which the government was insisting was a political assassination by a radical communist splinter group. No one had been arrested.

The following Wednesday the post office was heaving as we pushed our way in and pored over the smeared newspaper photographs of the funeral, wide-eyed at the deluge of people lining Ulaanbaatar's Enkh Taivan as the hearse glided slowly towards the cemetery. A headstone proclaiming Sanjaasurengiyn Zorig as the Mongol Father of Democracy had already been carved and erected on a pedestal for him, above his grave.

The villagers passed the papers slowly from hand to hand, shaking their heads and saying little. We were so distant from

Ulaanbaatar that the whole tragedy had a surreal quality about it, but the title of an article I read months later in the *Far Eastern Economic Review*, 'Death of Innocence', hit the metaphorical nail on the head. Something in the Mongol psyche fractured when Minister Zorig died. The violence of his death sent shock waves reeling across the whole country, and I could sense the grief and fear in Tsengel. I think part of the villagers' collective mourning was bound up with knowing that in some way their nation would never be the same place again . . . an indelible lifeline had just been crossed.

Tuya and I sat on the bank of the Hovd one evening, drawing our jackets close. It was impossible not to be affected by the sombre air still hanging over the village in the wake of the death of Zorig, and we talked in low voices and chuckled, whereas a week or two before we probably would have laughed out loud.

My friend was in a wistful mood that evening, reminiscing about her five years at university in the Tuvan capital, Khyzl. She'd been there at the same time as Gansukh and Sansar-Huu.

'Ah, it was wonderful. Great fun. There was always a party to go to, good food and places to visit in the evenings, not like here . . .'

She and Gansukh had both proudly shown me glamorous photos of themselves posing in leather coats and sunglasses in the centre of Khyzl, precious mementos of their previous urban lives. Now Tuya shivered a little in the chilly riverside dusk as she recalled the paved roads, well-stocked shops and elegant restaurants of Khyzl.

Finally she said with great feeling, 'I want to move back there as soon as Gerele and I marry, but I don't know, maybe we will have to wait.'

I'd stopped asking her when the wedding would be, because she didn't know herself and felt harangued enough about getting married as it was. 'I am the only Tuvan daughter in the village who is twenty-five and still not married,' she'd confided, trying to look as though she couldn't care less.

Tuya claimed her parents still knew nothing of her and Gerele's love affair, but I'd finally realised this was more of an unspoken agreement than anything else. Gerele was obliged to wait until a decent mourning period for his father was over before he could marry, and though Tuya hadn't actually announced her betrothal, it was hard to believe her parents still had no idea at all about what was going on. Everyone just seemed to be biding their time until the right moment.

When she'd finished talking about Khyzl there was a lull in our conversation, and we sat in silence for a little while, gazing over to the other side of the river where the man from the post office with the wonderful name, Buyan-Tok-Tok, had built his cabin. It was a feat of great ingenuity, this home of his: built on a narrow bank that backed on to a colossal wall of overhanging rock. It looked impregnable and I wondered how on earth he managed to cross the fast-flowing Hovd every morning to work. In winter it would be easy, of course, but there was no boat to be seen now, and the only bridge was more than thirty kilometres upstream. I was idly pondering Buyan-Tok-Tok's means of transport, and what his fabulous name meant, when Tuya quietly interrupted my thoughts.

'Louisa, London *yamar bain*? What is London like?'

In all the months I'd known Tuya she'd never asked me this, and I had to think about the question for a minute before any words came to mind.

'Oh . . . well, it's . . . a huge, crowded city. Very exciting. There's so much to do, and everyone's always in a great hurry, going out to work and arranging to meet people afterwards . . .'

And so I went on, happily reminiscing about my half a dozen years in London, recalling good times, old friends and fond memories. I'd actually spent a lot of my time in London working with young homeless people. I'd enjoyed it, though it definitely had its stressful moments, as did living in London itself. But though I mentioned my work to Tuya, and also told her London was noisy, polluted and could be violent, I know I described a very romantic version of my old life there. I don't think I even did it on purpose.

I wasn't trying to impress her. I was just recalling what I wanted to remember about the past. Like I guess most of us do when life feels hard.

'Are you going to go back there when you leave our village?' she asked when I'd finished. 'Where are you going to live when you go home?'

I shrugged. 'I don't know. Maybe in London again.' I'd tried not to think about what I was going to do after Tsengel, because I wanted to spend this final season living each day in the village as it evolved, instead of constantly plotting ahead and distracting myself from where I was right now. I knew I could immerse myself back into urbanity if I wanted, or move on again and explore new terrain. After the narrow contours of the village the world beyond would offer a host of temptations.

For Tuya, though, there were far fewer choices to be made. She was restless here, and made no secret of the fact she wanted to leave Tsengel for a new life in the city with Gerele, but she was stymied by her own and especially Gerele's family.

'I came back here after university because of my mother and father, you know.' She pursed her lips for a moment. 'They're getting older now, my parents, but they will be fine if I leave because they also have my brothers living with them, and they've got plenty of *mal*. Gerele's family, now that's a problem. They have no one to help them. His mother is alone with four children, and they're all still at school except Gerele, so no one works and they've got no money. He will have to stay here with them for several years. We'll both have to wait until one of the brothers can go out to work. Ah, I don't know! *Khetsüü.* [It's difficult].'

We were getting cold, so we stood up, stamped our numbing feet and tramped slowly towards home. Amraa had moved away to Olgii with her parents, and Gansukh and Sansar-Huu were at home with their children, and were also looking after two raw-cheeked young girls from the mountains who'd just started school, so Tuya and I were spending a lot of time together these days. Either one of us visited the other for part of most evenings, and sometimes we just sat around together and didn't even say very much, but it always felt very comfortable. Now I bade her farewell at the gate, and she teased me again about using the word *bayartai*, which we both knew I did jokingly because neither of us was actually going anywhere.

'One day soon, Louisa, you will have to say *bayartai* properly because you'll be leaving and you won't come back! But you know you'll see me again tomorrow, so why *bayartai*, eh?'

I grinned and waved as we went our separate ways for the night.

I usually visited Abbai's cabin for a while in the evenings too, because it was warm and cosy and I liked ending my day talking with him and Guul-Jan while the kids scurried around. I'd got used to the fact Tuya never came into Abbai's house. She would wait for me outside my door if I wasn't at home, or send one of the kids over to fetch me. Tsengel was a strange, old, familiar place to me now, but I felt adrift this evening and just wanted to sit alone by my stove and ponder my own thoughts. Tuya had invoked her halcyon days as a student in Tuva, and I'd responded by recalling my time in London, and igniting a slow-burning nostalgia, which I rarely succumbed to in the village. We'd both draped our pasts in reverie.

Several hours later, when I would usually have been well wrapped up in my blankets and sound asleep, I was still perched by the side of my stove, with a candle melting beside me and a goatskin-lined *deel* wrapped round my shoulders. I was slowly examining my hands, peering at my palms and fingers as though I hadn't seen them properly before. The skin was dry and tough. Horny, yellow calluses were cracking at the tops of my palms, my nails were chipped and dirty and the fingertips were frayed. For the first time in my life I had working hands.

CHAPTER TWENTY-SEVEN

And so our village lives continued, quietly, with their own small comedies, dramas, arrivals and departures. Trucks still rumbled into Tsengel as yet another family returned home late from their long summer sojourn in the mountains; cabins were whitewashed, spruced up and repaired before winter. The crack of axes striking wood resounded across the village, and the snapped electricity cables were once again strung along from house to house by a team of local men, who blithely clambered up the poles as whole families came out to watch.

Gansukh and I worked together at school, we continued deciphering the bizarre *Blue Sky* text, and I spent the majority of my time between the school, Abbai, Tuya and Gansukh's *hashas*. Just occasionally I realised how much my world had shrunk, how I knew almost nothing of what was going on outside my own tiny sphere of existence, and I'd quietly fret and pine about all the things I was obviously missing out on, before reassuring myself that it would of course all still be there when I got back.

Given these occasional cravings to connect with the outside world, it was rather odd that when Guul-Jan came into my room and announced a foreigner was coming to visit Tsengel, I didn't feel thrilled at the prospect.

'*Yamar gadaad-neen hun?*' What kind of foreigner? I asked her, suspiciously.

'An American doctor. He's arriving at the clinic this evening.'

'Why?'

She shrugged. 'I don't know. But you must meet him, you can tell him all about the village.'

Abbai later explained that the American doctor was coming over from Olgii for just one night with a couple of the city hospital doctors, but he also didn't know why they were visiting or which organisation the American worked for. Abbai, of course, thought it was splendid. But I reacted like a xenophobe.

'He's probably a bloody missionary,' I muttered viciously to myself that afternoon, 'and why the hell does he have to come here anyway? It's not as though there aren't any other remote villages in Bayan-Olgii. Why can't he find somewhere else to visit?'

I knew this was a snotty response to someone I'd never met, and who might offer the village funding or new medical facilities, so I did keep these rants strictly to myself, but it was interesting how territorial I felt about Tsengel. I had unconsciously claimed the village as my own, and felt as though I'd earned my niche here after months of grafting, which, of course, I had chosen to undertake in the first place. I hated the thought of anyone just wandering in here and maybe dismissing the place out of hand, or, if I was honest, threatening my position as the only foreigner. I loved having Tsengel to myself, and resented the idea of sharing the experience with anyone, for even one day. If another foreigner had ever come to live in Tsengel while I was there, I knew I'd have felt as though I had to leave, which is no doubt as unreasonable as it sounds, and unfortunately says far more about me than the villagers, who would have loved the idea of a well-funded foreign doctor moving in.

That evening Abbai and I trekked from our *hasha* to the clinic, which was on the other side of Tsengel, but the doctor and his entourage were nowhere to be seen. However, by the time we'd returned home, someone had rung Addai and Szandrash's phone, and explained the jeep had broken down and they'd all be here tomorrow.

The following afternoon I'd finished teaching with Gansukh for the day, and was writing my journal in my room when a jeep braked outside the *hasha*, and, moments later, three people strolled towards Abbai's home. As I peered out of my pink curtains covertly, like a snoop, it was obvious which one of them was the American doctor. And even from where I stood, he looked absolutely gorgeous.

I was soon invited over to Abbai's to meet the trio. They were sitting round the table, which was laden in their honour with plates of sweets, biscuits, *buurtzug*, bread, and bowls of steaming tea. The children kept coming in with more snacks, and then being abruptly shooed outside by Guul-Jan, who stood next to the table, hovering and flushed. All Mongols place a great emphasis on hospitality, and the arrival of the foreign doctor was causing panic in the *hasha*. Foreigners had visited Tsengel before I moved into the village, but not often.

I exchanged Kazakh greetings with his companions while the American looked on with that baffled smile most people use when they've heard certain foreign words before, but don't have a clue what they mean.

'Hello,' I said to him afterwards.

'Hi there.' We smirked because there was something slightly comic about the stilted air of deference and expectation pervading the room. He and I were obviously meant to sit and converse together for hours while everyone watched us. *Sain yerekh*, as the Mongols say: have a good talk.

After ensuring we were engrossed in conversation, Abbai, Guul-Jan and the doctor's escorts left us to it, talking together in rapid Kazakh, and glancing over as the doctor and I asked each other fairly unoriginal questions.

He was indeed an American, and he looked even better close up. His dark skin was smooth, and his thick curly hair swept back beautifully and shone as though it had been polished. He worked as a consultant for one of the big aid agencies, and was spending a few weeks in Mongolia.

'What sort of consultant are you?' I asked.

He grinned, flashing fluorescent white teeth at me. 'I work in HIV and Aids, but we look at all aspects of sexual health, y'know, plus infant and maternal mortality.'

I told him one of the few things I knew about local family planning, which was the number of women who'd had IUDs fitted, and the problems these implants had caused, from heavy bleeding to sterility. I'd learned about this from a late-night conversation with Gansukh and Tuya et al, where we'd compared methods of contraception and I'd realised they had very little choice about what to use.

'Did you bring any supplies of contraception for the clinic with you?' I asked him. I'd brought a couple of dozen condoms to the village with me, but had long resigned myself to the fact I was never going to use them while I was here, and had given them away instead. I was sure my friends would be glad of more, though, because you certainly couldn't get them in Tsengel.

'I don't have any contraception with me to distribute to locals.' He winked at me slowly through heavy lashes. 'I just brought some condoms with me for my own use.'

The American's companions, a middle-aged Kazakh couple called Aplom and Zaurich, wanted to take their guest on a jaunt through the river gorge, and invited Abbai, Guul-Jan and I to go with them. They both spoke Mongolian and Aplom also spoke English. He was acting as the doctor's translator.

'We come from the big Olgii hospital,' he told me, as we all squeezed into their jeep. 'The American, he came here to Bayan-Olgii to see hospitals in Mongolian countryside, and he said, "Now you must take me to a small clinic in the mountains, so I can see how they work."'

I glanced over at our guest to confirm this, and he nodded. 'Yep. I said take me to the wildest place you know, so I can see how good or bad things are.'

'And how good or bad are they?'

'Infant mortality is very high here, though the birth rate is dropping, and from what I've seen of the clinic they have very little medicine and few facilities. It must be a real struggle.'

The jeep bashed its way south for a few kilometres, until we came to a camp erected on the river bank, and then, of course, we stopped for tea. I recognised a couple of the nomads from the summer camp, greeted them and made to introduce the American, but he was already glancing over my shoulder towards the river.

'Louisa, look at those horses! D'you think they'll let us go for a ride?'

I was used to the stocky Mongol horses by now, but he groaned as he swung his right leg over the horse and into the stirrup. 'God, these creatures are tiny! I ride an Arab in the States, and he's a *big* horse. OK – shall we go?'

We trotted out of the *ail*, and I couldn't resist glancing behind us, where Guul-Jan, Aplom, Zaurich and half a dozen bemused nomads stood silently watching us depart, and then all started talking together at once.

This must look like a clip from a bloody TV mini-series, I thought.

It was a beautiful ride. The air was cold but the sun shone and the river gorge, with its dark walls of rock and canopy of brilliant sky, was spectacular. I'd hardly been alone in the company of a man since I'd arrived in Tsengel, and it was a real novelty to be with this attractive foreign doctor, who seemed genuinely interested in what I was doing here, and in Tsengel itself. I finally relaxed my guard, especially when he roared with laughter and assured me, 'Hell, no! I'm not an evangelist! I hate those freaks!'

We let the horses walk and talked for a while as the river slid past. I told him about summer in the mountains and life in Tsengel, he told me about life in Kansas where he lived and he gave me his card. We both laughed at this, then turned the horses around.

When we arrived back at the *ail*, Aplom was contentedly fishing with some of the nomad kids, clasping a rod made of a branch and a length of twine. '*Balakh!*' He triumphantly held up half a dozen fish and thrust them into my hand. They were neatly snagged on to a thin stick. 'For you, *bagsh*. I don't eat *balakh*.'

Most of the people I met in Tsengel didn't eat fish, which seemed a shame as it was one of the few edible alternatives to boiled mutton, goat or beef. But they thought it a poor man's substitute for meat, and though I quite often saw children fishing for sport on the river, I was never offered fish at anyone's home. Now I accepted the catch gratefully. I'd been given fish before because people knew I liked it, and though I really hated scraping, gutting and cleaning the slimy fillets, they tasted fabulous fried in butter.

'Now we must go,' announced Aplom, already striding towards his jeep as the others slowly filtered out of the three *gers*.

'Where are you going?' I was amazed they were planning to leave so soon. In the village guests came to visit for days, not hours.

'To Ulaan-Huus. We must meet one doctor in the village and we will stay there tonight.'

Ulaan-Huus was the village that lay equidistant between Tsengel and Olgii. Surrounded by a broad river valley and colossal red sandstone rocks, it looked dramatic at first, but as you drew closer you could see that it was in fact a weary, ramshackle settlement, with rubble-strewn dirt tracks, marauding stray dogs and half-ruined cabins. It was very easy to believe there would be plenty of sick people to attend to in Ulaan-Huus. But the doctor wouldn't be seeing any patients. He'd already told me that he'd come for just a glimpse of the west of Bayan-Olgii.

'Hey, Louisa, why don't you come with us? Surely someone could arrange to bring you back here afterwards. Come on, come and stay the night with us in Ulaan-Huus.' The American fixed his gaze on me, beaming expectantly, and I averted my eyes.

It wasn't his words or the invitation itself, but the underlying tone of his suggestion – and his slight leer. The handsome doctor was away from home for a few weeks, I thought cynically, and he was trying to pick me up. I'd forgotten how presumptuous men can be.

I smiled broadly back at him, shaking my head firmly at the same time. 'No, no, it would be difficult getting back and I have work here, you know.'

He arched his eyebrows, brushed his outstretched hand down my arm and said quietly, 'C'mon, Louisa.'

And that made up my mind. Apart from getting recklessly drunk a few times, I'd lived a remarkably virtuous life in Tsengel, and that, unfortunately, would have to continue until I returned to the city. The thought of sneaking out of an Ulaan-Huus cabin with him late at night for a brief bout of chilly, outdoor sex, and hoping we weren't witnessed by anyone, or attacked by one of the local rabid dogs, didn't tempt me at all. Not even after eight months of celibacy. He could get lost, I thought irritably. I could do better than that.

We drank more tea back at the *hasha* before our guests set off for Ulaan-Huus. I made conversation with the doctor about nothing much at all, because I suddenly couldn't be bothered. I'm not sure that he noticed.

As we escorted him and the other doctors out of the *hasha* and back towards the jeep, Guul-Jan nudged me. 'Louisa, where is he from, this doctor? Is he Indian or American?'

'He's American.'

'Is he coming back here?'

'I don't think so.'

We all stood around saying goodbye for a few minutes. Abbai was asking the American to please return to Tsengel and spend some time at the clinic, when the American reached forward and embraced me tightly in full view of everyone.

'It's been great to meet you, Louisa. Hope I see you in Kansas one day.' He kissed me full on the lips and I stepped back from him, my arms stretched out in front of me, blushing and angry. For God's sake, I thought, leave me alone. How dare you do that in front of everyone here, it's just embarrassing.

If I'd met this man before I came to Tsengel I've no doubt I would have seen his behaviour as a mild flirtation, nothing more or less. I would probably have enjoyed his attention, and might well have responded to his invitation. After all, he was very attractive, I was a single woman and we were both available at that moment. But my parameters had shifted. I'd moved into a remote and extremely conservative society, and had conformed to local notions of decent behaviour. I had changed in order to adapt to my environment, because it made my life easier. From where I was choosing to stand now, his careless suggestions and easy touch were out of order. They, and by implication he, didn't belong here. I was glad to see the back of him.

CHAPTER TWENTY-EIGHT

One of the things I hadn't realised about the onset of winter in Tsengel was that the local population swelled. Some of the elderly nomads moved from the mountains into the village itself for a few months, until the worst of the weather was over. Most nomadic families had already moved with their animals from their summer *ger* camps into winter cabins built high in the mountains, and complete with corals for the *mal*. Some but not all of the eldest relatives then left their *mal* in the safe-keeping of their grown-up children and trekked off to other family in Tsengel to enjoy the relative ease of village life for three months or so.

Tuya's parents hitched a lift into the village and moved back into their daughter's home. Tuya's mother was called Gurov, which means 'three' in Mongolian, presumably because she had eight siblings and her parents had already run out of names by the time she was born. Amina's sixty-five-year-old mother, Apam, also moved from her summer camp in Tsergal to a site near the village. She and her son, Quartz, erected their *ger* on the opposite side of the Hovd from Tsengel. When the river froze, Apam would cross the ice and also move into the village for a few months.

Since school had started, a young boy called Irlaan had been staying in Szandrash's home. Szandrash often sent him over to mine, smiling and timid, his small hand unsteadily clutching a bowl of warm milk or a plate of bread or cheese. Irlaan was Quartz's eldest son. He was eight and in his first year at school. I'd always presumed that Irlaan's parents were herding in the mountains, but when I finally asked Szandrash, she told me Irlaan's mother was dead.

'She died three years ago, so Quartz lives with Apam. Irlaan has a little brother as well, you know.' She tutted. 'Quartz has two sons but no wife. The other little boy is called Nuurlan, and he lives with Quartz and Apam too.'

Every weekend Amina, Szandrash's daughter Nuur-Guul and Irlaan would ford the Hovd on horseback, and spend two days milking Apam and Quartz's goats, and collecting dung and crusts of dead wood for their stove. They invited me to spend the weekend with them. I was longing to meet Apam, whose name simply means 'Grandmother' in Kazakh, and who was always talked about with great affection, so I was glad to join them.

After school on Friday we traipsed off to the river together. Quartz was already waiting for us, poised at the water's edge with a spare horse to ford the swift deep waters. He was a large, solid man, with red skin that was heavily pocked, and a deep voice that was quiet and sad. I wondered what had happened to his wife, as he could only have been in his mid-thirties. Quartz greeted me formally and embraced his young son with great affection. Then, sharing two horses between the five of us, we waded in convoy across the Hovd, our mounts forcing their way through the treacherous downstream currents.

Apam's *ger* was less than half an hour's ride away. The wind screeched as we rode into her camp, which had been set up next to a small tributary of the Hovd and was concealed from Tsengel by a thin copse of orange pine. The ground was strewn with their brittle needles.

Apam stood at the door to her *ger*. The mother of fourteen children, she was a tiny, shrunken widow whose skin had been so ravaged from a life amid these elements she looked at least several centuries old. Experience was gouged in creases across an ancient face, her rheumy eyes blinked in deep sockets of loose skin, and her neck had long collapsed into narrow, hunched shoulders. But she chortled gleefully as she greeted us all, and grasping my hand with strong dry fingers, led me to her warm stove.

That evening, while Irlaan and Nuurlan tussled and giggled, Quartz strummed the plaintive *dombra*, and women from nearby *gers* came to visit and sing. Apam's *ger* was near the edge of a wide valley set back from the river, where families of *ails* were still clustered, and herds of Bactrian camels roamed. After the nomad women had finally left, we all slept curled up close together in folds of summer felt, coarse blankets and thick, hairy *deels*. When I slipped out late to pee, the stove embers were still glowing.

I always loved waking very early in a *ger*. Dawn streams through the roof in ribbons of dust-moted light, and the air is tinged with dew and smoke. The blankets tucked around you feel comfortingly heavy, and you can hear the resonance of other people breathing beside you. Over the last nine months I'd learned to love sleeping with six or eight or ten other people, forgetting about personal space and enjoying this intimacy that has nothing to do with touch but everything to do with being very close to other people.

Apam was the first out of bed. She was kindling the fire as I awoke, and I lay and silently watched her kneeling stiffly and pressing dry cakes of dung into the stove. Like most elderly Kazakhs she didn't speak a word of Mongolian, so we talked together in slow Kazakh as the camp slowly roused itself for morning tea.

There are several questions you should never ask an elderly woman here, including her age, her name, and when her husband died. I knew Apam's age because Amina had told me, but, like everyone else, I addressed her as Apam. She had spent her whole life herding in these mountains, raising her troupe of children, first with her husband and then alone in the splendour of the Tsergal valley, only moving nearer Tsengel village in winter.

'Do you have livestock where you come from?' she asked me, and I nodded, smiling because I'd been asked that question many times.

The children and I spent the afternoon collecting sacks of dung, wandering along the Hovd as a large herd of Bactrian camels watered themselves and grazed on the dry yellow grass. The weather was crisp and getting colder. Later Amina and I stole Quartz's horse while he lay snoring, and cantered off together, giggling as we sped over rocks and across the rough steppe. When we clattered back, Quartz was outside the *ger* placidly waiting. I felt ashamed about our prank because you shouldn't ever borrow a nomad's horse, and certainly not without asking. I apologised to him, though Amina said nothing, and he nodded passively as I handed back the reins.

The next morning I rose at the same time as Apam, and after she and I had shared a quiet couple of bowls of tea together, I told her I was going to fetch another sack of dung. She shook her white head, muttering as she limped over to an ancient chest, and dragged a colossal sheepskin-lined *deel* out of the bottom drawer. She stuffed and belted me into this immense garment, cackling with merry laughter at the sight of me smothered in the interior white fluff. It was so thick I couldn't put my arms by my sides. She also insisted on my climbing into a pair of traditional Mongol *gutal* boots, which were knee-high and had upturned toes, but were nonetheless incredibly comfortable. By the time I finally got away Amina and Nuur-Guul were awake and giggling at the sight of me. I've always thought foreigners look daft in indigenous costumes, and had to console myself with the thought that no one else would see me anyway.

But it was quite amazing how many locals there were still pitched in their *gers* and scattered across this valley opposite the village. As I was foraging in the cold sunshine, one of my students, a teenager called Kaerat, waylaid me. I remember him as a long-limbed teenager with startling bright blue eyes, which looked divinely out of place on this brown-skinned Kazakh boy. Kaerat insisted on carrying my almost-empty sack, and escorted me to his *ger* for tea, where his gaunt, smiling mother insisted on cooking me lunch, 'Because you are his *bagsh*, *bagsh*.'

I spent a happy hour eating tasty beef noodles and talking with Kaerat, his mother Rina, her four daughters and an infant granddaughter. Their *ger* was very poor and cramped with sticks of rickety, ancient furniture. It was patched up where the canvas had torn or eroded. There were six women and girls living in it even when Kaerat was away. No husband or father materialised during my visit, and I didn't ask Rina where he was because I somehow suspected he'd been gone longer than that afternoon.

Eventually I said I must go, because it was late morning and I'd still barely collected any dung. Slinging the sack over my shoulder I waved, but didn't say *bayartai*, and set off to forage once more. Minutes later I met someone else I knew, a woman called Ilig, whose family photo I'd taken that summer just after her second child was born.

'*Sain bainuu*, *bagsh*. Drink tea with us,' she insisted, 'my *ger* is very near.'

This is the Mongol way: they are outrageously generous and welcoming people. Ilig laughed off my protestations that I was *tsaatsun* [full] and led me to her *ger*, which was perched in an idyll on a small plateau overlooking the river. Once inside someone's *ger*, it's rude not to taste something of the food you're offered, and Ilig and her husband, who was none other than Gold Teeth from my spring adventure with Princess and her grandfather, fed me with meat and bread and bowls of tea until I thought I would explode.

I finally waddled back to Apam in the early afternoon, sated with food and hospitality, the *deel* open and flapping in the suddenly warm and brilliant afternoon sunshine, with the still half-empty sack slung over my shoulder.

We left Apam late that afternoon and rode back across the river with Quartz. It was cold and windy as we left him on the bank of the Hovd and trekked over to the *hasha*. Amina suddenly stopped dead in her tracks, then streaked ahead of us, bellowing something over her shoulder as she fled.

'What is it?' I turned to Nuur-Guul, who made no attempt to follow her.

'I think maybe someone has arrived from Kazakhstan,' she replied shrugging.

As Nuur-Guul, Irlaan and I pushed the *hasha* gate open, Amina was at the door of her house, frantically beckoning us over. 'Come on in! We're waiting for you! My sister Elia and her family have returned from Kazakhstan!'

These days I wasn't quite sure who was and wasn't Amina's sister but I quickly followed her inside, eager to meet these new arrivals from that other land over the mountains.

CHAPTER TWENTY-NINE

It was getting very late, and we'd been talking for hours, Elia and I. Bent over our bowls of cooling tea, with apple cores, sweet wrappers, jars of pickles and clods of salty white *aaruul* strewn on the table around us. People constantly interrupted as we started, stopped and wilfully resumed our exchange of life stories. We were mutually intrigued. Elia wanted to know where my family lived in England, what the fashions were in London, and 'Why on earth did you come to live here, *bagsh*?' And I wanted to know all about Kazakhstan.

Although she'd been away for a long time, Elia's Mongolian was still much better than mine, and we talked with our heads quite close together so that we could hear and understand each other properly. Everyone in the *hasha* was crowded into the room: Abbai, Guul-Jan and their children; Addai, Szandrash and theirs. It was a din.

'Why did you leave here to live in Kazakhstan?' I unwrapped another gooey Russian caramel from the mound in front of us while Elia frowned deeply, as though trying to remember. She was a handsome but fraught-looking woman of about my age, with an equally handsome and boisterous young son, and a cheerful florid husband called Marat-Khan.

'I didn't go to Kazakhstan from here, *bagsh*,' she said. 'No. I went to live in Erdenet city first, when I was nineteen, to study electrical engineering. There are many Kazakhs in Erdenet, and I stayed there with some relatives. That's where I met him.' She nodded towards Marat-Khan, who turned round and beamed when he heard his name mentioned. 'I was nineteen when we got married – my husband's a pharmacist. The year we both graduated was the year Kazakhstan declared independence from Russia, right at the end of 1991. And as soon as our new President Nazarbaev took his place, all of Marat-Khan's family said, "*Zaa*, let's go to Kazakhstan." Because things were always a little bit difficult in Mongolia for Kazakhs, and we all knew life in Kazakhstan would be better than trying to find good jobs in Erdenet, or returning here to be *malchin*. So we all left together, thirty of us from babies to grandparents, to live in Akmola.

'Nazarbaev and the Kazakh Government, they wanted us Mongol Kazakhs to go back to the homeland, and they offered us places to live and work and pensions for the old people. You know when we went there, there were thousands of other Mongol Kazakhs arriving and finding places to live and work. We were all visiting Kazakhstan for the first time, all wanting to live in our own country, because now at last we had a country. No one wanted to stay in Mongolia. It was like coming home.'

'Do you ever miss Mongolia when you're in Kazakhstan?'

Elia shook her head with almost violent certainty. 'No! Look at this place. It's so difficult just to live. In Akmola we have electricity and hot water and black [paved] roads. No. I just miss my mother.' For the very first time her frown lifted and her face broke into a wide smile. 'A daughter will always miss her mother, and I have not seen Apam for seven years. I haven't been back here for seven years, *bagsh*.'

There is no physical border between Kazakhstan and Mongolia. To travel from one to the other you must first cross a slither of Russia. And, ironically, according to what the local Kazakhs told me, the first of their people to roam the Mongol steppe didn't even come from Russian Kazakhstan. Apparently they were Chinese Kazakhs from the north-western province of Xinjiang, who trekked over the Altai mountains sometime around 1860, and whose motive simply seems to have been searching out fresh pasture for their animals. These remote central Asian frontiers had long been crossed back and forth by nomads who cared nothing for national boundaries, and left only the indent of their *gers* as evidence of having ever pitched a camp. The Kazakh pioneers swiftly found what they were seeking: horizons of ungrazed steppe, and few people to disturb them. Abbai's local history tome, a solemn navy-blue book scribed by the Russian historian G.H. Potanin, claims that Kazakh patriarchs with splendid names like Kojamjar, Samur-Khan, Kulku-Shuu and Kobish-Butumsh erected their tall *gers* along the deserted banks of the Hovd river on the Xinjiang–Mongol border, and herded their livestock in isolation. They and their families came into contact with only a smattering of Halkh Mongol herders, and a small nomadic community who were then known as the Urianhai, but, after the 1921 Mongol Revolution, were renamed the Tuvans.

As news of this barely inhabited Mongol steppe filtered back to China, so more Xinjiang Kazakhs joined Kojamjar and the rest. Gradually Kazakhs from the Russian Altai also began to trek towards Mongolia – fleeing the October 1917 Revolution. By 1924, the year Mongolia became a sovereign state, there were more than 10,000 Kazakhs in Bayan-Olgii. And during the 1930s thousands more Xinjiang Kazakhs fled over the border to escape frequent riots in their volatile Chinese province.

For the Mongol government these new Kazakh settlers were ironically welcome, as they served a strategic purpose. They represented a buffer zone between Mongolia and China. The Mongol government was concerned about the possible break-up of western Mongolia, having already ceded territory to north-western Xinjiang. The Russian and Chinese Kazakhs were encouraged to remain on the western Mongol cusp, and in 1940 the Mongol government declared Bayan-Olgii a Kazakh autonomous area. The name Bayan-Olgii means 'Rich Cradle'.

Inevitably, as the Bayan-Oligii population expanded, some Kazakhs began an intrepid new urban life in Mongol cities and then in the capital itself. They arrived in Ulaanbaatar during the early 1950s, settling in city enclaves, and in the mining town of Nailakh, which lies 35 kilometres from the capital. Nailakh was a microcosm of Kazakhstan – the Kazakhs constructed their own wooden homes and a distinguished silver mosque. This was originally a thriving proud community with a burgeoning coal mine, but when that industry slowly collapsed, 20,000 Kazakhs were forced to survive and forage in a ghost town. The mosque was tattered and tourists accelerated past Nailakh towards the nearby Terelj nature reserve, repelled by the bald gaping hillside and the scars of the mine, gouged out of the dry, heavy earth, which was now useless and obscene. By the mid-1990s most of the coal seams had been exhausted or abandoned and few Kazakhs were needed to descend the shafts. Nailakh became a slum ruined by boredom, dereliction and despair.

The Kazakhs of Nailakh, Ulaanbaatar and Bayan-Olgii have always lived uneasily alongside their Mongol neighbours. Many of the Mongols, agitated and threatened by Kazakh patriotism and especially their religion, casually branded the Kazakhs as dirty, potentially dangerous Muslims. In response to this insidious contempt, the Kazakhs made little effort to integrate with the Mongols, choosing to remain separate linguistically, culturally and religiously. Despite spending more than a century in Mongolia, the vast majority of Kazakhs have remained in Bayan-Olgii, as far from Ulaanbaatar as possible. In Ulaanbaatar the Mongols usually refer to Bayan-Olgii with a grimace. 'It's a foreign country to us,' more than one of my Mongol friends told me before I'd even thought of moving to Tsengel. 'We don't trust those Kazakhs. *Zowan* [dirty]. If you ever go there, you'll be kidnapped and taken as a bride for a Kazakh herder, you know. It's a dangerous place.'

When the Kazakh government dramatically appealed to its Mongol brethren to return to their newly independent homeland at the end of 1991 and boost the Kazakh population, the response was momentous. The temptation of finally belonging to a land of their own had a magnetising effect on the 120,000 Mongol Kazakhs, and by 1994 almost half of them had flown, driven or trekked to Akmola and beyond, abandoning their fragile Mongol inheritance for a new life over the mountains. It's easy to understand why they left: they'd never had a homeland before, the newly

democratic Mongol economy was floundering in comparison to
Kazakhstan, and most of the Mongols had never wanted the
Kazakhs in their country in the first place. Elia, Marat-Khan and
their extended family had all reinvented their lives in that better
land, which every Kazakh I had met in Mongolia referred to as
his or her spiritual home.

Over the last nine months I'd slowly become used to hearing
the scathing comparisons between Tsengel and Kazakhstan,
between Mongolia and Kazakhstan. Even, and maybe especially,
those who'd never set foot outside Bayan-Olgii province, assured
me Kazakhstan was the land of plenty. Alma-Ata means 'City of
Apples', and long before I spent that evening talking with Elia I'd
often listened to other Tsengel Kazakhs lovingly describe the wealth
of fruit and vegetables, motor cars, apartments with colour TVs,
stocks of lavish food and laden market stalls of Kazakhstan.
Zulmira, Princess, Abbai, the teachers at school, the shopkeepers
and the Imam himself had all told me the same sublime tale.

But in spite of this abundance, these apparent opportunities
and this potential new life in their own nation, the brutal irony
is that so many of the Mongol Kazakhs who left Mongolia in the
early 1990s have already returned. Bruised but unashamed they've
trekked back over the Altai mountains to their barren refuge on
the edge of Mongolia. After their long expensive pilgrimages to
Kazakhstan, after uprooting their families and abandoning their
homes, they discovered that even in their own land they're still
considered a minority, and not a particularly liked or welcome
minority at that. Of the approximately 17 million people living
in Kazakhstan, just under half are ethnic Kazakhs, with the rest
of the population made up of mainly Russians and Ukrainians,
plus Germans, Uzbeks and Tatars.

In Kazakhstan the Mongol Kazakhs are still widely regarded as
immigrants. Initially encouraged by the Kazakh government to
settle and work in the underpopulated, windswept northern
Kazakh oblasts, where mainly Russians lived, they were immediately regarded with suspicion and treated not as Kazakhs but
Mongols who spoke Kazakh. Foreigners laying claim to a land

which was not theirs by right. The Russians, Ukrainians, Uzbeks and Tatars already owned part of the history of Kazakhstan, and had nothing to gain from living amongst newly settled Mongol Kazakhs. When the Kazakh economy began to flounder in 1996, many of the Mongol Kazakhs, who like immigrants everywhere were employed in low-paid manual work, quickly lost their jobs. And as Nazarbaev's government struggled with a crippling and unpopular reform programme, state pensions also dried up. But most intransigent and ironic of all, the Kazakhs' nomadic herding life, which has thrived in the harsh Mongol Altai since the middle of the last century, has been almost curtailed in Kazakhstan itself.

Long before Kazakh independence the Russians were already intent on urbanising this land and exploiting its vast mineral resources. The compulsive building and then expanding of factories and surrounding new towns and cities has reached endemic proportions since 1991 as Kazakhstan has sought out industrial wealth. The nomads, who've stoically continued with traditional herding lives in the face of this concreting over of their land, have found themselves increasingly living on the edge of a nation that does not value them any longer.

'No, there aren't many herders left in Kazakhstan,' Elia told me that evening. She sounded pragmatic, there was no trace of regret in her voice. 'Most of us live in the cities. Most of the Kazakh nomads live here you know, in Bayan-Olgii [the Rich Cradle].'

I mulled over Elia's story and the fractured history of the Mongol Kazakhs for days, while Elia and her family were hosted by the Tsengel Kazakhs, visiting *hashas* across the cold village.

As I staggered from the Hovd with my buckets of water one afternoon that week – the communal well at our end of the village was being dredged so we had no choice but to ferry water from the freezing river – it began to snow gently as I headed back, so I stopped for tea with our neighbours Merim-Khan and Aimak on the way.

I knew them well by now and we frequently drank tea together. They were one of the poorest families in the village, and sometimes we drank black tea because they owned only a handful of goats and were often short of milk. They'd also stayed in Tsengel throughout the summer because they didn't own herds to graze or have a *ger* to move into, and when they invited me to stay around for dinner that evening, we ate boiled mutton on its own, without bread or flour noodles, because the sack of flour was finished and they had no cash to buy another one.

'*Möng backo,*' said Merim-Khan, shrugging his shoulders, weary but unembarrassed, 'We have no money.' He and Aimak had no income at all, and I imagined they were forced to rely on the generosity of his brother, the Imam.

As we sat crouched around the table over the meat, I casually asked Merim-Khan if he'd ever thought of moving to Kazakhstan. What I meant, though I didn't actually say it, was wouldn't life be easier for them there?

Merim-Khan wiped his long fingers on a clean shred of rag, and shook his head. 'No, *bagsh*. We can't. We have no family over there. I would never find work.' He glanced around his small dark home, and I was sure his expression resembled mine when I'd glanced around my despised first home in the clinic all those months ago.

'Look at this place,' he said quietly. 'We've got nothing here. I've got no work, we've got no electricity and we can't buy medicine if we need it, or even flour. But,' he sighed, 'it's not always easy in Kazakhstan. You have to know people and to have good connections to make a life over there.'

The Tsengel Kazakhs never told me they were disliked or even ostracised in Kazakhstan. They never confided that Russian Kazakhs treated them like immigrants or settlers. They only told me how good life was Over There. It was the Tuvans and, after I'd left the village, Mongol and expatriate aid workers in Ulaanbaatar who told me of the contempt the Mongol Kazakhs confronted when they returned to their homeland.

The Russian Kazakhs don't like the Mongol Kazakhs, the Mongols told me, almost gleefully. 'They don't want them there, so they don't treat them well.'

'They don't think the Mongol Kazakhs are real Kazakhs,' the

Tsengel Tuvans murmured. 'They don't welcome them, so it's hard for them to find work and settle down, because even though it's Kazakhstan, it's still not really their country. You can see how many of them have come back here.'

But I never directly asked any of the local Kazakhs why so many of them had returned to Tsengel from Kazakhstan. At the time I just accepted that many of them had come back because they still had extended family in the village, and their recent history was here and not there.

It felt as though the subject wasn't up for discussion and that if I persisted in asking these unwelcome questions I'd be applying pressure to a trapped nerve. The longer you live with a community of people, the more you take certain aspects of who they are for granted. You also inevitably learn of the local taboos, and this was definitely one of them. But the evidence was all around me: literally hundreds of Kazakhs who'd moved to Kazakhstan, then returned to resume their lives in diaspora.

This experience contrasted sharply with the situation and attitude of the Tuvans. Tuya, Gansukh and Sansar-Huu had all lived in Khyzl, but apart from a handful of other Tuvans who'd studied at Khyzl university, most of the Tuvans in the village I spoke to hadn't even bothered crossing the border from Mongolia to Tuva. I remember Deri-Huu and Bash showed remarkably little interest in visiting Tuva when I asked them about it, and Gansukh, who was officially the sole Tuvan language teacher in the whole of Mongolia, was now very anxious to specialise in English.

'My students don't want to go to Khyzl any more,' she'd lamented several times, 'they all want to study in Hovd or in Ulaanbaatar now.'

The young Tuvans especially didn't harbour the same cravings to visit their homeland as the Kazakhs, because despite speaking their own distinct tongue, they already felt very much at home in Mongolia. They moved effortlessly between the two languages, gave their children Mongol names and simply seemed to enjoy the best of both worlds. I never heard a Mongol utter a bad word about a Tuvan.

If I hadn't spent months living alongside Abbai, Guul-Jan, their family, friends and neighbours, learned to speak hesitant Kazakh and taken part in the everyday life of their *hasha*, I don't think I could have fathomed why most Tsengel Kazakhs seemed reconciled to the idea of living out their lives in a remote enclave surrounded by tangible hostility from both Tuvans and Mongols. Unlike the Tuvans, whose culture is barely distinguishable from Mongol culture, the Kazakhs thrived within a cultural cocoon: they basically had nothing to do with the rest of Mongolia. Many of them, especially those herding in the mountains, spoke little or no Mongolian, and as a people mainly confined to Bayan-Olgii they didn't even have to acknowledge their Mongol citizenship. They could hear Kazakh radio news transmitted from Bayan-Olgii every evening, the wealthier Kazakhs could occasionally visit Alma-Ata or Akmola, and they could all continue to recall this better land over the mountains, which from a safe distance was something akin to my mirage in the Gobi desert en route to Ulaanbaatar – a self-deceiving illusion.

But having spent these months with them, I finally concluded that the Tsengel Kazakhs were relentlessly patriotic and traditional not only because conservatism is sustained by isolation, but also because they were acutely aware that their village and nomadic traditions now barely exist in situ outside Bayan-Olgii province. Beyond culture, language and religion, the inextricable difference between the Tsengel Tuvans and the Kazakhs is that nomads still thrive in Tuva, and the Tuvans are welcome to join them if and whenever they choose. For the Kazakhs I lived among, Tsengel village on the windswept edge of western Mongolia is the only real home they have left.

But each summer another trickle of Kazakh families sell up, pack up and depart in pursuit of a new life in Kazakhstan. They clasp the grace of optimism.

CHAPTER THIRTY

Elia and her family had driven from Kazakhstan to Tsengel in the final throes of autumn, so they could arrive safely before the winter set in. They seemed to have made it just about in time, because now the intense cold was really starting. Some mornings the very first sensation I was aware of when I opened my eyes was my almost-numb face. In an attempt to insulate my rickety room properly, and to keep the freezing draughts at bay, Abbai had nailed a thick blanket of felt over the outside of my door. Meanwhile Guul-Jan and I had sealed the crumbling window frames with glue made from a paste of flour and water, over which we'd plastered shreds of newspaper. But my room was basically an outhouse, with thin walls and a loose-fitting door. It hadn't been built to be lived in, and especially not to shelter anyone from the onslaught of an approaching Mongol winter. I'd already started sleeping with my hat on, and when I woke the temperature was unbearable until I got the stove going.

There were occasional mornings in that room when absolutely everything that could go wrong, did. These I called Mornings From Hell. On a Morning From Hell I'd have no clean clothes – they'd be either crumpled in a grimy sack or frozen solid on the washing line outside – I'd hurriedly dress myself in several stained layers and try to light my stove as fast as humanly possible. But the kindling would be damp and I'd drip candle wax on to the smouldering sticks and then blow on them until my throat rasped and my head was light. All that effort would earn me a pathetic stuttering flame that was barely worth it, because I felt even colder just looking at it. My water bucket would be sealed with a thin layer of ice that then had to be broken by hand or shattered with a knife just so I could fill the kettle. But because the kindling only smoked instead of igniting, the kettle wouldn't boil anyway, and then my room would reek of smoke, as well as being coated in a layer of the gritty dust that filtered in under the door and through minute chinks in the window panes. I had unearthed a broken half of a small mirror when I'd moved in, and I'd take a glance at my smeared reflection, groan out loud at my greasy lank hair, cracked lips and dry flaking skin, and resolve to throw the bloody thing away.

And it would get worse. As soon as I stepped outside and strode towards the trench toilet, the wind would rise, whirring and hurtling dust in my face. The toilet would, of course, be occupied, and when I finally squatted down I would either find that my period had just started, or I'd miss the gap between the slats, wee on myself and stomp off to school with ankles frozen in piss.

It was on one of these hellish mornings, when I privately cursed life in 'this stupid barren village' that I slammed my flimsy door shut and heard a pane of glass pitch to the ground and shatter. On a better day I would have laughed. But instead, I clenched my fists like an enraged child and swore as I marched out of the *hasha*, refusing to even see the broken window behind me.

Those vengeful, springtime dust storms briefly resumed, and the winter snow was flung back into the sky. I usually rose at around half past seven, and lit a candle until dawn blanched the sky, but one morning I was violently startled while still in bed, by a roaring that sounded like the mountains themselves were toppling into the village. It was still dim inside so I knew it was early, but I desperately needed to go to the toilet. When I unlatched my door, I couldn't see even to the *hasha* fence – everything was smothered in a thick, seething blanket of dust. I tried to wade across to the gate, but when I peered upwards all I could see was what looked like a beige hurricane blasting towards me. Squealing, 'Shit!' I bolted indoors and crawled back into bed as the windows rattled and I breathed in and tasted the dust infiltrating my mouth, nostrils and every crevice of my room. It was the most ferocious dust storm I'd ever witnessed in Tsengel, but it was also the grand finale and for the rest of the winter we were spared.

A week later, at the end of October, the snow fell again, thick and slow. Overnight Tsengel transformed into a rustic, turn-of-the-century film set. Chimney smoke plumed upwards into the descending flakes, as *hasha* fences, cattle and people were draped in white. The Hovd glistened under a thin veil of ice. Bullocks and snow-crusted young yaks tiptoed through the riverbank drifts. At school the stoves had just been lit and the classrooms were cramped but cosy, the teachers swathed in fur. On days like this, enchanting, clear and brilliantly cold, when my cheeks glowed, my stove roared and I laughed out loud with my friends as we drank bowls of steaming tea in each other's homes, I could not have cared less about Mornings From Hell. On days like this there was nowhere on earth I wanted to be more than where I already was. In between lessons I loitered in the snug school kitchen where the Gang of Three fed any teacher who wandered by, or I strolled round the village square with Tuya and Gansukh, who cheerfully assured me it was soon going to get much colder than this.

But the weather had been strange and unreliable all year, and even now, when the nomads were expecting and prepared for winter, the temperature suddenly rose a little. The Hovd river thawed, froze and then thawed again, as though pondering her next move. These brief flushes, which melted the ice on our windows and left clothes limp and dripping on the outside rack, were rare and extremely unwelcome. The nomads depended utterly on the continuity of the seasons, and winter was now overdue. They didn't want an unexpected wave of mild weather. It was time for snow and ice.

'Ach this is no good, *bagsh*,' complained Merim-Khan, squinting in the sunlight as he paused from splitting logs in his *hasha*.

We were standing at the side of his house: Merim-Khan with his axe clasped in his hands, me with my usual two pails of water at my feet.

'In spring we need this sun to melt the snow, you know. That's
why the animals starved this year, because spring was too cold and
the ground stayed frozen – they couldn't feed. But look, we need
snow to cover this steppe and stop the *mal* from grazing, or next
spring will be like this year, another big disaster. If the *mal* keep
grazing now, there won't be pasture left to grow in spring. They
will have eaten everything and the steppe will be ruined until
summer, which is too late.' The situation was becoming serious,
and, like all the other local men, Merim-Khan was impatient for
the river to freeze over. 'As soon as the Hovd is frozen, all of us
are leaving for the mountains, to collect the *mal*. We always
slaughter the animals at the beginning of winter, while they're still
fat from grazing all summer but it's cold enough for the meat to
freeze. Then we'll all have plenty of meat till the end of next spring,
when the *mal* can feed again.'

The carcasses are hacked and then stored and frozen in minute
rooms like old-fashioned larders that are built on to the back or
side of every village cabin: a home-made refrigerator, which is also
used to store the summer dairy surplus. But the exceptionally mild
weather was delaying the slaughter. Merim-Khan shook his head
with the lethargy of a man who has been anxious and unwell for
a long time, and beckoned me inside for tea.

'*Tsai oh, bagsh*. You went to the countryside recently, eh? You
know the herders have all moved from their *ger* camps up to their
winter cabins. They thought they would have snow to melt for
water up there in the mountains. But there is very little snow, and
they are struggling. Did you see those trucks down at the river
the other day?'

I nodded, bowl in hand. I'd watched groups of the men on a
shallow frozen river tributary, shattering the ice with their axes
and hauling jagged milky slabs on to the back of a truck.

'They have taken the ice up to the cabins because this is the
only way they can have water. Some are taking their camels down
to the river to carry the ice back home. Ah, *yanaa*. We need the
snow now.'

CHAPTER THIRTY-ONE

In the mail that week I received an unexpected letter from a friend of mine called Jo. We'd known each other for years, but had rarely written to each other since I'd been in Mongolia. I guess we assumed that when I came home we'd just pick up where we'd left off. I had sent her one or maybe two letters from Tsengel telling her about village life, and she'd occasionally written back with news and gossip from our mutual friends.

But now Jo had important news to tell me: she was in love. She scribbled half a dozen pages about this man she'd met and how they were both struggling to find enough time to spend together. She said he was the most wonderful, sexy, caring beautiful thing that had ever happened to her; that she really wanted me to meet him when I got back, so I could tell them both about my adventures. Her happiness sang from the pages. She concluded by saying that she admired my managing out here in the village all on my own. She didn't know how I did it; she already felt a little lost when her new lover wasn't beside her.

I read her letter in the afternoon, spent the early evening with Tuya, and after she'd gone home to her parents I went to see Abbai and family. Their house was as crowded and noisy as always, and I felt more than usually reluctant to leave them that night when it got late, but eventually came back to my own silent room, stoked up the fire and clambered into bed. I left the candle burning down and thought about Jo, and then I thought about my other friends and the men and women they loved, the families they were starting to have, and of course it brought home my own situation far more than I'd have liked.

I had never really minded about the fact that I was the only person in Tsengel who slept on her own. Here I was, surrounded by homes full of families: adults and children sharing beds, curling up together, smelling each other's skin. Even the bigger cabins in the village, like Abbai and Guul-Jan's, only ever had one real bedroom, which everyone shared, including guests. I really appreciated the luxury of my single room, and much of the time I did love having it to myself after my visitors had gone for the evening. It is difficult living in a foreign community, even when you know their language and customs, and I've always needed time alone to think my own thoughts, write or read or just pass several hours quietly. But that night I really felt the gulf.

It had been a long time since I'd shared my bed with a man and felt the closeness of falling asleep and then waking up with him beside me. It wasn't only the pleasure of sex that I missed, so much as the thought of someone holding me, stroking me and keeping each other warm by the heat from our naked bodies. I found myself stroking my own arms that night, touching myself because there was no one else there to do that for me.

I had come to the village assuming I would have to be celibate while I was here. I didn't want to be entangled in a messy affair where I didn't understand the rules, or be expected to marry and settle here, which I knew I could never do. I wasn't interested in a life of drudgery, and that was the life almost all the women led. As the months passed, I'd come to associate having any sort of sexual relationship while I was here with being even more immersed in the village than I already was. I knew I was eventually going to leave, and so being celibate let me keep the distance I thought I needed. And I didn't, frankly, want to be hassled by local men thinking they could all get me into bed just because one of them had. So I didn't behave like a woman who was available. I sometimes had a laugh with the men, but I'd rarely flirted with any of them, and in return very few of them had ever flirted with me. Maybe they could see there was no point. Maybe they didn't find me attractive. I don't know because I never asked.

I'd had this notion that being celibate would give me some sort of clarity, that I wouldn't be distracted by romance, or bind myself to someone and miss out on seeing as much of life in Tsengel as I could. I also thought I'd look back on my past relationships, see them for what they really were, and maybe never make the same awful mistakes again.

But that didn't happen. Instead of embarking on clever and fruitful self-analysis, I'd gradually become aware that part of me was very lonely, and that living alone like this was not in the end what I wanted at all. I didn't want casual sex, because I thought that would make me feel even more alone. That was why I'd rejected the American doctor's unspoken offer of an hour or two together. I didn't want to be picked up. What I really wanted was to make love and to be loved. It was that simple really.

CHAPTER THIRTY-TWO

Autumn died the following week and winter arrived, as it does in Mongolia, with the force of an unforeseen blow. The temperature plummeted and fetching water from the freezing Hovd became a freezing ordeal – slushy river floe numbed our hands, the pails clinked with ice. Now clothes froze solid as soon as they were hung, steaming, on the outside rack. Life suddenly got much harder. Guul-Jan looked exhausted. Elia, Marat-Khan and Toktal-bek were staying in her home, which now had ten occupants plus visitors day and night. While Abbai held leisurely meetings at home with posses of the village men, Guul-Jan split logs with a huge blunt axe, hauled 25 litres of water at a time, cleaned the house, cooked huge communal meals, brewed and served tea constantly, and worked at the clinic throughout the night delivering babies although she hadn't been paid for the last four months. She even passed Abbai his radio as he sat at the table drinking his tea. He just pointed in the right direction.

This was my only prejudice against the Kazakhs. I loved the sound of their language, a rich guttural tongue that could come from nowhere else but the mountains, while the tragic plaintive melody of the *dombra* could make a bareknuckle fighter cry. Their Islam was pragmatic, even casual, and they were generous people with a great sense of humour: we laughed a lot in Abbai's house. But the women did everything. And it still galled me.

So while Guul-Jan was stooped over the stove in the evening, Abbai sat at the table patiently twiddling the knobs of his radio as it spat out words and static. Occasionally he'd snare an English channel and brandish the set triumphantly as I struggled to hear what was being said and translate it into Mongolian for him. Once or twice we even tuned into the BBC World Service, and everyone listened, fascinated by the clipped English vowels.

Though I did sometimes still boil up thick meals of rice and meat in my own room, I was invited to eat with Guul-Jan or Szandrash and their families every evening by now. I always offered to help them prepare the meal, but either Abbai or his brother would tut, shake his head and tell me to sit down and relax.

Guul-Jan's temper did occasionally fray, however. I was entering the house one morning when I heard her bellowing at Abbai, who was obviously trying to shout back but couldn't get a word in. He suddenly ducked his head as though something was being thrown towards it, and fled past me out of the house, clutching his hat.

Addai and Szandrash's home had two rooms: a front room with the stove, a large circular table and the famous chipped red phone, and a dark but cosy back bedroom where I usually gave the children their daily English lesson by candlelight. On 11 November we were just packing up for the evening when the light bulb dangling from a wire above us that I'd long stopped noticing, suddenly lit up. Everyone clapped and cheered and we blew the candles out. Seconds later the bulb flickered and the light died. As though on cue we all groaned dramatically together and relit the tallows. But about half an hour later the electricity was back and narrow panes of glass were ablaze across the village.

We moved en masse over to the other house, where Abbai unveiled and solemnly switched on the *hasha* television for the first time since spring.

'We had electricity all last winter until the week you came, *bagsh*, and then when you arrived the lights went out. Now you are going to leave and the lights have come back on again!' Abbai grinned at me and we all laughed together. Finally we knew each other well enough to banter.

The electricity was a revelation. It made life so much easier. Small things that got dropped and then lost in the shadows just beyond the strain of candlelight could suddenly be seen easily, picked up and used again straight away. Carelessly placed buckets of slops weren't accidentally kicked over, things lying round the *hasha*, like axes and sawn-off logs, weren't tripped over en route to the loo, and I could read without peering at the words, or sitting so close to the candle that wax dripped on to the page. There were no light switches anywhere in the village, because obviously no one ever wanted to turn off their light. The TV and lights would just blip and cut out at the end of the evening and that would be it until the next day.

The electricity ran from about 6 p.m. to 10 p.m., and it was surprisingly reliable. There were frequent black-outs, but they were usually very brief and power resumed almost every evening. The people who had TV sets enthused about this new lease of life, which helped pass the yawning long winter evenings for them. In Abbai's house we watched grainy Russian TV, ancient Charlie Chaplin films, and once, a juddering, dubbed episode of *The X Files*, which I stared at open-mouthed for about fifteen minutes before there was another power cut and we lost it for good. That was very strange. Meanwhile Gansukh and Sansar-Huu had a television that could only receive one Mongol TV channel, and another Tuvan family, much to their chagrin, could only get Kazakh TV. It was the mocking irony of watching the box in the western Altai.

As Tsengel indulged in this daily dose of electricity, so the mountains finally embraced winter. The sun was languid, climbing into a bloodless sky after eight in the morning. The land was bleached and frozen. Everyone stayed indoors as much as they could.

Halfway through November the mountains were obscured by bulbous clouds, which emptied themselves of flakes as though shedding their skin. Our small world was smothered. This was the juncture of the year. Each of the seasons, from the arid spring, through the lush summer and the flaming autumn, had in turn surrendered to the next. Now the nomads welcomed the boreal dark winter.

The Hovd also surrendered and froze overnight, white and

jagged, stacked like a landslide. I stood at the river's edge with buckets in my hands, gazing at the floe. It was incredibly beautiful. The river had erupted, ice rearing in crests a metre and a half above the bank. I set down my buckets and walked downstream, along the edge of the village. There was hardly anyone around. It was Saturday or Sunday, the shops and kiosks were closed, and the streets deserted. I paused just beyond the final *hasha* at the other end of the village, and looked out across the white valley. Here the Hovd was at its most turbulent and the ice at its most spectacular. Bergs tilted recklessly, like buildings after an explosion; waves had been frozen as they sprayed downstream. How, I thought, could all this have evolved in just one cold night? But it had, and now two locals clad in long dark *deels* faltered across it towards me, inserting a long thin branch into the ice before them as they clambered over the glinting debris.

It wasn't only the river that froze. Toothpaste, shampoo, the dregs of hot drinks: everything congealed in my ever-colder room. My face cream was so frozen it was like smearing ice-cream across my cheeks. My water bucket was a solid block in the mornings. Abbai and Guul-Jan asked me to move into their house several times, but it didn't seem fair because they already had so many people living with them.

Guul-Jan was brought home from work in the medical jeep one morning and laid out on the small bed in the living room. We all sat and watched as one of her colleagues inserted a limpid drip, which slowly drained vitamins into a vein in her arm as she lay there, pallid and silent. I'd never seen Guul-Jan lying or sitting still before.

'My wife is very tired,' said Abbai, motioning for Amina to pour me a bowl of tea.

While Guul-Jan was resting, Amina immediately assumed responsibility for running the whole house, and literally raced home from school to chop wood and haul water, cook dinner for everyone and scrub their clothes. Now that the river had frozen, Apam was also due anytime. She would be staying in the *hasha* until spring, sharing the spare room with Elia and her family, who had just calmly announced they were also staying until the spring, four or five months later.

Tuya came over for dinner, shivering as she scuttled inside my room. '*Yanaa* it's cold!' she exclaimed, leaving her thick jacket and hat on as she crouched by the stove. She looked healthy and rotund: maybe that was what being in love did for you. As I set down our plates of tomato paste-flavoured mutton and rice she caught my eye and arched her brows.

'We're getting married in the next couple of weeks,' she beamed. 'Gerele will choose the date and it'll be a very small wedding because of his father . . . no *khurim*. But I don't care, I just want to be his wife.'

I pulled her to her feet and hugged her fiercely. I knew Gerele was a rogue, but I also knew that this marriage was what Tuya wanted more than anything in the world.

'I haven't got any *arikh* for a toast,' I moaned. 'Maybe Gansukh and Sansar-Huu have got a bottle. We could go and see them.'

Tuya, who didn't drink much *arikh* apart from our occasional binges, pulled a face. 'No. We don't need *arikh*, we can celebrate at the klub on Saturday instead. Kultii just told me a pop group from Olgii is coming to play. Let's go and dance!'

So Tuya, Gansukh and I got the lipstick out of retirement and happily returned to the klub for the first time in months. I knew this would probably be the last time we went out for the night together, because Tuya had already told me that once she was married she wouldn't be attending the klub for quite a while. Newly married women stayed at home, they didn't go out partying with their friends, and by the time she did go out again, of course, I'd be gone. It was an unsettling reminder that our lives were soon going to be taking very different paths.

Throughout the year, Bayan-Olgii pop and folk bands had occasionally turned up to perform at the klub, and I must admit that even as starved of entertainment as I was I still thought most of them were bloody awful. I never tired of listening to the *dombra* at home in the *hasha*, but found the klub concerts stilted and boring recitals, lacking the soul of music played at home for its own pleasure.

But that night was the extravagant exception of the year. A posse of handsome Bayan-Olgii boys with their own drum kit and keyboard blasted out raucous Kazakh covers all evening and, for once, the motor didn't let us down. The packed Tsengel klub rocked! Whirling, stamping and cheering, people paused only to strip off another layer of clothes and then got straight back on the dance floor. It was terrific and we three were giddy and excited all night. We hadn't danced together for ages and we made up for all that lost time with a delighted vengeance.

After several encores Kultii turned the tape deck on and the party continued. I spun round the dance floor with a young Kazakh named Alibi, who'd just returned to Tsengel from university in Alma-Ata. He was handsome, but there was vodka on his breath and his eyes shone as though he was slightly delirious.

'Louisa, stay away from him. I went to school with him and he's no good,' Gansukh warned me, her mouth pressed against my ear. Alibi repeatedly asked me to dance, and I reluctantly partnered him. As we waltzed unsteadily he squeezed my hand and hissed, 'Take me home with you, *bagsh*.' Somehow I wasn't surprised. I shook my head, assured him I was betrothed to a possessive Englishman and declined his next invitation on to the floor. He left, alone, before the end of the music, lurching down the uneven klub steps on his way out.

At the end of the night we avoided the traditional post disco punch-up, and walked home together under the cosmos of a billion freezing stars. Tuya and I parted just over the bridge, metres from our respective *hashas*. As I fumbled at the latched gate, a whisper echoed over my shoulder, 'It's me, *bagsh*. The one from Kazakhstan.'

He emerged from the thick shadows and tried to take my gloved hand. I kicked the gate open and swore at him in Kazakh as I strode to my door, swift but calm, knowing he was startled and I'd warned him sufficiently that it wasn't worth following me. I heard him crunching back towards the bridge as I lit my candle.

*　　*　　*

Guul-Jan called in the next afternoon while I was sitting along-side my stove writing my journal. She sometimes popped in for a hasty bowl of coffee, which she loved, and to relay the latest gossip.

As she worked at the clinic Guul-Jan always kept me up to date on the accidents and gruesome injuries people sustained in Tsengel. I knew about the young boy who'd chopped off half his little finger as he was splitting logs with his father's axe, the two locals who'd crashed their jeep in the gorge and had to be dug out by herders and then galloped back to the village on horseback, and the tragedy of a young man in the village who had been struck over the head with a jeep starting-handle (the long L-shaped iron pole used to jump start all the jeeps). The victim was twenty-six and married with two young children. He'd been attacked by one of his own friends, after they'd both been drinking and an argument had raged out of control. The victim, whose name I didn't ask and never knew, had passed out, but soon regained consciousness and appeared to be none the worse for his blow. His assailant had swiftly sobered up and apologised profusely. He'd also paid for treatment at the village clinic.

'We thought he was fine,' said Guul-Jan, sipping at her coffee. 'But a couple of weeks ago he passed out and we had to send him to Olgii, to the big hospital. They couldn't do anything.' She tapped her scarved head. 'It was here – the problem was inside his head. And now he has died. Alibi has to pay the family a lot of money – or he'll go to prison.'

'Alibi?' I repeated. I hadn't told anyone in the *hasha* what had happened after the disco, because I absolutely knew that Abbai, who lived in quiet fear for my physical and moral welfare, would either argue I shouldn't ever go out alone in the evening again, or even worse, would insist on escorting me. 'You mean Alibi who just came back from Kazakhstan?'

Guul-Jan nodded and drained her bowl.

'Do the police know?'

To my amazement she shrugged and said, 'I don't know. Maybe not.'

I asked Abbai about it that evening, hoping I wasn't overstepping the mark but too fascinated not to find out more.

He drank his tea slowly and paused for thought before carefully answering me. '*Zaa*, of course our police know all about it, Louisa. But you see, the important thing is that now this man is dead his wife needs to have money to keep her children. It is terrible what happened, we all know that, but the police did not ask any questions yet because they are giving the family time to talk with this man and see if he can give them enough money. No papers have been signed. Our police don't usually work like this, but this time they are letting the family make their own decision. If Alibi can pay enough money no one will talk to the police, and then yes, he will be able to stay here in the village.'

And so it was. I saw Alibi several times after that, though we never acknowledged each other, and each time he was walking through the village, hunched and alone. The pragmatism of the villagers astounded me. No one mentioned Alibi again. It was all very quiet and very bizarre.

On the last day of November it happened at last. Tuya and Gerele married. Neither Gansukh nor I attended the discreet wedding. Tradition dictated only relatives could be at Gerele's home that day, and of course no *khurim* was celebrated. Tuya simply packed her bags and left the house she had grown up in and would now never live in again. Escorted by Gerele, her mother and father, she crossed the threshold of Gerele's *hasha*, and he became her husband.

Two days later, to my confounded delight, she gave birth to her first child.

CHAPTER THIRTY-THREE

'We can't go into the clinic, Louisa. Algaa will not agree,' whispered Gerel-Huu, as we both stood hovering in the narrow clinic doorway. 'We have got to ask permission from Algaa before we go in to see Tuya. You never go in to see a mother just after the baby is born, and you know he's the clinic boss.'

But for once I didn't care. Algaa could go hang. I stepped inside and tugged at Gerel-Huu's arm. When she hesitated I abandoned her at the door and brazenly pushed my way through other smeared glass doors, peering into several of those filthy, empty wards before I found Tuya and her baby alone in a tiny but brightly sunlit room.

Even she was alarmed at my unplanned visit. 'Louisa! What are you doing here? Did you ask Algaa?'

I shook my head, grinning like a delinquent. Tuya was the most brazen person I knew in Tsengel and I was surprised by her panic. Her new daughter lay in her arms, a small, swaddled bundle with a cradle of dark curls. We shared a furtive hushed conversation as she strained to hear Algaa coming to throw me out.

'How was the birth?' I asked, giving her a bag of the nicest sweets I could find in the village, which looked misshapen and pretty horrible.

'Not so bad.' Tuya shrugged almost casually. 'It was all over in a few hours.' We looked at each other.

'Tuya, why didn't you tell me you were pregnant?' I burst out, trying not to sound as hurt as I already felt. She and Gansukh were my closest friends here. As Gerel-Huu and I had raced down to the clinic together to find out if the scandal about Tuya was actually true, I'd recalled the last few months with astonishment: Tuya hacking recklessly at huge ragged stumps of wood, walking miles through the countryside back to the village after we'd visited her relatives, dancing like a fiend at the disco, and the endless manual tasks she'd taken on in seeming defiance of her body and the healthy child she'd been carrying. It seemed no one had noticed her changing shape. I certainly hadn't. But anyway, why hadn't she told me?

She stared straight at me. 'I thought you would be angry, Louisa,' she said. 'I couldn't tell you. You kept saying there was plenty of time to have a child. You said I should not have a baby right now, that I should wait for a year or two. I just couldn't tell you.'

I hung my head and almost burst into tears on the spot. Damn it – how arrogant and stupid of me. How could I just have marched in and told someone how to live their life like I knew best? And here I was, bursting into the clinic as if I owned the bloody place.

I was guilty as charged. I could remember telling, in fact, insisting to Tuya that I knew what was best for her. I've never been more ashamed in my life than at that moment when she calmly pointed out the height of my arrogance. Is this really how I've behaved here? I thought miserably. Have I done this to other people as well? Maybe that's why Menke didn't want me back at school, why Zulmira didn't want anything to do with me, and why Princess stopped visiting. Had I been acting just like one of those imperious foreigners I always said I hated so much?

'I'm sorry, Tuya,' I said. 'I am so sorry. I should go. Gerel-Huu is waiting outside. She said I shouldn't come in but I did because I wanted to see you and the baby. I'm sorry.'

Tuya smiled. With the grace of so many of the Mongols I've known, who speak their anger and then peacefully lay it to one side, she held her daughter out to me, and I rocked her gently, amazed at the tiny new life breathing in my arms.

Gerel-Huu had given up on me, and I walked slowly home from the clinic on the quietest track at the edge of the village. I

had so little time left here now. I didn't want the villagers to
remember me as someone who never listened, but just forced her
own opinions on everyone. I honestly couldn't recall any other
time I'd given unasked-for advice to anyone here, but that didn't
mean it hadn't happened. I felt really ashamed and embarrassed
by what I'd done, but I was glad Tuya had told me. In fact I
wished she'd told me months ago, because she might have spared
me from myself. There's no such thing as a new beginning, I
thought. You take all your own defects with you wherever you go,
and this is obviously one of mine. You do have to live with who
you are. But I won't ever do that again.

Tsengel basked in the scandal of Tuya for days. She had escaped
the supreme stigma of bearing her child out of wedlock, but Abbai's
manifest disgust seemed to reflect the general village consensus.

'Is that right? Is it correct – two days after the wedding?' he
snapped at me when I told him of Tuya's daughter. I flinched.

'You just don't understand, Louisa. They really hate it here when
a woman has her child just after the wedding,' Gansukh told me
when I moaned about the incessant gossip. 'People do understand
that she would have been married in summer if Gerele's father
had not died, but they are still very angry.'

I couldn't bear to ask Gansukh whether she had known about
Tuya's pregnancy all along. The news of the birth had blazed across
the village in hours, and though I knew Tuya would combat the
sniggering and pious criticism aimed at her, I just wished she didn't
have to face it all in the first place.

So, thank God (or perhaps I should say Allah) for Apam,
Szandrash, Guul-Jan and Elia. Apam had arrived a couple of days
earlier with Quartz and his youngest son, Nuurlan, and that
evening I joined the women in Szandrash's house. The men were
watching TV as usual. After telling the kids to scarper, all four of
them bombarded me with questions about Tuya and her new baby.
What happened? Had I seen her? How was her daughter? Two
days after the wedding – what good luck! They howled with
laughter at the sublime timing of the marriage, until Szandrash

and Guul-Jan were wiping their eyes, and Apam was rubbing her stubby hands with glee.

'We've got to see that *okhin* [daughter] soon,' exclaimed Guul-Jan, 'because if she looks anything like Gerele then she's beautiful!'

They all roared. I'd never seen them so raucous, and found myself joining in, more through relief than anything else. I wanted to hug them all, because they hadn't a bad word or a gloat about Tuya's fall from grace between them. They were just genuinely thrilled about the arrival of a new child and cared only that Tuya and her daughter were both healthy. I learned something about the public façade of the village that night. I knew our conversation would never have gone on in front of any of the men. This display of moral outrage was a male preserve, and the women kept their integrity and pragmatism to themselves.

Ironically, while Tuya was still immured in the dingy clinic recuperating from the birth, Algaa unceremoniously sacked Guul-Jan as the senior midwife. Guul-Jan was given no notice and was still owed three months salary. She was furious at Algaa but delighted to have lost her job. After seventeen years of full-time work she was exhausted, and welcomed a long break at home. She and I sat and drank tea together and spent a happy half hour calling Algaa lots of awful names. I was surprised when she then told me she was planning to go to Olgii to petition the provincial health director about her dismissal. But Guul-Jan was calmly and stubbornly determined.

'I have worked in that place for seventeen years, Louisa, and Algaa owes me money,' she said. 'I don't want my job back. But I want an explanation.'

It was so cold now, water could only be fetched mid-afternoon, when the temperature rose a little. Every day narrow shafts were hacked through the Hovd ice with long-handled axes, and every night, as the temperature plummeted below -30C, they resealed, thick and cloudy as marble. Every afternoon they were smashed open again. Young children streaked along the now compressed ice on blades bound to home-made, knee-high felt boots, or squatted aboard square slabs of wood with the same narrow blades welded underneath. Their cheeks were raw, and they shrieked with laughter as they floundered and tumbled on the clouded ice. Some of them also had sacks strapped to their backs, and paused from games to forage for cakes of dung amid the snow.

The well opposite our *hasha* gate had been dredged, but was so solid that the rocks I hurled down the shaft to break the ice only cracked the opaque surface, and sent shards ricocheting from the frozen depths. When Abbai came into my room, shivered and said, 'No, Louisa. No, you can't stay in here. Come to our house', I finally gave up my wretched room and moved into their home, where I slept on the bed in the living room, cosy and snug.

In the mornings we arrived at school with numb, flushed cheeks. The teachers now shed their hats but not their coats during classes, and during breaks we all hovered round the staff-room stove and everyone teased me about leaving before the coldest time of winter, at the end of December.

'Ey, Louisa *bagsh*, it gets much colder than this!' grinned Gerel *bagsh*, who was wearing an immense sheepskin jacket. 'Sometimes it's minus forty-eight here at the beginning of January!'

'*Yanaa*!' I laughed, rolling my eyes. 'And this is the village they call Delight!'

I remember stumping home from school one afternoon, needing to collect something from my room, which still had some of my stuff in it. The room was locked with a padlock, and, impatient to get into Guul-Jan's warm house, I pulled off my sheepskin glove and clasped the padlock with the fingers of my right hand. My warm, dry fingers stuck to the frozen metal like an adhesive, and I panicked. I couldn't loosen or remove them. Wincing, I had to peel my flesh from the lock, hearing and feeling the skin slowly tear. There was no blood, but a thin layer of several finger tips was plastered on to the metal, like tufts of shrivelled cloth, and my hand tingled and throbbed as though it had actually been scalded.

When I got into Guul-Jan's, she was clearing up after yet another crowd of guests. 'They came from the mountains,' she said, grinning at me slyly. 'Eight of them, on their way to Olgii. They all asked about you. How is the foreign *bagsh*? they said. I said, oh she's fine, but you know she does a lot of work at our school, and these foreigners, they need a very quiet place to stay, they are not used to everyone sharing and sleeping together. Oh, they said, oh maybe we shouldn't sleep here tonight and disturb her. So they've all gone to stay in someone else's house tonight.'

'But Guul-Jan, I don't mind! It's not a problem for me, honestly!' I've done it again, I thought. Now they'll think I'm a snotty foreigner who has to have a room to herself.

But Guul-Jan started laughing. 'No! I know you don't mind, but I do! I don't want to cook for eight more people tonight, and now they've all gone. *Sain bain!*'

We laughed together at her cheek as we drank a pot of tea. That evening Abbai was out and I helped her cook dinner for the family.

The next morning, as ice filmed the window panes and bridles cracked and split, scores of the village men mounted their horses and rode into the Altai to claim their livestock for the slaughter.

CHAPTER THIRTY-FOUR

For the next week or so, flocks of sheep and goats were driven down from the mountains by scores of local men, all riding horses crusted in frozen sweat. During the short daylight hours they herded their animals across the frozen Hovd river, and soon Tsengel was crammed with livestock passively waiting to die. Families and neighbours got together en masse to kill all their animals in one day. They feasted on the fresh meat afterwards.

Quartz and his handsome younger brother, Oraz, arrived in our *hasha* late one morning with two cows, a couple of dozen sheep and goats, a camel and a pair of geldings with thick, tangled manes. Only the camel was to be spared. The rest would be killed and eaten. I was curious about the slaughter. I couldn't picture exactly what it was going to be like, but I wasn't worried about it. During these last nine months I'd seen plenty of animals being killed, and it always seemed to be the same quick unsentimental death by one smooth slash of the throat. In fact, a week or so earlier, just before winter had finally set in, I'd been perched on a log in the sunny *hasha* writing a letter home to my sister while several feet in front of me Quartz had killed a sheep.

'It's at moments like this that I feel as though I've been living here for a very long time,' I'd written as the basin on the ground filled with blood. 'I can't be bothered to move, because I'm comfortable and the sun is warm. It's bizarre to feel so casual about death.'

I presumed I was used to seeing the men killing our food by now.

Each of the village households started their own slaughter

without ceremony. In our *hasha*, Quartz and Oraz first bound the two geldings by their legs. I was outside at that moment, chopping wood with numb fingers, even though I was wearing thick gloves. I didn't look up, but I knew exactly what was going on because the geldings started screaming in wild terror. And I dropped my sticks and ran straight into my room because I could not stand there and listen to them. Instead I sat cringing on my bed, swallowing dryly and biting my lower lip. When the geldings were silent, I busied myself with anything to distract my attention from the sound of Quartz and Oraz raising their axes and breaking the bones. When I did venture out, a little while later, the two men were skinning and chopping up the carcasses. Szandrash, Guul-Jan and Elia were rinsing the two large stomachs and the ropes of yellow intestines.

I stood near them, flinching as the two moist horse skins were staked out on the ground and slowly scraped free of blood and sinew, as they steamed and then froze. Then I went back inside my own room, feeling jumpy, unnerved and shocked by my own reaction. I hadn't expected it to be like this at all.

A few hours later Oraz shouted me over to Abbai's cabin for dinner. 'Eh, Louisa! *It jey, it jey!*' Eat meat!

A whole crowd of people were in the main room, crouching round the stove and drinking strong brown tea while the vat of dark horse meat simmered. Merim-Khan, Aimak and other neighbours had helped out during the afternoon, and everyone had been invited to eat afterwards. Guul-Jan and Elia set down two huge dripping platters – one for the men and Apam sitting round the table, the other for us, crouching on the floor. We prayed and then ate the very soft, oily meat. The head of one of the horses was perched next to our platter, its eyes wide open. I glanced at it a few times. 'Oh, we'll eat that afterwards,' Szandrash said as we chewed. I nodded with my mouth full and carried on dunking chunks into the salty juices. I had no problem eating the horse – I just couldn't have watched it being killed.

When we had finished the meal and were wiping our fingers, Quartz gestured to one of his sons to bring him a bridle. Taking

the cracked leather between his greasy hands, he nourished the
bridle, softening the frayed straps with his glistening fingers as he
talked with the other men.

I watched him silently. The villagers never seemed to waste
anything. Everything served a purpose here. Maybe it sounds
romantic now, my watching this man doing something he had done
for years and finding it somehow touching and exceptional. But
life had been harsh for a while, and it was a gentle reflective moment
that made me think of how differently we all live, even now.

Guul-Jan and Elia had already started hacking up the rest of
the horse meat, and stuffing it in handfuls inside the horses' own
intestines. They made dozens of thick crimson sausages two or
three feet long, and sealed them with small wooden splints. That
night Apam hung a rack of these bloody stumps over a pole
suspended across my ceiling. The meat had to congeal and her
room was too warm. I whacked my head on them several times
as I stumbled out of bed before sunrise, and they dripped clots of
dark blood on to my floor. It was like waking up in the butcher's.

The morning after we ate the horses, I arrived home from school
to find the ground outside Szandrash's cabin strewn with fresh
skins. They'd obviously been at it again. I opened Szandrash's door
to see what was happening, even though I wasn't sure I wanted
to know, and froze in the doorway with my mouth agape. The
main room had been transformed into an abattoir. The bare
wooden floor was smeared with puddles of congealed blood and
littered with decapitated heads and hooves. A trough stood in the
centre of the room half filled with blood and lumps of floating
offal. Above it, a fresh carcass hung from a thick hook that had
been punched into the ceiling. The table was piled with bulbous,
cream-coloured sheep stomachs like ruptured footballs, and long,
thin, white intestines were draped over all the chairs and nailed
to the walls. The place reeked of carnage. I was mesmerised. Silent.
Only my head moved from side to side, as I gazed from one corner
of this bloodbath to the other.

'It's too cold to work outside,' said Szandrash wearily, wiping her damp brow with the back of her blood-stained palm.

'Are you going to help us, Louisa?' grinned Guul-Jan, as I stood there, fixated by this medieval slaughter-house. But I couldn't speak. Only when Quartz pushed past me as he hauled in a rasping goat that kicked feebly, did I finally move. I shook my head violently and backed out of the doorway as though I'd just been pelted with rotten fruit.

'My God,' I heard myself say as I pushed open my own door and sucked in several large gulps of clean air. 'My God, I really have seen it all now.'

CHAPTER THIRTY-FIVE

December. Two weeks to go. God. Whenever I thought about leaving Tsengel, which was starting to be most of the time, my emotions were in conflict. I've no doubt it would sound far more poignant to say I was utterly loathe to go, that I suddenly knew I needed to see out the bitter splendour of the Tsengel winter and to continue living in a *hasha* learning more about the villagers and the nomads and so on, but the truth is that I was almost ready to leave. I was very, very tired. Months of gradual weariness had crept up on me like a virus and I suddenly felt worn out. I was sick of hauling water and ice, chopping frozen wood and scrubbing my clothes. I couldn't bear to crouch, shivering and naked in the tin bath any longer, and I hated that outside toilet, which was now slippery with black ice and sprouting stalagmites. Going to the loo at night was absolutely lethal, so I just squatted outside the *hasha* gate like the children, clenching my teeth and buttocks against the cold. This constant, intense cold was the most exhausting thing of all. Our whole lives revolved around staying warm. Apart from when bathing I never took my clothes off, and didn't even change them very much any more. I pulled layers on top of more layers till I looked like the circus fat lady whenever I went outside. In the mornings the temperature made my eyes smart.

Guul-Jan's house always felt warm, for she had already rekindled the stove before anyone else rose, and by the time we were up the ice was melting from the windows and tea had already been brewed. In the evenings I always stayed at home, because it was just too much effort to brave the dark and freezing village at night.

There was light in the houses, but of course there were no street lamps and the tracks were black as pitch and silent as the cemetery on the hill. I was longing for life to be easier: to eat fresh fruit and vegetables, to lie in a full-sized tub of hot water, see my friends, take a lover, and be reunited with my mother and twin sister.

But these last couple of weeks in Tsengel were in many ways the most precious time of the whole year. I coveted every single moment, from the pale dawn sky to the noon of glinting ice and nights of frescoed stars, because every part of every day felt as though it was all I had left. After school I visited my friends and acquaintances across the village, then walked alone in the mid-afternoons, skating to the other side of the river and wandering through powdery drifts, to be as close as I could to the scattering of trees draped in snow and the white mountains rising directly in front of me against the outrageous sky. I remember those long rambles so well. A gang of my male students would wave and holler, '*Bagsh*!' as they skated past, and I'd wave back absent-mindedly, immersed in every stride I was making. And then I'd notice an eagle spiralling in the sky or tracks from a nomad's horse indented in the snow, and that would be enough to make me think that when I did leave I'd realise what it had all been about, how incredible it had been. The village was still my life and my normality, and only when I had left and half the world lay between me and Tsengel would I really understand and appreciate it.

Now all I knew was that I couldn't stay here much longer, because it was too damn hard, and I was eager to re-enter life Out There. But I didn't kid myself that it was going to be easy to extract myself from this intimate world, and once or twice I stopped and cried, tears freezing on my eyelashes, laughing as I cried because all these thoughts were so confusing. I couldn't celebrate leaving Tsengel, because this was the end of the most remarkable time of my life and it had been beautiful but occasionally hideous, lonely, intimate and profound.

Ten days before I was supposed to leave I got a letter from my friend Javhlan in Ulaanbaatar. '*I reserved your ticket*,' she wrote. '*Sorry, but*

you have to sleep one night in Moscow on the way back to London.
You leave UB on 22 December.' I showed the letter to everyone in
the house, and they all beamed and said I must be so pleased to be
going back home to such a warm place, and how lucky I was.

I desperately wanted to return to the mountains once more
before I left, but couldn't ask Abbai because any trip in winter was
tough and now people only ever travelled into the mountains for
a good reason. But I was lucky, because one of Abbai's many sisters,
a young woman called Sanya, had just been discharged from the
clinic after giving birth to her first child, and Abbai and Guul-
Jan were taking her back to her *ail* beyond the river gorge.

Sanya was delicate and bashful, with freckled pale skin and
wisps of fine dark hair. She knew no Mongolian and was so shy
she hardly said anything, even in Kazakh.

'Sanya needs to go back home with her new daughter. We will
be taking her together tomorrow afternoon. If you want to come,
Louisa, then you can meet her father-in-law. He has one of these
eagles our people hunt with,' Abbai invited me, over the din of
the TV screen.

I practically jumped up and down with excitement. This was
the one thing I had been longing to see before I left the village:
the Kazakh men who caught, trained and then hunted with eagles.

'*Rakhmid, rakhmid,*' I thanked him warmly in Kazakh.

Abbai chuckled. He knew me well by now. 'Yes, Louisa, I know
you want to go! I know you won't say, no thank you, I will stay
in the village. It's OK, we have room for you in the jeep.'

'Abbai, tell me about the eagles.'

'What do you want to know? This Kazakh will explain everything when we go to the countryside. But this I will tell you now.
We Kazakhs are the only people in the world who hunt with eagles.
All those other men, they use the falcon to hunt. No one else uses
the eagle . . .'

I hung on to his every word, restless to go.

We left at noon, driving upstream as the sun shone fierce and
cold. It was strange driving on the ice again and reminded me

that another cycle of the seasons had turned over here. After a while we lurched up the bank on the far side of the Hovd, and drove through deserted white valleys where camels foraging in the snow stared over at us in apparent disgust, and it made me laugh all over again. It was a jarring, beautiful journey.

Sanya's *ail* was surrounded by steep hills, flanked by mountains and already banked by deep drifts of snow. This settlement of three cabins, plus a sturdy stone corral for the huge herd of livestock, was home to the Kazakh patriarch Sistem, his wife Amantei, their thirteen children, numerous grandchildren, hundreds of sheep and goats, a large herd of horses – and a hunting eagle. Sanya's husband was one of Sistem's elder sons.

As Abbai swung and parked the jeep, a fresh horse carcass lay steaming in the snow, its coiled yellow intestines thick as a hefty man's arm.

The main cabin was solid and gloriously warm, and adults and children were constantly coming and going. In one corner slabs of horse meat were being carved up by some women while cauldrons of snow were thawing on the large stove. A small flock of either very late or early lambs were tethered and bleating in another corner.

'*Sain bainuu, bagsh?*'

Sistem shook our hands firmly. He was a short, broad, smiling man, wearing an embroidered Kazakh skullcap. His hands were heavy and his smile wide. I warmed to him straight away. He and his wife were delighted with the small whimpering addition to their already huge family. The babe was lain on a cot, but scooped up every two or three minutes by a passing parent or child.

While meat was being simmered for our lunch I wandered outside into the white sunshine. The snow was so spangled I had to retrieve my sunglasses. Untrampled drifts already reached to the corral roof.

While we were eating, Abbai talked with Sistem, who regarded me carefully and finally nodded his consent.

'*Zaa,*' Abbai said to me, 'we are going back to the village soon, Guul-Jan and I, but if you want to see this eagle properly you will have to stay here tonight, and then go out hunting in the morning with Sistem's eldest son, Kilden. He will take you into the mountains with the eagle. You know our women do not hunt, but Sistem has agreed that Kilden will take you with him, because this is the one chance you have to see the Kazakh eagle work. He will also bring you back to Tsengel on horseback tomorrow.'

One more night in the mountains, a morning's hunting with an eagle and a journey back to Tsengel on horseback: I could have asked for no more.

Abbai and Guul-Jan left, and I spent an easy afternoon drinking tea with Sanya and the other women, then wandering alone around the valley. Nowadays I felt a slow ease unfold inside me whenever I was in these mountains. There was nothing to achieve, nowhere else to go. Life was immediate.

The evening dinner was a large, boisterous affair with the entire family eating together. We knelt in a huge circle, prayed, then tucked into horsemeat. I was sitting next to Sistem, who was an entertaining and erudite dining companion. He asked me scores of questions as we chewed. We talked of politics, religion, England, the break-up of the Soviet Union, Kazakhstan – and dogs.

'Now I think you Europeans have a very interesting attitude towards animals,' he commented thoughtfully at one point. 'I think you have *mal*, yes, but you also keep dogs as companions.'

I could hear the amusement in his deep voice, and I nodded, trying not to snigger as I explained how we English love our pets; because by now the thought of keeping a dog inside a house instead of outside in the yard did seem quite disgusting to me as well. Here in the countryside a Mongol would never allow a dog inside their home unless lightning strikes. As a nation they harbour a collective, almost religious terror of lightning, and during an electric storm even the dogs, which are routinely kicked around and fed only on scraps, are pitied as they cower.

'Yes, we do love our dogs, and we even let them live in our houses,' I admitted to Sistem, suddenly feeling embarrassed about coming from a nation of such slobs.

'Hmm . . . I've heard that about the English,' he replied, shaking his head gravely before adding with a completely straight face, 'but the Russians, you know *they* even let their hounds sleep on the beds!'

The entire packed cabin erupted with laughter at the thought of Russian dogs being put to bed with their owners. It was really quite lewd.

After we'd eaten, Sistem rolled a cigarette in a twist of newspaper and leaned back against one of the narrow beds. 'Five generations of my family have been born here, *bagsh*,' he said slowly. 'My father lived and died in this valley, and so did his father, and now our children have their own families. We've always herded our *mal* here. This is our land.'

'Have you ever been to Kazakhstan?' I asked him.

I wasn't surprised when he shook his head and smiled. 'No. I don't need to go anywhere further than these valleys to herd my animals. This is the only land I know. My children, well, maybe some of them will travel far and then that's how it will be. If they want to go, then I will say, "*Zaa*, go." But I will stay here with the rest of my family.'

I realised why I'd warmed so much to Sistem. He was happy with what he had. Surrounded by his large family, over which he was a gentle patriarch, he owned almost a thousand livestock, so he was financially secure and could provide amply for his whole clan, including the babe his middle-aged wife was breastfeeding as we sat and talked. Sistem didn't yearn for Kazakhstan because he didn't need a vision of a better place to sustain him. He was exactly where he wanted to be.

The next morning I woke very early as I always did in the mountains, driven outside in spite of myself to greet the dawn. As the sheep and goats surged out of the corral, the steam from the heat of their confined bodies surged into the dry air.

After breakfast I mounted a white horse as Sistem's eldest son, Kilden, strode out of his cabin with his blindfolded eagle on his arm. She was larger than I expected. Her feathers were dull dark brown and when she opened her wings they spanned more than a metre either side, the cartilage joining them to her torso sturdy as a branch. Her blindfold looked like a pair of ancient black motorcycle goggles. Though she could see nothing, she rotated her small head almost 360 degrees and cauled repeatedly, urgently, revealing a sliver of white tongue inside her hooked beak.

Abbai had already told me that Kazakhs prefer to hunt with female eagles as they're considered better predators. It takes five years for an eagle to mature, and an adult female weighs about twelve pounds. Kilden's right hand and wrist were protected by a thick felt glove that reached halfway to his elbow. His bird gripped on to him with five immense black talons.

'My little brother is coming with us,' was all Kilden said to me before we set off. He looked the strong silent type and this image was only slightly offset by his extravagant crimson felt hat, lined with frothy-looking fox fur that draped the back of his neck. It was stunning. His little brother, Kaerat, casually vaulted on to the back of my horse as we were about to leave and just held on from behind.

We took the thread of a steep trail straight into the mountains, Kilden leading and his right arm now resting on a small 'A' frame of short thick sticks, which supported the weight of his eagle as he rode. My stomach was cramped with tense excitement; I'd never been hunting before, and there was an element of illicit danger about setting off into the mountains in deep snow, riding into this white wilderness.

We slowly climbed so high that my breath tinkled as I inhaled through my nose, and it was only when we finally paused on a broad ridge that I realised why young Kaerat had come with us. He slithered from my horse and slid himself down into the steep rocks below us, cauling like the eagle herself to entice some creature from the security of its frozen burrow or crevice for her to snatch. Kilden said nothing, just motioned for me to stay in my saddle, and *huulej* – wait.

So we waited.

There was only Kaerat moving below us, no other sound in the whole world. I could feel my horse breathing beneath me.

Eventually, Kilden lifted the eagle's blindfold, and she turned her head slowly round and then back again. '*Zaa*,' said Kilden, '*zaa*', and we moved upwards. After a while we stood silently poised on another higher ridge and waited again as Kaerat made his eerie, beautiful caul a second time. I didn't even know what creature we were hunting and it didn't matter. I'd never wanted to be anywhere more in my whole life than right where I was.

My horse was slightly in front of Kilden's and I could see the eagle's yellow and brown eyes darting like a fiend. 'Her eyes are so much stronger than ours,' murmured Kilden. 'If she sees it, she will go.' She wasn't tethered now. But she gleaned no kill, and we climbed on, the horses' sweat freezing into crystals that glistened over their necks and bellies. We finally dismounted on a ledge that was so high it seemed level with the gleaming peaks beyond us. Kaerat was beneath us again, and way below him the sheer rock splayed into an untrodden white valley.

'Climb down there and wait.' Kilden signalled where I should go, and I led my horse down a little, scrambling over icy rocks and then gazing back up at him and her poised against the rock. His headdress resplendent against the dark ridge and lazuli sky. The eagle on his gloved arm. The sun so brilliant it looked wet.

I crouched, trailing Kaerat's slender shadow. My feet and face were numb, but I could feel sweat dripping down my sides.

Kaerat screeched a triumph and I glanced down and then upwards, just as the eagle launched herself from Kilden's outstretched arm. She didn't plunge, but swooped slowly down towards the shadow hurtling across the empty valley. She flowed as though diving through water, streaming slowly towards her skittering prey. I could just see the moment of impact, when she ripped the creature from the earth.

Suddenly Kilden and I were waving and shouting to each other, elated and cheering. When I climbed back up to him, he was beaming. '*Yamar bain, bagsh?*' How was that? And I grinned back. He could see I was thrilled. We led our horses slowly down the escarpment, through knee-deep drifts, the horses gulping mouthfuls of snow as we clambered gradually down towards the eagle and the corpse she stood over. I thought she would fly straight back to the glove, but she displayed a sudden streak of rebellion when Kilden raised his arm, and stayed her distance on the snow.

'She's killed her meat and it's a beautiful day. She doesn't want to come back to me,' said Kilden placidly. But the blindfold and her captor's discipline had ultimately broken her spirit, and when he held his arm out to her again she did fly back, with the corpse in her talons.

'She can eat it now,' said Kilden, glancing at the small rabbit. 'We always hunt with hungry birds. If you feed an eagle before hunting then it's lazy. When I take her over there,' he gestured to the wide mountains beyond us, 'then she takes foxes and even young wolves. We only hunt after the first snow has fallen. It's easier for her to see her prey then.'

This small valley suddenly didn't feel cold compared to the ridges we'd scaled, and we sprawled luxuriously out on the snow, the sun warm on our faces as we talked about the eagle, who stood between us, cleaving her rabbit into shreds of meat.

CHAPTER THIRTY-SIX

I rode back to Tsengel with Kilden, and when we got to the *hasha*, Elia, Merim-Khan, Amina and all the children were there, but Apam, Abbai and Guul-Jan were nowhere to be seen. They didn't come home until late in the evening, and when they did finally return, long after dark, Quartz was with them. There was something about all of them that made me suddenly wonder where they'd been. Abbai often went away for the day, but Guul-Jan and especially Apam rarely left the *hasha* at all.

I asked Guul-Jan where they'd been as we sat at the table.

'We went to see some relatives,' was all she said, glancing over at Abbai, and for a little while at least I probably would have been none the wiser, except that Abbai decided to tell me what was going on.

'We went to find a wife for Quartz,' he said, when Quartz wasn't in the room. He was a man who moved quietly and he'd slipped outside somewhere almost as soon as they'd all got back.

'Really?' I said. I had no idea how the Kazakhs sought their wives and had just presumed each man visited, courted and then married a local woman. But, of course, it isn't always that simple.

Quartz had lost his young wife three years earlier to an infection that had engulfed her stomach and killed her swiftly. Her boys clung to their father, especially young Nuurlan who was always by his dad's side.

Quartz was now thirty-seven, which was old to be seeking a wife, but too young to be a widower. He had wanted to find a second spouse for himself and a mother for his sons, but he'd never met the right woman again. After a couple of years Apam had finally taken matters into her own hands. Friends and relatives across the whole of Tsengel, the village itself and the countryside beyond had all been asked if they knew of any available women who could marry Quartz and care for the boys. Unknown to me these stealthy enquiries had been going on for months, and only now had an apparently suitable woman been found: a young divorcee of twenty-three with no children of her own. She lived more than 100 kilometres away in a village called White Lake. Abbai, Guul-Jan, Apam and Quartz had just been there to meet the woman and her elderly mother for the first time.

'What did Quartz think of this woman?' I asked. I couldn't help it, I really wanted to know.

Guul-Jan laughed out loud, the skin round her eyes crinkling like dried leaves. 'Oh, he thought she was lovely! Beautiful, he said! But the woman, she wasn't sure. She said maybe he was a bit too old. We're going back there next week to see her and her mother again, and find out if she's going to accept him. Her elder brother will also be there next time, and if he likes Quartz he might just give her to us anyway.'

I dropped my spoon. 'Guul-Jan – you can't do that!' I spluttered. 'She'll be completely miserable if she's forced to marry Quartz and live in the mountains – and she'll be horrible to the boys!'

Before I left Ulaanbaatar to come to the village, my Mongol friends had assured me that the Kazakhs still kidnapped their brides, and never bothered with the courtesy of obtaining a woman's consent to her own marriage. But in Tsengel even the local Tuvans had conceded that this just wasn't true any more. There are still reports of isolated bride kidnappings in Kazakhstan itself, but in Bayan-Olgii bride-snatching finally died out in the mid-1990s. However, it is still perfectly acceptable for a woman to have her husband chosen for her by the men of her family. Kidnapped or not, some local Kazakh women are still married against their will, and despite my determination to respect and accept Tsengel for everything it was, I couldn't wholly contain my sense of outrage. It was a purely instinctive reaction to the idea of a forced or coerced marriage with its implications of violence, neglect and abuse. The stereotypes kicked in and left me no room to doubt this was an utterly cruel and barbaric practice.

Abbai and Guul-Jan took my brief outburst in their stride.

'Sometimes we still do this,' said Abbai calmly, making no attempt to appease me. 'But we will all talk about this wedding a lot before anything happens. Because of course we want everyone to be happy, including her.'

For Quartz this second visit to Tsagaan Nuur was crucial. Abbai, Apam and Guul-Jan would negotiate his potential marriage, and though he would go to Tsagaan Nuur with them, neither he nor the woman herself would take part in the discussions about their possible future together. All that was up to everyone else. And if everything went according to plan, Quartz would be returning to Tsengel the day before I left, with a new wife.

My freezing, abandoned room was hastily scrubbed down and decorated by Guul-Jan, Amina, Szandrash and Elia. New beds, rugs and crockery were dragged inside, the windows cleaned and fresh bolts of felt hung over the inside and outside of the door. For this was hopefully to be Quartz's new marital home. When the room had been spruced up, Guul-Jan and Amina went shopping and came home bent under the weight of huge bags of rice, sugar and boiled sweets. Between them the women then fried mounds of *buurtzug*, baked wagon wheels of crusty bread, and hung up joints of meat to thaw. It was a frantic week that somehow reminded me keenly of the frenzy before Christmas in a big city. By the time the wedding party were due to leave for Tsagaan Nuur again, the whole *hasha* seemed to be stuffed with food and static with anticipation. I was very grateful for the distraction of the wedding, because I did not want to be reminded by anyone, including myself, that the day after they all came back, I'd be gone.

The next morning, just before they left, Quartz and I chopped wood together. Or rather, I was struggling with a tough, knotty

log and the blunt *hasha* axe when Quartz held out his hand for
the axe and split the wood for me. He was dressed in smart new
breeches, his jacket had been brushed and his boots shone.

'Are you bringing your new wife home today?' I asked him as
I bent down to gather up the sticks.

'Yes, I'll bring her,' he said quietly.

I felt a sudden hot rush of affection for this gentle sad man with
his red, raw-looking skin and dependent young sons. I wanted to
put my arms round his neck and embrace him, wish him luck,
insist it would all be fine. I really wanted this marriage to work for
him, even though I hated the idea of a woman being driven back
here silent and resigned to a marriage she didn't want.

I don't know exactly what I felt for Quartz, but I do know that
when he glanced at me I smiled at him with more tenderness than
I'd felt towards a man all that year, and maybe much longer. I
knew he would be a good husband. He was a real grafter and never
flinched or showed a trace of resentment about the way he was
treated by his brothers Abbai and Addai. He was the youngest of
the three, and in both their houses he placidly knelt to eat on his
knees when other men were in the room, because he wasn't usually
offered a stool. While his elder brothers worked in their respective
offices, Quartz chopped wood, rode to and from the mountains
with supplies and herded the family livestock. I thought he was
treated like a lackey. After these three years without a spouse he
had a lot to lose at White Lake. It was obvious that having a new
wife would improve his status and earn him a lot more respect.

We all stood in the *hasha* and waved the party off. They were
taking gifts with them: a sack of flour, another of salt and a bundle
of sweets. This was my last full day in Tsengel, and we all hoped
it would conclude with the traditional Kazakh *betashaa* ritual of
removing the wedding veil and introducing the bride to her new
family before a late-night feast of meat and music.

It was a disquieting day. While everyone in the *hasha* went about
their business, I traipsed round the village in a quiet panic, visiting
Marat-Khan and Aimak, Gerel-Huu, Shinid and Bagit in the
kitchen and then Sansar-Huu and Gansukh, who were all horribly

cheerful about me leaving and seeing my family again, while I became increasingly maudlin about the road ahead of me. I had no real plans about where I was going to live or what I was going to do when I got back to England, and I knew I'd be shell-shocked for a while and would have to ease myself very slowly back into my old life. The fact that I was going to be in Ulaanbaatar for a week before I flew to Moscow and then London would definitely help, though even the thought of landing in the Mongolian capital was unnerving me now.

It felt weird that hardly anyone in the village asked me what I was going to do back home. It was as though my time in their lives ended the day I left Tsengel, and they were comfortable with that. Only Gansukh quizzed me, and when I shrugged numbly she smiled and took my arm for a moment. 'You will be fine, Louisa,' she said, and I nodded though I wasn't sure.

At dusk Gansukh and I wandered to the shops, and I later returned to Abbai's *hasha* clutching bags of sweets, tubes of thin orange biscuits, and a bottle of local vodka the store keepers had given me. Bless them, no wonder they never made any money. They were too damn generous. I had already shaken many hands that day, and now evening fell, a steady trickle of people came to the *hasha*: students with their parents, acquaintances and friends all sat down, drank tea and quietly slipped Togrog notes into my palm as they were leaving, 'For your journey home, *bagsh.*' This was *zam mŏng* – road money – to provide for me on my way. I smiled and hugged every single one of them and said *bayartai*, because this was farewell. It was hard.

The wedding party had said they'd be back about six, and though we expected them a while later, by six o'clock we were all sitting in Abbai's home, drumming our fingers and waiting. Szandrash cooked soup, but no one ate much. Everyone just fidgeted and looked at the clock. I finished my packing and walked over to Tuya's new home to say goodbye to her and Gerele and their daughter. I'd only seen her once since she'd left the clinic. She was still in confinement after the birth, so people only visited when invited, but she'd sent a message asking me to come by this evening. Their cabin was tiny, and they were sharing it with Gerele's mother and four brothers and sisters. Gerele looked healthy – and sober.

Tuya insisted on opening a bottle of *arikh*. 'This is because you're leaving, though I know you're going to write to me,' she bantered, 'and we also need to celebrate because we've just given our daughter her name.'

We toasted each other and little Davaa-Bayar, whose name means First Celebration of Many, and I promised that of course I'd write.

As I was leaving their cabin, Tuya waved as she held her daughter to her breast. 'Hey, Louisa! Come back and see us next summer in the mountains,' she called cheerfully, and I nodded gratefully. She'd been a good friend.

I returned to an empty *hasha*. The jeep hadn't arrived yet. The electricity came on late that evening, but even the television provided little distraction as we listened for the rasping engine. Quartz's two boys looked bewildered and fretful, especially Nuurlan, who'd already asked if it was his real mother who was coming home. The two boys were pampered this evening, though I'd seen them often scolded by Guul-Jan and Amina, and sometimes mercilessly bullied by the other *hasha* children, who sensed their frailty and happily tormented them because of it.

The lights went out. We lit candles. Addai peered at his watch and shook his large head. 'It's not so good. They should be here by now.'

But they didn't come back until after eleven, and when we finally heard the jeep hacking into the *hasha*, we all stood and pushed through the door together without bothering about jackets or hats, although it was below -30C outside. The headlights illuminated the *hasha* as the party clambered wearily from their seats. Abbai, Guul-Jan, Apam and Quartz. There was no bride.

We crowded back into the house. Abbai and Guul-Jan were already explaining what had happened, what had gone wrong. Apam and Quartz said nothing. I could understand some of what was said: the woman's elder brother had over-ruled his mother, who had urged her daughter be swiftly remarried. The brother said Quartz was too old. And his decision was final.

'Oh, we ate and drank and talked all day,' said Guul-Jan, yawning as she rose to her feet and crossed the room to her stove to make a late-night supper.

'But on the way back we heard of another woman in Olgii city who's a little older,' said Abbai. 'So we will visit her later this month and maybe she or her family will agree.'

They talked so candidly about how they could negotiate a marriage for Quartz, who was sitting on the ground against the wall with both his sons in his arms. His boots were scuffed and he was staring at the floor. Irlaan and Nuurlan wrapped themselves around him. They'd already forgotten whoever else might have come home now that they had their father back. I'd bought Quartz a token wedding present, a packet of cigarettes, and I pressed the carton into his hand and then fled into the spare room before I burst into tears, because he looked so dejected.

The day of 14 December was a clear, freezing, beautiful morning. Everything I did registered itself as being the very last time I'd do it here. I stood on the stack of logs at the front of the yard and gazed out for a long last look over the village. It was early, but I could see Gansukh heading over to say goodbye, again. As soon as she walked through the gate, we hugged each other, hard.

'*Bayartai*, again. You know you need to see your family,' she told me, smiling. Gansukh has such a beautiful smile. 'We have been your family here. But we are not your real family. They are waiting for you.'

'I'll miss you a lot,' I told her, shaking my head because I just didn't know what else to say.

I watched her walking away, back towards her home. I hadn't spent so much time with her recently, but there was something there, some kernel of friendship that would last. Because for a while we shared a life together.

EPILOGUE

Dear Louisa

Thank you for your letter from Scotland. I send my greetings to your mother and your sister and to her family. I know your book is nearly finished. What will you do now?

We are all fine here. I don't know if you heard the news from Mongolia, but our last winter was very hard, like the one before. We had too much snow and we lost many animals.

But in our village everything is easier. Things are different here now, Louisa. We have electricity all the time and the school is warm because we have a new furnace. And Sansar-Huu has a job as the school accountant. Our life is better.

After you left, another English teacher came to live in Tsengel. He is from the American Peace Corps. He came in the autumn and he will stay for two years. He is very funny!

Our American teacher lives with Abbai, in your old room. I know you want to know about Abbai's brother Quartz. Well, he has a new wife. Yes! She is from our *aimag* and also is a widow. They married at the end of last winter.

OK, Louisa – no more 'gossip'! Tuya is fine. Her daughter is three now. And Gerele is OK. And my little 'Hooligan' is asking about you.

Write me many letters!

Love,

Gansukh

APPENDIX

Names

While I was living in Tsengel, I was commissioned to write a series of 'Letters from Mongolia' for the *New Internationalist* magazine. In spite of my appalling handwriting, and our once-a-week postal service to and from Tsengel, my letters always arrived at the *New Internationalist* office on time, and were legible. After several months, the commissioning editor wrote me a letter from Oxford, saying how fascinating she found the names of people in Tsengel, and suggested I write a letter about them.

I was unenthusiastic at first, mainly because I hardly knew what any of the names meant, and so it was more work for me and I had quite enough to do as it was. But as I slowly unravelled the translations, with Gansukh's help, I realised how right she was. The local names told their own stories in decadent, mighty and tragic prose.

To start at the beginning, Gansukh's name translates as Steel Axe. She told me it was given to her to strengthen and protect her. Sansar-Huu means Son of the Cosmos, which is a splendid name heralding the arrival of a first-born son. Their two children have equally vivid names: Yalta means Victory and Opia is the name of a healing plant.

So I delved further, and found out that my students at the school had some brilliant names. In one of my classes Odgerel (Starlight) sat between Buuta-Kooz (Camel Eyes) and Amer-Huu (Boy of Great Strength), who was a girl. Chudruk (Fist) and Zolbin (Stray) sat behind them. Meanwhile Sasug (Smelly) sat near the back of the class. I am not making any of these names up, I assure you. Two of my students, a boy and a girl, were both called Enkhjargal (Great Happiness). And finally there was young Neer-

Gui, whose name literally means No Name.

I asked Gansukh why anyone would call their daughter Camel Eyes.

'Have you never seen a camel's eyes?' she retorted. 'Go and look – they're beautiful!'

It was true. Tsengel was home to many a camel with deep, sexy brown eyes, framed by the kind of thick gorgeous lashes that models can only dream of. This name was a true compliment.

'So what about Chudruk?' I asked her, oblivious as to why you would name your child after a body part.

Gansukh smiled and clenched her fist at me. 'That name is also given to protect him from harm, like mine. And you know the boy down the street, the one called Buuga (Bull)? His name is the same, it was also given to him to protect him and keep him strong.'

So far the theory was fairly simple. But Sasug was a bit more difficult to fathom, though Gansukh explained that it's an antonym, and actually implies he smells nice. She also insisted that, in spite of *his* name, Zolbin the stray was a very loved child. 'You know, these names all mean the opposite of what you think they say. They are good names. Zolbin's little brother, now he has an interesting name! Zerleg. It means . . .' She flicked through her dictionary, and we both howled with laughter when we found the translation. Zerleg means Savage or Barbarian. 'It's because . . .' Gansukh tried to stop laughing. 'Louisa, listen! He is a bit crazy, that child, but his parents believe his name will make him peaceful when he gets older. Honestly!'

We laughed and bantered about local names until I asked about Neer-Gui, the girl with no name. Then she suddenly frowned and her voice dropped to a lower, more serious pitch. 'That girl, Neer-Gui, her parents had four or five children before her, you know, and they all died very young. So when she was born they took her to the Olgii Lama and asked what name could they give her that would not anger our gods. He told them to call her Neer-Gui to please the gods so they would spare her.' In other words, it's a very passive name that cannot give divine offence.

Enbisch (Not This) is the male equivalent of Neer-Gui, and is given to a sickly or frail son for the same reason. There are many children and adults with both these names.

I never found out very much about the origins of Kazakh names, so I don't know if they apply the same principles. But the Tuvans often give their children classic Mongol names, with their predominantly revolutionary or religious origins. Baatar means Hero. Huu is Son. Baatar-Huu is a very common male name, as is Sukhbaatar (Axe Hero) or Enkhbaatar (Great Hero). Despite Gansukh's fierce name, many Mongolian women's names are traditionally gentle and reflective, like Narantsetseg (Sunflower), Munkhtsetseg (Silver Flower), or, my own favourite, Altan-Duul (Golden Flame). But, to complicate matters further, there is also a host of androgynous Mongol names. You cannot predict whether someone called Odgerel, Enkhjargal, Jargal-Saikhan (Beautiful Happiness) or indeed Gansukh is male or female before you speak to her, or him. In a society as conservative as Mongolia, it's also interesting that traditional male names are sometimes given to girls. This is another parental method of petitioning the gods for their next born to be a son. That explains how my friend Gerel-Huu (Son of Light) got her name and why Amer-Huu (Son of Great Strength) might be a daughter.

Mongols have two names: their own given name, and their father's, which they use as an initial before their own name in official circumstances, for example, B. Baatar. Recently the government has tried to promote European-style surnames, but the Mongols have continued to use just one name. The initial is applied for identity purposes only.

ACKNOWLEDGEMENTS

To start at the beginning: thank you to Sue B for helping me get to UB and housing and feeding me when I got back. To Baatar, for the invitation to Gandan, to Jargal-Saikhan and Sodnam for my welcome: to Javhlan, Masimo, Piara, Donna, Giovanna, Namie and Grace for good UB times, especially at the Matisse. To everyone at the UB post for giving me a chance. To Bilguun, for New Year in Bulgan. To dreadlocked Gulliver, for rhythm – we owned the dance floor! To Rob, for beer and skiing. To Clare, *la reine noire*. *Y Gracias Jorge, para todos.* To Greg – it's all your fault. But thanks anyway!

Thank you to Nikki VDG for taking a chance and commissioning me to write letters from the village – let's get together for G&T! To everyone in Tsengel, especially Abbai, Amraa, Gansukh, Sansar-Huu and Tuya.

Back at home, many thanks to Bill and Caro for a room in their Orchardton castle where I wrote this: there was no better place. To Chris, Siri, Fred and Jiff. To my co-scrubber Alice, and to Dave, Jo, Kate and Rob. Close your eyes and race to the beach! Thanks to you, Geraint, for early inspiration. And to Dumfries & Galloway Business Enterprise, for a crucial grant.

I want to thank Dr Alan J K Sanders, for sharing his extensive knowledge of Mongolia. His reference book, *The Historical Dictionary of Mongolia*, (Scarecrow Press) was an invaluable tool. So too was Melvyn C. Goldstein and Cynthia M. Beall's, *The Changing World of Mongolia's Nomads* (The Guidebook Company).

To my agent David Grossman, for picking up the phone on a Saturday and laughing at all the right moments, to Alan Samson, and Sarah Shrubb for being a great editor. To Nevil Thomson for encouragement. And to Rob Gilliat, for being the best damn proofreader there ever was.

To those who keep me sane and laughing: Deb Corcoran, Adam (Darling!), Bertie, Derek, Rahul, Carmella Rose (*je ne regrette rien*, eh?), Machete Jo, and the Bath St Coop. Thank you Tam, Tim, Manda and Lyn. For living with me.

To Ma and Ami. I love you both.